The Red Sea Bride

by

Sylvia Fowler

Grassroots Writers' Guild

1

Dedication:

To my sons

Table of Contents

4

Chapter 1

Part 1

Dream by the Red Sea

My eyes fluttered open on thin streams of sunlight filtering onto the foot of the bed through filigreed wood balcony shutters. I was not alone. Near me—so close, one of my arms draped over her shoulders— was my husband's new wife. Her face lay in shadow. She was my replacement.

The bedroom was on the top floor of a whitewashed limestone structure of old Jeddah. A balmy, moist breeze tinged with brine fluttered in off the Red Sea, stirring the light muslin window curtains and bedsheets. I sat up, pushing hair out of my eyes and noticing splintered, foot-sized holes that mottled the floor. Strands of what had once been finely woven Indian rugs littered the spaces between.

"Look!" I nudged the sleeping girl so she would awaken.

She blinked and sat up, leaning back on one arm.

"You can't walk on the floor without being careful." I pointed at the gaps. "You might fall through and break your neck."

I got to my feet. Sensing the woman was an invalid, I lifted her in my arms, surprised at my own strength, and held her carefully. Such is the nature of dreams. She murmured something into the cotton scarf that I used to cover my head in prayer but which had fallen around my shoulders during sleep. Her words seemed to be of consent, even thanks, and I felt sad.

And suddenly I knew, as sleepers do while dreaming, that the dream was over.[1]

* * * *

---

[1] When I had this dream, I had returned to the West after nearly two decades in Saudi Arabia. Later, I learned that my husband's new wife, whom I never met, had been diagnosed with multiple sclerosis.

Part 2

Lessons of Childhood

The number of young, independent Western women who meet and marry Saudi men, flying far from their homes to make a new one in an isolated desert Arab land, is more calculable today than it was in the pre-internet age. Before the internet, each young woman thought she was alone in throwing caution, like fine grains of romance-bleached sand, into the winds of fate.

And she was.

In the late 1970s, I was one of those girls. Every Western bride of a Saudi has found herself, in childhood, on stepping stones leading away from home. Our culture teaches us to be friendly, open to new experiences, and to follow our hearts.

I got to Saudi Arabia through a love of languages, which my mother had depended on to win me back to herself. She made a great sacrifice—separation from her child—to break the spell put on me by a woman who taught at my high school.

Like most parents, she never saw that need arising. Mom spent her young adulthood trying to get over the pain of my father's departure with another woman. My parents' divorce came early, disorienting my little brother and me in ways we were too small, and my mother too emotionally hurt, to understand.

Mom got remarried to a man named Ted, twelve years her senior. He became a father figure to my mother, who could never please her own. I was four when Mom announced we would have a new daddy. She gave me the news at bedtime.

"Mommy, why? I want to keep my old daddy."

She assured me I didn't; this one would be better.

Being adopted is great if you don't have a parent, if the one you had was crushed by a rhino or lost in outer space. No one wants a new parent if the old one is somewhere to be found and made you laugh. We were told the old daddy was gone and we had to suck it up.

7

My maternal grandmother, "Nana," wanting her daughter to be happy, bankrolled the construction of a car dealership for Ted. It was luxurious, with a shower in his office bathroom. Ted drove home a new car for Mom (Marcia) to "break in" every few months. He also brought home a battery-powered miniature children's Chevrolet that I drove down the sidewalk to see my friend Arlene, two houses away. The tiny car didn't stay long, for it was meant to entertain clients' children at the dealership.

My playmate Arlene and her brother, Barry, had been adopted by a kind Jewish couple who worked 60-hour weeks. While Ted contracted a construction firm to build a swimming pool in our backyard (sending the bill to Nana), Arlene and Barry's backyard was full of tumbleweeds, bugs and lizards. Our swimming pool was the only one for blocks around. My little brother, Steven, and I became popular with any child who could walk to our house in a swim suit with a towel over their shoulders, rubber sandals slapping against the concrete sidewalk on a hot summer's day.

Arlene and Barry's parents had little time to give to their children, who fended for themselves at home after school. I had watched Barry drink salad dressing from his refrigerator. No one was there to tell him salad dressing was not juice.

When not playing with Arlene, I visited my adored grandmother, whom I had been named for, in the nearby city of Pomona. Nana lived with Papa on a green hill surrounded by all types of trees. An avocado orchard lay on the property's upper reaches while a fecund pomegranate tree dropped fruit not far from the back kitchen door.

I liked Jimmy, the respectful gardener from Japan who had two green thumbs, and I loved Rosie, the black maid who took me on her lap every time I came over. She made frozen bananas dipped in chocolate, fried chicken, and apple pie. I discovered, when I was older, that she took a number of foster children into her house and legally adopted as many as she could.

One day my mother asked Rosie to take me to a black Baptist church, where the entire congregation was ignited to praising God in hand-waving, clapping, stomping and swaying musical jubilation. That visit offered two powerful spiritual lessons: it was fine to accept other people's ways of worship and music had the power to sweep away boundaries.*

Nana had bought tricycles for my brother and me to ride at the sprawling red brick hilltop home. We slept in the two poster beds in my mother's childhood suite with its own bathroom. Nana and Papa slept in separate beds in the master bedroom where the windows afforded a panoramic view. Ceiling-to-floor niche shelves, running the expanse of most walls throughout the house, were crammed end to end with books. My grandparents and mother were avid readers.

In the mornings, after waking up at Nana's house, I slid out of my poster bed to tiptoe into her bedroom and climb up next to her. In the afternoons, she read stories to me until a frog crept into her throat.

"Nana, please let me see the frog!"

She shook her head. The frog stayed hidden.

She was willing, however, to show me geese. Nana saved scraps of bread so we could feed those wildfowl at the local park. They were as tall or taller than I was and their exuberant honks scared me. When I cried and reached up to be held, she lifted me to the safety of the car's hood.

As a young woman, Nana had gone to the Julliard School of Music. A living room grand piano stood with its top open. Pages of etudes, nocturnes and mazurkas by Chopin cluttered the sheet music stand above the keyboard. Whenever Nana finished performing, I liked to sit on the bench and touch the keys, making pretty sounds. On my last visits, the piano top was shut flat to hold Nana's bottles of medicine.

My grandfather, Papa, became grumpier. I saw his face turn red at night. He yelled about money and papers needing to be signed. Nana's illness upset him. He snapped at her to get out the room he was in because she "stank." The colostomy bag she wore hanging under her clothes at her side, he claimed, had a bad odor from the bile it collected.

Nana went to the hospital to get better. I couldn't see her when I wanted. I tried to be patient. We spent more time at our home, in our pool, and with Ted.

Our adoptive father had a tricky habit of throwing his arm out at the dining table, like he planned on punching Steven in the head in the same manner he hit his punching bag. Steven cringed and flinched because half the time, Ted *did* slap him upside the head. The other half, Ted jerked back his arm to look at his watch, chortling that he had tricked Steven, making my brother jump in his chair.

"I'm army-training the boy," he explained to Mom.

Mom grew quieter around Ted until after Steven and I went to bed. Then their arguments woke us up or gave us nightmares, and sometimes there was a hole in the door or a wall next day, where Ted had punched his fist the night before.

One morning, when Ted was not in the house, Steven and I found Mom at the breakfast dining table. "Eat your breakfasts," she said. She had set out cereal and cold milk, not French toast or scrambled eggs like she often made.

We sat down and she drank coffee, not talking. Suddenly Mom stood up, her lower lip quivering and her brow furrowed. She threw her coffee cup across the breakfast nook. The porcelain shattered in pieces against the wall, we jumped, and coffee dribbled down the flowered paper.

My brother and I stared at each other, aghast, as our sobbing mother ran out of the room.

"What shall we do?" asked Steven. I felt helpless, shaking my head and lifting my shoulders.

Days later, Steven and I woke up to find our neighbors, the Forbes, at our house. Teenagers Terry, Larry and Linda Forbes were our babysitters. One of the kids and their mom got us dressed and took us to their house for a breakfast of French toast. They made quite a fuss over us. I thought it was a nice way to start the day and almost wished we could be surprised this way more often.

"Don't worry; your mother is fine," said Mrs. Forbes reassuringly.

When I came home after school, my mother was sitting with red-rimmed, dark-circled eyes, staring out at the backyard. I got the feeling that she wasn't really noticing anything in it. She didn't hear me walk in. I thought she was hypnotized until my touch made her notice me. She pulled me close, smelling like flowers, and then flipped the world over by saying Nana had died.

My mother's words were a hideous vacuum cleaner, sucking every bit of happiness out of the house. Now I saw how the garden didn't matter. A huge, dark void had been following my mother around for weeks: it was the reason I couldn't go to Nana's house. The dark chasm started following me too, outside when I went to play (but not really playing), and with me to school and to bed. The darkness engulfed me and my brother, and swallowed our mother like a cocoon.

Not long after, I asked Mom to please explain why God took Nana away. She was the best Nana in the world.

"The good die young," my mother said, haltingly, "because God misses them."

Papa cried at Nana's funeral and visited us every day for a month. He had stayed at his wife's deathbed until he got her signature on a new will. If Ted had known the contents of that legal document, he would have dragged Papa out into the street. After the 30-day waiting period to allow contest from aggrieved family members, Papa stopped coming to our house.

Ted's dealership went bankrupt right after Nana returned to God. Ted blamed the bankruptcy on a shadowy "partner," who must have been Death, and decided we should move to the beach on my mother's dime.

All I grasped about this change of residence was that I was losing Arlene. She was a gentle girl who had taught me about Hanukkah, a superior holiday to Christmas because she and her brother got presents every single day for eight days.

Arlene often stood under my bedroom window after I had gone to bed. There, she was shielded from view by landscaped shrubbery. During the setting of the summer sun or in the cold early dark of winter, she stood, perspiring or shivering, and shared the problems she had at home. If we moved, I would have no one to play with or talk to after I went to bed.

At the conclusion of weeks spent visiting ornate mansions facing the water, Ted settled for a slender, white-washed house sandwiched into a block on one of the man-made islands in Newport Beach. Mom could afford at least that.

A spanking paddle, purchased by Ted on a summer trip to Illinois, was packed inside the moving boxes and hung on a hook at the top of the stairs. The paddle was thick wood and had a picture of a little kid with his pants down and a red burning butt. Flames came out the child's buttocks to emphasize pain. The illustration was scary, but Ted thought it was as hilarious as the crack in the wood caused by hard whacking on Steven's posterior.

The spanking paddle's position on the wall at the doorway leading to our bedrooms was a warning to be good or our adoptive father would beat our naked butts until we cried and screamed and blood appeared.

Steven got the worst of it. Even going to bed was no escape, for Ted was capable of pulling a child out of bed to get what he or she deserved.

Living at the beach was more expensive than living inland. Mom was a small heiress but she had to get a full-time job because Ted no longer brought in an income. He studied at home to be an insurance agent and most of the time he was in a bad mood.

I tried to avoid him when he was grouchy, but sometimes he trapped me. He grabbed my fingers to yank over the dusty tops of wall paintings. Cinderella wasn't doing her job. Mom went to work every day while Ted made notes in books at home, slurped coffee and dunked his cream cheese-slathered toast into the same brew while eating eggs covered in ketchup, just like in the army.

Mom left a list of after-school chores written down on paper. I made sure that Steven and I got our chores accomplished so Ted wouldn't yell at or spank us. Ted made a chore list for us too, but he kept it in his head. We were supposed to ask, "What do you want us to do, Daddy?"

Then he rattled off the tasks Mom had asked him to do before she drove off to work. I tried my best to protect Steven, but Ted liked to torment my brother at day's end. Sometimes I tried claiming credit for whatever "wrong" Steven had done so he wouldn't get hurt. It was hard to watch my little brother be spanked, or hear him cry all alone in his bed.

Strangely, when he was not mean or hateful, Ted tried hard to bond with me, if not Steven, and Mom most of all. One morning, as she

12

was on her way out the door to work, he grabbed her and French kissed her, the two of them swaying—and Mom struggling—next to the dining table where Steven and I were trying to eat our breakfast cereal. I almost spit out my corn flakes.

Soon after, Ted asked if I wanted to see my grandmother. My jaw must have dropped. He claimed peculiar things at times, like when he insisted tadpoles would grow in rainwater caught in a bucket. My third or fourth grade teacher had debunked the concept of spontaneous generation, but Ted insisted it was real science.

"I mean *my* mother," he said.

A mother? Where had he been hiding her? On that summer trip, when we had visited his cousins on a farm in Illinois, catching fireflies to keep in glass mason jars, there had been no mother among the family members, at least not one belonging to Ted. Now he had one?

"Sure," I said. "How come I haven't met her before?" After all, he had adopted us. His mother must be an adopted grandmother. He mumbled something about her not being often present. Okay, so she traveled a lot? Maybe having a new grandmother would fill in the painful loss of Nana.

We went to a trailer park and he told me to call the lady, whom I would meet in a moment, "Oma."

"That means 'grandmother' in German."

"Does she speak only German?" I asked.

Ringing the trailer doorbell, he assured me she spoke English. An elderly woman wearing bright red lipstick, a skirt and a sagging bra with no blouse or shirt covering it, opened the door.

"Hi Mama," said Ted.

"Hi Oma," I said.

Oma had dementia and couldn't remember how to get properly dressed. I felt sorry for her and for Ted. No wonder he had kept her hidden. Ted seemed to be reestablishing his family ties while trying to keep his marriage to Mom together. I was too young to say whether his efforts were reasonable. Being grouchy so often was definitely not helping.

I entered sixth grade in Newport Beach. The school was situated on the peninsula, and kids could see the waves crashing on shore through the wire fence while we played foursquare or shot baskets.

When the teacher asked who would show me around the school, Patti raised her hand. Patti was the butt of jokes for her brains, with jealous enemies like Ann, who taunted her. The wise teacher chose Patti from among those who raised their hands because as a stranger untouched by festering schoolkid prejudice, I was a good candidate to be Patti's friend. She needed one.

Patti came from brilliant parents—a father aerospace engineer who worked on the Apollo project and a mother anesthesiologist. It is hard to make friends when you are so smart studying takes all of five seconds. Patti had a photographic memory and could look at any page and remember it. Ann hated her, as did a few other mean kids.

I found Patti amazing. She became my 6th grade guru, and we solemnized the spirituality of our friendship by giving a full burial ceremony to a dead seagull found on the beach one foggy weekend morning.

She introduced me to musical wizards like Peter, Paul and Mary, the Mamas & the Papas, and Donovan in the temple of her little bedroom. While the record spun, she showed me the window next to her bed where a male hand once slid in, trying to grope the prepubescent female who lay there.

Together, we did arm pumping exercises, imagining the results would be a Sophia Loren hourglass figure. Patti chanted, "We must, we must, we must improve our busts!" Both of us stayed parked at "A" cup size for an eternity.

For the 6th grade talent contest, Patti talked me into accompanying her in singing "Jamaica Farewell," the two of us swaying in grass skirts while she strummed away on her guitar. Ann competed against us. Later known as "the voice," Ann won first place while Patti and I won third, helped by our parents' ballot box stuffing.

Ann stared down her nose at both Patti and me all that semester. I tried to avoid her on the playground, but one day, I found Ann, flanked by her toadies, standing in front of me. She smiled into my face.

"You're going to hell."

"What?" Disliking me or my choice of friends didn't give Ann the right to pronounce my eternal damnation. "What makes you say that?"

"I can tell by your eyes."

"What can you tell?"

"I am a born-again Christian," Ann explained, "and I have been taught what to look for in people's eyes. I can see you haven't been born again, so you are going to hell."

Someone could teach a kid how to do that? I was impressed even if this was not a conversation I wished to prolong. I went straight to the girls' bathroom and looked in the mirror, trying not to be obvious to anyone who walked in. I studied the pupils and corneas of my eyes closely but didn't see anything to indicate eternal damnation. No inflammation or dark spots. Surely hell clues weren't in the whites of the eyes? They weren't bloodshot or yellow. I looked healthy.

If being born again meant being cruel, I could do without it. Being born once was enough.

My family's narrow two-story house, from which I heard the surf breaking at night from my window, was right across the street from Ann's. That was at first an uncomfortable proximity to the girl who made claims to seeing souls. I preferred entering and exiting by our garage door, taking Via Palermo rather than Via Orvietto up or down the street to get somewhere.

In seventh grade, we students were told we could dress up for Halloween. I forgot about that permission until the morning arrived. Then I turned to the woman who knew everything, to save me.

"Mom! What shall I do? I don't have a costume!"

My mother gave it a thought, then reached into the foyer closet and pulled out an overcoat and hat belonging to Ted. She drew a mustache on my upper lip with charcoal. I was either Ted or a hobo. I looked idiotic.

Yet I was pleased. In chill autumn morning air, the coat sagged off my shoulders, and it was all I could do to keep it and the hat on while carrying my books. In those days, students did not use backpacks. On weekends and in between classes, all unnecessary books were kept in

15

lockers. Our books must have been thinner than nowadays because I do not remember my back or shoulders hurting.

At the bus stop, a bunch of kids were already waiting: Patti, the handsome and identical Baduini twins (with one of whom I was quietly in love for a good six months), my brother, Steven, Ann (who pretended not to see me or Patti), and a handful of other kids. Most wore an attempt at a costume.

I stuck my hand into my Ted the hobo right pocket and was surprised to find a metal item. It was an oblong silvery object attached to a black plastic handle with an on/off switch.

"What is this?" I asked of no one in particular, holding up the strange useless product. I pushed the switch "on." The metal object started vibrating. It struck me as quite funny.

"Well there's a useless item!" I said, watching it jiggle in my hand.

Patti grabbed my elbow hard and pulled me aside. Ann was staring at me with her nostrils flared, ready to throw her head back and laugh like she always did. A tall boy snickered and elbowed another kid whose lips raised to show his teeth.

"Put that away," hissed Patti. "Hide it. Put it back in your pocket."

"Why?"

"It's a dildo. A vibrator." Her breath tickled my ear. "Put it back and talk about something else."

I was mystified. "What is a dildo vibrator?"

Patti had never looked so stern. "I'll tell you later," she promised, "in the bus."

I slid the metal thing back in my pocket, and Patti kept her word.

Indeed, the school bus was an extracurricular classroom where brilliant Patti expounded fascinating theories about what made people the way they were. She gave me the lowdown on every kid living on Lido Island. There was a boy, for instance, who had gone from genius to

16

retard because his father made him study too much. He was reduced to making motorcycle noises.

After Patti explained vibrators, I was embarrassed and sure my mother had not known what was in the pocket. She had given me the coat Ted wore to work when it was cold. Why did Ted need this thing? According to Patti, it did not work with male anatomy.

The rest of the day was nerve-wracking, as I was preoccupied with trying to decide what to do with the metal vibrator. I secreted it in my locker, only to find Ann and her saintly associates watching me narrowly every time I went back to that stash for a change of books. You'd think they could find some weary travelers' feet to wash.

"Got your little sex toy?" I heard behind me as I climbed in the bus after school. Snickering followed. Patti was in front of me. I still had the metal thing deep in the coat pocket. It was the safest place for transport.

Seated next to Patti, who was conversing with someone, I opened my history book, suddenly keen to know more about British tax policies on the New World colonies. I did not look up until the bus came to my stop.

Getting off, I let Ann have a good lead before proceeding down Via Orvietto. I passed several houses before realizing I should have walked down Via Palermo. Too late. My gaze remained on the ground. That is when I saw the student paper lying on the sidewalk. It looked clean, as if it had just slipped out of someone's binder.

I saw the name "Ann" and picked it up. It was a returned vocabulary quiz with an A on top and doodling on the sides.

Oh wow.

She had written, "I repent."

At what point in the day had she written "I repent"? Was she sorry for making fun of Patti and me? Of assuming God's role?

I folded the paper and slipped it into my pocket. If a steamroller had been cruising down the street, I could have taken out the metal vibrator and tossed it to be smashed, but no such luck.

At home, a list of items Mom wanted from the store waited for me. Inspired by Ann's quiz, I hopped on the bike, still wearing the coat.

Right off the island was a church I had to pass before getting to the market. I left my bike in front and walked in. The place was empty, thank God.

After walking up the nave, I laid the metal vibrator upon the altar. Inspiration struck again, and I pulled out Ann's quiz, laying it next to the vibrator. She deserved a little credit with the Almighty.

Who knows what the preacher thought.

The winds of religious revival had whipped through our house as they had through Ann's. Ted and Mom had invited representatives of various Christian sects to speak to us on weekends. I remember Mom getting flustered because the Mormons wouldn't drink coffee, tea or wine. She couldn't think what to offer. Coffee, tea or wine were the best times of her day.

My brother and I were required to be present for each religious presentation. Sitting cross-legged on the floor while visitors from a new church droned on about stuff that wasn't Edgar Allen Poe or the Beatles might have been my most boring childhood memory if Ted hadn't come up with the idea of buying a large boat. It seemed a natural course of events subsequent to going bankrupt and moving to a beach town. There were boats in the bay around Lido Island, where Ted had moved us, and where Patti, Ann, and lots of my new schoolmates lived.

Boats became an obsession with Ted. He and Mom took their wine coolers to the end of the street and watched the weekend parade of sailboats go by. Mom knew how to sail from when she was a kid, visiting Balboa Island on weekends.

My brother and I were given a sabot, a two-seater dinghy (small boat) designed for young people. I did rather well in sailing lessons taken with Patti. She and I went out in the sabot, loving the spray of ocean water in our faces and our hair swirling in tangled energy masses. Sailing is fun on windy days, when weight placement in the vessel means everything. In a high wind, we had to sit on one side of the boat, sometimes leaning out to keep from capsizing, and of course we ducked when tacking (turning) so as not to get hit in the head by the moving boom. Patti pointed out strange vessels like Catamarans and named people sailing them.

Other times Patti and I lay on our surfboards, paddling them slowly around the island under lucky people's waterfront piers, where everything smelled like brine and mollusks until we got under the main bridge to the island, where the stench of Sulphur made us pinch our noses shut. We often forgot to apply sunscreen, burning the backs of our lily white legs bright red, so they hurt to bend when we sat in the classroom next day.

Ted had grander plans than a kids' sabot or the Lido-14, a six-seater sailboat, he sailed with my mother and friends. He wanted a cruiser to go deep-sea fishing with. To that end, we should all learn how to navigate. Then Ted, still unemployed, could buy the cruiser and in case he and Mom were occupied in the hold with the door bolted, Steven and I could navigate the ship.

If anyone thinks gym, chemistry or grammar is boring, they should try a navigation class at the age of twelve. The classes lasted three, four or fifteen hours each and were all held at night after dinner, when hastily consumed food was digesting in my stomach. Steven was considered too young to attend, but I had to since Ted said I inherited his IQ. Apparently it came with the adoption papers. Ted bought a captain's hat at the first class and wore it to every lecture. I wish the dreariness of those classes could be sold in pill form. Insomnia would be wiped out forever.

Meanwhile, music tamed savage beasts. In junior high, Ann, Patti and I found ourselves together under the direction of the junior high choral music master, Mr. Lynde.

A passion for music made us sing while the rock revolution, gripping the world, preached loving the one you're with. We all three had pianos, which we practiced. There was too much uniting us to keep us foes any longer. Pronouncing religious judgments upon others is an unrewarding undertaking, and I think Ann wanted friends, as most kids do. She let the matter of my damnation slide.

Condemnation has a similar bad effect on marriages. Ted was a jealous man and caused my mother much suffering. More than once, the morning light displayed how he had put his angry fist through the back of a chair or door. As their marriage deteriorated, he attempted to play the kid card. I came into my own room one day after school to find him sitting in my rocking chair, crying.

"Why are you crying, Dad?" I had never seen a grown man cry before, and certainly not the very man who wielded a paddle so sharply he could draw blood. Tears rolling down his cheeks were a phenomenon that didn't match my experience of his army personality.

I knew Ted to be a crafty crocodile, unexpectedly driving up to my summer school (right before 7th grade) with a toothy smile on his face. Patti and I had just returned from a full day of playing hooky, and I was relieved for having gotten back before Ted could notice. As soon as I got in the car, he smacked me hard across the face. My head hit the opposite window. At home, I was grounded for six months (made to stay at home except for school). All the Beatles posters I made with pastels were thrown in the garbage. My subversive hippy music was hidden in the foyer closet (where the coat came from) next to Ted's scores of *Playboy* magazines.

Still, this was also the man who claimed credit for saving my life, driving me to the hospital when I woke up in a sweat from a nightmare that an army was marching across my stomach. In the emergency ward, the doctor said my appendix had swelled up like a grapefruit and was ready to burst.

Ted's tears were deeply disturbing. I went downstairs to find my mother. "Why are you divorcing Dad? You made him cry!"

On a stepstool in the kitchen, Mom turned her head to look at me, her expression one of defeat.

After Mom left Ted, I was ill for almost a month in the eighth grade. We had moved off Lido Island to a less posh neighborhood. Mom worked full time, and the sailboats were sold. Luckily, I was still at the same school. Mr. Lynde took a song I had written, titled "Like Lovers," about the divorce my mother and Ted were headed for, and wrote it out for the entire choir. When I came back to school, he surprised me by having everyone sing it.

"It's your song," he said. "Which do you prefer for the spring concert? Do you want the choir to sing it or for you and Ann to sing it alone?" Love of music and proximity of houses had pulled Ann and I together.

"I prefer to sing it as a duo with Ann," I said. Mr. Lynde kindly allowed us to record that song on that year's record LP. Now I wish I had opted for his choir version. He was a gentle soul.

Mr. Lynde soon after announced that a whirlwind of musical influence, the indomitable Mrs. Galbraith, would appear on our campus the next week to audition candidates for the choral department of Newport Harbor High. Ann, Patti and I bit our fingernails in anticipation. What if one or two of us was accepted and the third not?

In our hearts, we worried that our trio would not survive the jealousy. Girls are silly to worry about such things. Friendships are like lizards' tails. They fall off and new ones grow.

The day arrived and with it, Mrs. Galbraith, her hair flaming red and steam rising off her skin from the passion for music that coursed through her veins. She had trained in New York, Vienna and other glittering cities. She was a madwoman of music.

Ann and I made it onto the list of new members for the "Chantelles." Not having a voice like Ann's, I do not know why Mrs. Galbraith chose me. Patti would be in the other two groups. On reflection, I realize that year's denial helped steel Patti's determination to become a lifelong creatively active musician, singer and piano teacher. Like her brother, Chris, born with a guitar in his hands, Patti has made a splash in her field.

If Mr. Lynde was a ray of light, Mrs. Galbraith was a blazing festoon of fireworks. She was a magnet, a Svengali who pulled anyone with an ounce of talent—not necessarily musical—into the choral music department to serve the greater purpose of performing vocal arts. She had studied opera somewhere, but managed to grow nodes on her vocal chords from over-training, the trauma of falling in love, smoking, or all three. Famous opera star Beverly Sills had been her classmate, but poor Mrs. Galbraith had not scaled the same heights (a point she glossed over). We heard her crooning along in her cigarette-lowered alto to all the arrangements she conducted.

Mrs. Galbraith had to hunt hard to get males to audition for the regular choir and the Madrigals. She allowed the talented males to do other things like conduct or accompany us on piano or guitar. For the years of her rule, Mrs. Galbraith pandered to student egos, choosing favorites for various projects. She made us all believe that no classes were more important than her extra-curricular ones.

21

With no children of her own, she usurped the position of many parents. By the end of my freshman year, if not sooner, Mrs. Galbraith became my mother's undeclared enemy.

Almost every teen in the choral music department lived for music and Mrs. Galbraith. Our parents became unimportant as Mrs. Galbraith oozed music from every pore of her body and made us swim in the stuff. She called rehearsals during weekends and early mornings before class. The wealthier parents were persuaded to donate their vacation homes for weekend rehearsal retreats, during which we sang and they bought the food, cooked and kept a respectful distance.

The Chantelles spent winter breaks at mountain cabin retreats our parents were forced to finance, but not allowed to visit. We did not ski or play in the snow. We sang. During the school year, Mrs. Galbraith shuttled us around, competing hither and yon. We were endlessly rehearsing on a bus going somewhere.

A girl who developed severe laryngitis was lambasted by Mrs. Galbraith for her psychosomatic illness. Apparently the laryngitis—though real—had been produced as an act of rebellion. The girl had to perform with us.

"How can she do that?" we asked.

"She will stand and mouth the words."

"What if she has a fever and can't stand?"

"Then two of you shall prop her up on either side. The show must go on." We felt like she was driving us straight to the Metropolitan Opera, stoking the fires of greatness. If she took our talent so seriously, by golly, so would we.

The only acceptable reason for not performing, Mrs. Galbraith said, was death. Cadavers did not look good on stage. In that case she excused us.

She found a way to have a special connection to every singer, so that the girl (or boy) in question felt irreplaceable. She assigned me the drawing of the program cover for our choral music department's winter performance of *Amahl and the Night Visitors,* an operetta by Gian Carlo Menotti. I made the paper mâché parrot that was carried by one of the three kings. Ann was given a singing lead.

Passion spun out from Mrs. Galbraith in luminescent threads. She could have been a Marvel Comics superhero, each one of us enthralled into submission. When she rehearsed us in singing *The Creation*, a rock cantata by David Bobrowitz and Steven Porter (lyrics adapted from Genesis in the Bible), Mrs. Galbraith shook her wild red locks and cried, "I don't care whether you are atheists at home, while you sing this gorgeous music, you *believe*!"

Her grasp caused us to neglect other abilities, other subjects. My English teacher, Mr. Ulander, had arranged visits to our classroom from television actors Anthony Zerbe and Roscoe Lee Browne, who enthralled us with poetry, and from science fiction writer Ray Bradbury. In my yearbook, Mr. Ulander wrote, "When are you going to free yourself from that diabolical music department and get down to some serious writing?"

In high school, teens are distracted by their friends. If I did not heed his words, it was largely Ann's fault. The apple of Mrs. Galbraith's eye took center stage wherever she went, even English class. In senior year, when Mr. Ulander selected students to be at his round table literature class (where he presided like King Arthur), Ann stole the show. She liked to cry out an author's name, then fling her upper torso into the center of the table, arms outreaching so that her fingers touched someone's typed papers. She lay with one cheek pressed down, dark tresses spread out like the floating locks of a drowned Ophelia. Mr. Ulander didn't stop her, so I guess her found her behavior acceptable.

Ann's amazing voice could be matched by her massive need for validation. Once she told a boyfriend (whom I met) that she had leukemia, just to see how he would respond. He broke down crying. She watched him stumble around red-eyed and shaken for a day or two, and then confessed she was fine.

When not emoting or singing, Ann invited groups of friends to eat at a Newport Beach restaurant chain her dad owned. She signed the check with her name and did not use cash. I thought she was going to be famous.

Being surrounded by so much talent was a dizzying, adrenalin-pumping sensation. To walk through any southern Californian neighborhood in the 70s was to hear fledgling rock bands practicing behind garage doors. Ann was a lead singer in the Newport Harbor High music department and with a rock and roll and blues band formed by

23

Patti's brother, Chris. Patti, too, played guitar and piano. Mrs. Galbraith's favorite male students, Joe, Gary, and Jerry, played various instruments, sang and composed and were so dazzling that the rest of us felt like turtles.

High school was cocooning me in an emotional turmoil. My mother realized she had to do something to help me regain my sense of self. She zeroed in on my fascination with languages.

As a small child, I had sometimes interfered with my little brother's cartoon craving. *George of the Jungle* is over? Good, click. Welcome Japanese soap opera. Scream. Kids didn't have multiple devices in the 60s. We had one TV in the living room and shared it.

When I enrolled in high school French, Mom started thinking about how to use that interest to help me. French class was the only place Mrs. Galbraith and Ann did not show up. The teacher was pleasant and un-pushy, and I received A's.

From out of thin air, my mother conjured a strange little woman with a heavy accent who knew people: European princesses and princes, daughters of international magnates, famed actors, film makers and South American coffee plantation owners. Mom took Patti and me to meet her. Patti dreamed of studying German in Austria, but her mother was too busy anesthetizing to attend the meeting and hear how to get her daughter placed in an Austrian boarding school. (How many children need a parent's attention instead of money? Patti said she might as well have been raised by wolves.)

The lady matched girls to appropriate schools in Europe. My mother warned me this European school broker would test us to see if we passed muster. We were all to have tea together. I had to hold my teacup properly, sit with my back straight and not slurp. I was to answer thoughtfully and articulate. Because I might not pass, you see.

Suddenly I wanted to. Oh, so much.

Madame was not very tall but towered over the tea party with her impeccable manners and bearing. She spoke to us in several languages. When Patti and I failed to answer in a heartbeat, she said, with sympathy, "If you are fortunate enough to go to Europe, you will learn to speak your second language *well*."

She might have been a German actress or impoverished aristocrat from Tsarist Russia, brandishing jewels and contacts. To me, she emphasized the desirability of attending a genteel girls' school in some converted castle of French-speaking Switzerland, where young European countesses, diamond mine owners' daughters and the offspring of sheiks came together. This was heady stuff. Suddenly Mrs. Galbraith's vocal music department seemed hopelessly mundane.

I realize now my great fortune. Up until that point, I was a typical high school kid plodding through life, distracted from my own abilities due to being hypnotized by a music teacher and overwhelmed by her favorites.

My mother bought me new luggage, warm clothes, and several pairs of gloves. Papa escorted me to Switzerland. Château Mont Choisi was everything this mysterious "Madame" had described it as and more. There, I was thrown in with girls from all over the world who spent, for a weekend's pleasure, the same amount as I received for half a year's allowance. To get me out of the grips of a teacher whom she saw as potentially harmful, Mom had to let me go free. In so doing, she taught me to pursue dreams on my own. I was not yet sixteen.

For almost three months, I spent long moments gazing out my bedroom window, looking up at the tall hills of Lausanne with tears rolling down my cheeks. The tears were not for Mrs. Galbraith; they were for my mother. I missed her cooking, her laughter, her prettiness, and her hugs. She missed me too. She was the only mother to bake cookies (some of them Italian, due to a new romance) and send them to Switzerland. Everyone on my floor of the château ate the cookies.

In addition to daily French classes and English with an American teacher who encouraged my writing, I took singing lessons with a Madame Goldenhorn in downtown Lausanne. Her father, Monsieur Goldhorn, came to our school to give piano lessons.

Mme Goldenhorn assured me that with six years hard work, I would be trained for the operatic world. My mother never contradicted this goal although it was a direct result of the steely Mrs. Galbraith controlling me from overseas. I intended to rejoin her classes in my senior year of high school, when I returned to Newport Beach.

My new best friend at the school was Suzanne, from Queens, New York. In the winter break, she and I went on an organized excursion with others of the girls to the German-speaking mountain resort of Zermatt. There we learned to ski.

I fell in love with one of the German-speaking Swiss horse-drawn sleigh drivers of Zermatt, named Matthias. He was handsome and smart, reading Herman Hesse and loving photography. The rest of the school year, I begged a German friend, Sybil, at the boarding school to translate my letters from English into German, which I painstakingly rewrote in my own handwriting, thereby learning a bit of German.

Suzanne was kind enough to accompany me by train to visit Matthias' village of Fiesch, founded in the 13th century. About 650 human beings lived there. As we walked through town, Matthias waved at half the people, all cousins.

Fiesch was so high in the Alps that in winter, the children either took the squeaking milk train down the slope or skied their way to school. Because it was spring, the mountainsides resembled green velvet, save for the highest reaches, covered in snow. White clouds moved across the sky, interspersed with sunlight that brightened the steep sides carpeted in wild flowers. Baby lambs leapt and danced in joy.

California seemed so different compared to Switzerland. This was what my mother wanted me to learn: "The world is bigger than Newport Beach."

I went home in June, leaving behind Alpine vistas and a unique young Swiss German man. Mrs. Galbraith was waiting. I had senior year before me. Mrs. Galbraith took it into her head that the Chantelles should dress like dancers in the *Folies Bergère*, wearing hot pants and kicking up their legs in unison. To this end, every girl was put on a diet and weighed once a week.

She asked me to teach French accents for songs we sang. Had Toulouse De Lautrec yet lived, Mrs. Galbraith would have manipulated him into the front row of the school auditorium, supplied him with a full bottle of absinthe and a sketch pad.

My lack of enthusiasm to be a showgirl was not lost on Mrs. Galbraith.

"Sylvia, would you come to my office after class?" she said in honeyed tones at the beginning of the semester, winking at one of her favorite male students, who held a baton in his hand.

26

"I want to hear all about your year in Switzerland."

I followed her into the office, naïve as a puppy enticed by a biscuit. She asked me if I appreciated her shift to all things Francophone.

"It was a choice made as a special acknowledgement of your return to the department."

"Thank you, Mrs. Galbraith." I hesitated, then decided to be brave. "Being a dancer in hot pants on stage isn't really my dream. Singing is fine, but I've always been the worst in ballet class because I can't balance on one foot." That was true. I had been terrible in ballet class in Switzerland. Suzanne had been great.

Mrs. Galbraith's neck and cheeks flushed as red as her hair. For a moment she was speechless with fury, then she blurted: "You are a *selfish* little bitch who walks on people to get what she wants!"

The hairs on the back of my neck stood up and my eyes widened. How could she say that? What had *I* done to her?

Mrs. Galbraith was sitting in a chair pulled out from the desk, kicking her leg. She yelled, her voice so shrill everyone heard, and at the same time, she blocked my passage to the door.

I suspect she mistook me for my mother.

The poisonous effect of her words penetrated my heart.

"I am sorry, Mrs. Galbraith." I remembered a lady does not get mad. A lady stays calm. "I will *not* be remaining with the Chantelles." The back of the chair felt hard with me pressed against it, regretting having followed her into the office. I stared down at my clasped hands.

For a brief instant, Mrs. Galbraith showed regret. "Don't leave," she pleaded. "I'll let you conduct!"

It must have been hard for her to make that offer since she reserved the honor for the guys. I cannot understand why she wanted me to stay. I had no great voice and performed no important service, save, perhaps, to her ego.

I withdrew from classes with Mrs. Galbraith and enrolled in choral music at the local community college. I tried to teach Mom how to say things in French.

27

Over the moon in relief at my break with Mrs. Galbraith, my mother reciprocated with knowledge on wine and cooking. She had recently married a man who loved cooking as she did. Their romance had blossomed over the gas range when Don came over to our house to make chili. Don's parents had both emigrated from Italy. Mom had joined my European experience.

After my high school graduation, Mom and Don got married. There were but a few tiny snags to this happy time. One was the news from Mom that my brother and I were illegitimate.

"How can you say that? You were married to Dad."

"In the Catholic Church," she said, "to which I have returned, that marriage doesn't count. I am very sorry."

She had converted to Catholicism as a teenager while living with nuns at Flintridge Sacred Heart Academy. If she wanted me to help shoulder her guilt for leaving the pope, she failed. Mom and the pilgrims on the Mayflower had taught me to believe in freedom of worship.

"Can't you just say you used to be Episcopalian? That your children were born in that church?"

"No, I can't."

Whatever floats your boat, I thought. She was still my loving mother.

Although Dad had reappeared in our lives, pressing Mom to remarry him, she decided they were better off friends. He accepted her choice of new husbands with grace. He came over almost every day to teach Steven how to fix cars. Dad said he loved Mom no matter whom she married. Steven got sent to a military boarding school for a year and he hated it. I went back to Switzerland to continue voice lessons.

Don was a cool guy. For a Halloween party he and Mom hosted, he wrapped himself up like a mummy and walked to our house, crossing a big street that way, because he couldn't bend his legs to sit in his car.

I believe he stopped traffic.

Don and Mom became co-managers of a restaurant called The Lost Mine in northern California and moved north, far away from the wiles of Mrs. Galbraith, whom I would encounter only once more, after I had become a Red Sea Bride.

Chapter 2
Changing Worlds

My potential as an opera singer was littered with cigarette butts. All the girls met at the Swiss boarding school had smoked. Ashtrays had been forbidden, but the girls let their cigarettes die out balanced on their filter ends. I had picked up the nasty habit.

My friend Suzanne, who smoked since she was 11, came back to Lausanne in the same year I did. She enrolled at École des Beaux Arts and I, at the Lausanne Conservatory of Music.

"You smoke," said Mme Goldenhorn during my second lesson. "I can hear it in your voice. You will have to throw away your cigarettes if you want to be an opera singer."

I imagined a burning desire to be an opera singer, despite Mrs. Galbraith no longer being my mentor. It would be cool to send her a little note from, say, a job singing at the La Scala Opera House in Vienna.

Mme Goldenhorn now presented me with my first challenge of self-discipline. Suzanne was no help. I walked down the hill to her flat from my boarding house, Château de Vennes, and told her the ultimatum

Mme Goldenhorn had given me. Suzanne contemplated my predicament, puffing out smoke rings.

"Want one?" she asked, pushing her pack towards me. Suzanne thought everything was funny. "It's no different than my not understanding what my teachers are saying in French."

I didn't laugh. "Why don't you work harder on learning French?"

"Why should I?" she asked. "You've always been around when we go out to eat. You order the meal, so I don't have to study."

Many of the young people at Château de Vennes smoked. Danielle Junod and her mother, two delightful ladies who ran the boarding house, were more focused on the rule about our leaving the door of our bedrooms open when male and female students were in the same room than on whether we smoked.

Except for opera singers, Europe felt like a world of cigarette smokers. French guys studying engineering in Lausanne walked around puffing on Gaulois, a cigarette so cool it didn't have filters.

My grandfather came to Lausanne to find me twiddling my thumbs, not attending the Conservatoire de Musique. He enrolled me at École Lemania to continue French studies.

Chips were falling into place. I liked studying French. Suzanne did not fare so well with art school, partly because of an anti-Jewish director and because she got sick as a dog during winter exams. I found her, one day, feverish in her apartment, with a temperature threatening to ascend beyond 104 Farenheit.

I called the hospital. A nurse instructed me to get my friend in the bathtub and give her a sponge bath in vinegar, wrapping vinegar-soaked rags around her extremities. It took days before she got better.

The art school director sent Suzanne a letter telling her to "find happiness in another profession," but my friend was tenacious. She reapplied and made it through to the end of the year at École des Beaux Arts, doing well, going on to study at C.W. Post College in New York. Like Patti, Suzanne was full of interesting information. Religions, romance and rock music were her favorite subjects.

I had never heard of Islam before meeting Muslims in Switzerland. "Oh, Islam is similar to Judaism!" exclaimed Suzanne, "Both religions focus on the concept of One God." Raised Jewish, Suzanne had fallen in love with a Christian. (Eventually she became Catholic. Then she married a Buddhist from Japan who moved her to California where she found a career in a private school working for an Iranian Catholic with a Muslim husband.)

At the end of that second year in Lausanne, my heart was broken by a French boy and I came home with a mention of « très honorable » (*summa cum laude*) on my Diplôme d'Alliance Française.

Tired of her daughter being so far away, Mom rejoiced to find the Monterey Institute of Foreign Studies only a couple of hours from her house. There I enrolled.

She and Don opened a French restaurant in Saratoga, California, both serving as chefs. They ordered langoustine (a slim, orange-pink lobster) from Spain and blue prawns from Maui. Don's Italian mother, Elvira, came in twice a week to make cannelloni and cannoli. The most popular dessert was Mom's French silk pie, intensely chocolate, which the restaurant served with espresso.

My mother read cook books like other people read detective novels. The restaurant was named *Le Mouton Noir*, "The Black Sheep," a term used to describe a disreputable family member. She hung my poem on the subject, in French, in the establishment's foyer.

Patti and Ann had both moved to northern California for college. Patti warned me, when I next saw Ann, to not go into shock. "The Voice" had anorexia in the wake of her parents' divorce and her father's remarriage, giving him new children and interests. She was no longer a star, but a waif.

For a few years, while Ann attended UOP in Stockton to study music, Mom consented to inviting her to our home on the weekends. I hoped accepting Ann into my own family would help her get over her depression. At the end of each weekend, Ann drove off to sing and I, to study French and world culture.

In my second semester at the Monterey Institute of Foreign Studies, a batch of male students arrived from Saudi Arabia to learn English. Two were princes. I had heard of Saudi Arabia.

A girl in my English class at Chateau Mont Choisi had been the daughter of Zaki Yemeni, the Saudi minister of petroleum. Later, at

Chateau de Vennes, two girls and their little brothers would prove to be my future Saudi husband's distant relatives. (I did not know that then.) In France, I had watched a bemused Saudi prince at a casino in France lose half a million dollars in thirty minutes. Employees had roped off the section so viewers could not get too near the prince and his lovely blonde companion. The smile had never faded from the man's lips.

Between classes at the Monterey Institute of Foreign Studies, six to eight or nine Saudi boys leaned on their sports cars just next to the school's mail office. Whenever female students walked to the mailroom, that group of Saudi boys meowed like cats and made kissing sounds in the air. We girls began waiting for them to go back to their classes before retrieving our mail.

One of my French teachers, a *pied noir*, had grown up in Algeria, tried to explain the culture gap to us:

"You cannot be too angry with them. They do not know how to act. They come from a rigid society where women seldom walk in the streets. In cities, women stay at home or go by car that a man drives to a doctor's office, shopping center or villa, and even then, it is with fabric covering them from head to toe."

That sounded very strange. None of the Saudis I met in Switzerland had told me about that. Maybe they didn't want anyone to know?

The *pied noir* French teacher added that the boys hanging out near the mailroom came from desert villages. "They feel like they are on another planet, seeing women moving around in society." We girls calmed down. Most of us were interested in other cultures; that was why we studied foreign languages. Of course our male peers in class didn't really care since the Saudi boys hadn't bothered *them*.

One day a group of foreign ESL students trooped past my French classroom. A bunch of Saudis were mixed in. The tallest of the young men paused to scrunch his eyes up through the window. I thought, "My Lord, who is that?" He was the most handsome of any of the young Saudi men, and in truth, of all the young men at the school. He resumed walking with his group, leaving a few of the girls in my classroom tittering in excitement. We had not seen him before.

"Do you know who that is?" I asked a classmate.

34

"No, but I can get his name!" she exclaimed. "I talk to one of the Saudi students a lot." Not long after, she told me the tall young man's name was "Malik." Malik means "king."

The name fit. He stood out for his athletic build, beautiful eyes and dazzling smile. Other Saudis clustered about Malik, competing for his attention. Yet his eyes were mine whenever I passed, blushing, and his voice remained stilled though a throng of compatriots pressed around with jokes and laughter.

One Friday afternoon he blurted, in a melodious accent, "Have a nice weekend, Sweet Angel." The young Saudi men near him (not the same who stalked the mailroom) fell silent. I murmured "thank you" and floated to my car.

He frequented my thoughts that weekend as I sunbathed under an apple tree in my tiny Carmel garden. My pretty little gray cat, Alceste, vied for my attention, hopping in and out of the cottage window. She was torn between me and her newborns. I had named her after a grouchy male human character in a French play even though she was female, friendly and furry. Alceste was so trusting and affectionate she jumped on the hood of my car whenever I slowed to a stop in front of my cottage. I tried to make her stop.

The next week, Malik called to ask me out. I do not know how he got my phone number and I was too distraught to care. The night before, Alceste had gone missing. Her kittens had been mewing for food for hours. I searched through the streets from dawn, feeling my heart race. At 8 am, I began dialing the numbers of veterinary clinics. At last a receptionist described a cat brought in from a hit-and-run. I heard a recognizable meow in the background. It was Alceste.

"That's her! I'll be right there." I scribbled down the address and hopped in my car.

The clinic was deserted and chilly, with a steely antiseptic odor. "The gray cat is mine," I said, leaning against the countertop. "Whatever you need to do, I'll pay for it." I knew my mother would help me with money if necessary. I wanted to see Alceste, so my pet could know I had found her and would take care of her.

The receptionist looked at me with big eyes, blinked and cleared her throat.

"I'm so very sorry. Your cat has just died."

I was eighteen year old. Alceste had been my dearest little friend. I sat down and cried. Soon, however, I stood up, remembering the tiny, motherless kittens that waited in feverish hunger. They would die if I did not nurse them.

It was definitely not the right day for Malik to call and ask me out. Yet he did. "I can't," I said, sobs choking my words. "Alceste died. I—I need—a few days to grieve."

"Oh!" his voice was warm. "I am *so* sorry. Who is Alceste?"

"My cat."

I was too naïve to understand the silence that met me on the other end of the line.

In Saudi Arabia, cats were all feral. In Malik's parents' generation, wild, mangy street cats snuck into homes. Their broods could be found under beds or staircases—wherever shelter from the desert presented itself to an expectant mother cat. The kindest people tolerated the creatures until the kittens were big enough to be shooed out.

Most Saudis of the 20th century found street cats as endearing as the pop-eyed pink geckos that hang by suction cup feet on walls. Few in Jeddah, Malik's home town, would get emotional about a cat except when kicking it out of the house. Malik wasn't sure if I was rejecting him or making fun of him. Much later I learned that he and his siblings grew up with a dog whom they loved. Unlike many urban Saudis, their father taught them to enjoy and care for animals. Cats, however, were not common pets during Malik's youth, so it was as if I had said I could not go out with him because a fish in my aquarium or a lizard on my front porch had died.

He almost didn't call back.

Despite these gaps in understanding, we fell in love. Our conversations were fascinating. Malik talked with me for hours on a subject many young Western men found dull, taboo or mythological— God and the unseen world. Malik's perspective was significantly different.

36

I had read about Islam in my 8th grade world religions class, but when I expressed interest in Muhammad, the teacher assured me that he was a false prophet. [2] Malik didn't try to convert me; he simply answered my questions. He told me about angels, created of light, who accompany us throughout life, recording our actions without interference. Jinn, he explained, were beings made of smokeless fire.

Like humans, jinn are allowed free will to choose their paths in life. In folklore and literature, the West knows them as devils or "genies," putting a fanciful spin on their supernatural abilities. The prophet King Solomon commanded jinn who were under his power. Jinn, like people, can incline to good or evil. (Becoming a devil is a choice of the soul, whether that soul belongs to a human or a jinni.) Angels, by contrast, are created by God to be obedient. It is not in their nature to choose rebellion.

When we didn't speak of the unseen, Malik spun an exotic cultural tapestry, narrating stories of his boyhood in Jeddah. We spent a lot of time introducing our cultures to each other through food. He constructed an outdoor underground oven using a large, high-fired, oval-shaped water container he found in a garden shop. After planting that container in a cement base, he surrounded it with bricks and mortar. Then he cut out an opening.

In this "oven," he made *sambusak*, a traditional Saudi meat pie. In return, I cooked beef stroganoff and veal Marsala. I taught him tennis so he could play with me. When he saw me painting, he asked to have a go, then painted a scene of Arab boys waving to a boat with a lateen sail in the Jeddah harbor.

Like many Saudi students who have come to the West, he took to cultural hobbies and interests as if born to them. He had physical courage that was hard to match. Once he swam across the Ubhur Lagoon in Jeddah on a dare. When at last I saw that lagoon, I was staggered.

One day we walked down the hill from the Monterey Institute to have lunch downtown by the water. Seagulls circled overhead, scavenging for discarded sandwiches or chips, while the faint bark of

---

[2] Peace be upon him. Muslims say these words when any of the prophets recorded in Scripture are mentioned, from Adam to Moses and Jesus, etc. Peace be upon them all and upon the prophet Solomon mentioned subsequently. Ameen.

seals floated off the bay. The sun had broken through the fog and we saw the ocean's sparkling blue waters sparkling. Such magnificent afternoons etch a permanent memory for college students.

I had chosen to wear a narrow red skirt and matching sweater. Malik seemed appreciative. "Do you know everyone is looking at you?" he asked. I wasn't sure if that was bad or good.

Malik had dated other Western young women before me. A Saudi Airlines scholarship had earlier sent him to the Midwest, and he had met a girl there who had changed his life, though I knew nothing of her at first. Now he was on a scholarship from the Saudi government.

One day I knocked at his door, as planned, to go to a movie. He answered, but went inside to answer the phone. I waited outside because the day was beautiful. When he did not come out again, I returned to his front door and opened, entering to the sound of sobs. What was this? Malik was a very manly sort of guy, not one given to weeping, yet his face was wet with tears, like someone whose dream has shattered.

"What is wrong?"

"She found me."

The story came out in broken bits: While attending school in the Midwest, Malik had attracted the obsessive attention of a young woman named Jean. Muscular, blonde and domineering, she had a black belt in karate. Seeing him in class, she stalked him to his room at the university and began a relationship.

Malik was Muslim, but he was also a male cut free from his country, desperate to run into the stereotypical "loose" Western woman his elders railed so angrily against. Jean offered herself as the real deal, and within a month or so, she was pregnant.

As tall as Malik when she wore heels and possibly as strong, Jean rarely left his room. She dropped all her classes halfway through the first semester. She was not inclined to studies or a job. An indulgent father paid her bills.

"I got tired of her always being there. I never asked her to move into my room!" he told me. Finally Malik insisted Jean leave, only to come back from class that day to find all his personal belongings on the rooftop.

Despite being pregnant, she was dressed in her karate clothes, ready for a fight.

"You can't get rid of me. I am the mother of your unborn baby!"

Jean's father, an airline pilot, met with Malik and asked him to give the child a name by marrying his daughter. He offered to buy Jean and Malik a house. Malik agreed to marry Jean, provided it was understood he wanted a divorce after the baby was born.

"That's why I gave up the scholarship," Malik explained. "I was willing to take legal responsibility, but I couldn't stay with Jean. I went back to Jeddah and gave up the scholarship. You don't know what she's like."

I soon learned. She threatened to come to California, wanting to live with Malik even though divorce proceedings went into effect after the birth of their daughter. She also wanted cash and lots of it. Money quieted her.

Over the years and despite the adoption of the little girl, Lujain, by Jean's father, Jean tracked us by phone, insisting on and demanding more and more money. She was strangely abusive to me, calling me "Snow White" for reasons I have never understood.

Malik visited his daughter, bringing gifts and spending all he had. He claimed there was nothing he could do about Jean's father adopting Lujain, for he could not afford a lawyer. I was a little surprised by what struck me as passivity. After a few years, Jean found another Saudi and did the same thing, having another child. Then she got a full-fledged pimp and had a third child.

While I felt sorry about Malik's experience, I couldn't help but wonder why so many young Saudi men insisted of thinking of Western girls as joy rides. Maybe Jean filled the bill, but I knew no other woman like her.

There were other cross-cultural love stories like mine and Malik's, but the general male Saudi student attitude towards women in the West did not seem romantic.

For instance, once while Malik and I sat with a few of his friends at a café, some girls walked by on the sidewalk. Malik's Saudi friends said, "*Lehem*" and laughed.

"What does *lehem* mean?" I asked.

"It means 'meat."

We were drinking coffees and teas, but no one had ordered meat. It took a moment to understand "meat" meant the girls. I wasn't happy about that. Malik said his friends were being silly.

I decided to learn Arabic. It was not offered at the Monterey Institute of Foreign Studies, strangely, though the school seemed to offer every language under the sun. An Arabic class *was* offered at nearby community college, taught by Professor Khalidy, a native of Lebanon. Professor Khalidy confided later that he had been driven out of the Monterey Institute by teachers who wanted Arabic taught by non-Arabs (or not at all).

Professor Khalidy introduced his students to Middle Eastern issues and counseled us when, in our dealings with Arab people, we could not grasp cultural differences. Like many Lebanese, he served as a bridge of understanding between Arabia and the West. He showed slides of his war-torn homeland. I became interested in world politics.

At the language institute, I took a class on Israel's kibbutz system and a second on the making of Palestine. I acquired a Turkish female roommate named Gizem, who taught her native tongue at the nearby Defense Language Institute for military personnel. Gizem was preparing a group of American students working for the CIA to infiltrate her homeland under Turkish identities.

When visiting home, I asked my mother for her perspective on the Israeli-Palestinian dilemma. She had trouble finding words and could not form an answer. I repeated my query, boiled down to basics: "From what you have heard, Mom, who are the good guys and who are the bad guys?"

"The Israelis are the good guys and the Palestinians are the bad guys."

Was it that easy to sum up? Loving my mother, I wanted to hear her say that all human beings deserve understanding and compassion.

My mother knew I was dating a Muslim, yet she had quickly stated that the Muslims—Palestinian or otherwise--were the "bad guys." Malik had warned me. He liked Americans very much, but he said we did not sympathize with Muslims in international conflicts. I had defended my culture's ability to be fair.

*   *   *   *

With a Bachelor's degree in French achieved, I made a round of sad farewells, none sadder than the one between Malik and me. According to plan, I was going to Paris to study international journalism. That career path thrilled, but I was heartbroken to leave Malik. We tried to be mature about breaking up. How could there be any other way for us?

A couple of Malik's friends had urged him to marry me. "My mother would never accept that," he explained to me sadly on our last meetings. "She would say you are not 'clean.'"

I stared at him. Really? Then what would she say about Malik's relationship with Jean, or for that matter, about Malik's younger brother Hisham, who had no sooner come to Monterey than he had started a relationship with our landlady, who happened to be his teacher?

"Don't feel bad," I responded coolly. "I was always planning on being a foreign correspondent. I never wanted to give that career dream up."

In Paris, I reconnected with old friends, made new ones, and took refresher classes in French. I met writers, including a young journalist conducting a series of interviews with the philosopher Jean-Paul Sartre.

Despite the intellectual stimulation, my heart and mind were distracted by the concept of God Malik had shared with me. I had begun to perceive myself as "Muslim," one who "submits" to God. I missed the stories of family and old Jeddah that Malik told so well, and through which he had ushered me into a vibrant, foreign past.

Malik missed me too, writing, *"To my only love, forever I am wondering, how should I start this letter? I don't know what to say except that I have just lost my pearl. My life has started to show a huge change. . . . Sylvia, everybody loves you here. Hossean, Aijaz, Essam—they all miss you, and Hossean even asked for your address, which I gave to him. I love and will never forget you, and I will help you whenever you ask (whatever you need, and at any time). Sleep well, relax and be sure that you are not forgettable. May the Peace of the Lord Almighty be upon you, wherever you go. Your slave, Malik."*

One day we spoke on the telephone while I was in France. It was the Muslim holy month of Ramadan, and I was trying to fast (abstain from food during daylight hours to develop spiritual enlightenment) and he was surprised at my effort.

Abruptly he proposed marriage, painting a prospect of bright possibilities: I could pursue a master's degree in San Diego after we married. Once he managed to obtain the elusive permission for our marriage, I could teach at King Abdul Aziz University for Women.

Everyone in Jeddah, he assured me, would love me as much as he did. What a fascinating future I would enter with this handsome, spiritual, funny, intelligent, and ambitious Saudi man!

His proposal felt like the answer to my prayer for guidance. I returned to Monterey without telling my mother[3] because I was afraid she would try to stop me.

Mom had been gracious about my having a Saudi boyfriend while I was studying at the Monterey Institute. Whenever I had driven back to the coast from her house, she had let me stop at Fishermen's Landing to pick up a lobster from her seafood supplier and put it on her restaurant bill, knowing I would share it with Malik. She had sometimes sent the odd bottle of fine wine or round of good cheese back for me to share with Malik.

However, I knew my mother would not like me to move to the other side of the world. Her dismay would be harsh. A future as an international journalist is not the same thing at all as a daughter cutting herself off in a backwards Arab kingdom.

---

[3] It was the era of the Moonies, when Sun Myung Moon, founder of the Unification Church, presided over mass marriages in the USA after allegedly brainwashing young people. American parents had begun resorting to kidnapping their own children to hold them captive until they were "deprogrammed."

My mother's joy had been palpable when I achieved a college degree, something no one in the family had done in living memory.

Malik was scared, too, because of a strict Saudi law banning marriage to foreigners. He could be imprisoned for years if our marriage was found out before he had permission. His family would blame me.

After being back in the States a week or two, I began writing letters to my mother, begging her forgiveness for changing my plans. Despite my difficult decision, I adored her. I explained that marriage to Malik was not only for love but because Islam was my new faith. Finally she agreed I could visit her.

When I got back home, Mom refused to go outside her house with me. She was embarrassed to be seen with a daughter who wore a scarf on her head like Queen Elizabeth on a foggy day. I understood her feelings. My conversion was so recent that even I was groping my way, trying to get used to it. I loved fashion, and scarves over my hair made me feel frumpy.

"How will Malik's parents like to have a spoiled Californian girl as a daughter-in-law?" my mother demanded.

Was I spoiled? I would try not to be.

My grandfather had a few questions to ask before disowning me: "Did Sylvia marry a prince?"

Malik, alas, was not a prince. My insurance-selling grandfather had feasted on grilled sheep eyeballs with a couple of royal Bedouin clients. Blue blood and wealth are a sauce that make anything palatable.

Lacking the regal connection, I was a disgrace. I wrote to Ann, still in Stockton, begging her to cheer and console my mother.

Ann, whom I had adopted into my family as a sister, replied, "Don't ask me to be there for your mother. I release you from friendship with my non-Muslim love."

We were back on the playground and I was once more condemned.

Mom wrote to me, "I do not want you to die, but I never want to see you again."

Dad wrote, "All religion is hypocritical and your choices are stupid."

To Malik's family, I remained a secret.

Chapter 3

Luck of the Irish

I was not the only Californian girl to wound her mother by marrying an Arab and converting to Islam. After Malik and I moved to San Diego, Kate, a first-generation American-Irish girl who dressed like a gypsy, showed up at my door. She was a statuesque beauty with long, flowing reddish-brown hair, freckles, an upturned nose and cornflower blue eyes. She had found her way into a Middle East that had taken root with its music, food, hookahs, and religions on Californian soil.

A few years older than I, Kate was a flower child who had married and had a baby at seventeen. Life as a young housewife of a big rig-driving husband swiftly lost appeal. Kate left with her child for a houseboat in Sausalito. There she studied yoga and modern dance and attended California's first Renaissance Fair.

When her daughter, Jenny, was a toddler, Kate enrolled in a community college. Her classes included a course in Russian language taught by a sophisticated Israeli-American named Paul. They fell in love and married. Here began Kate's fascination with Middle Eastern thought and culture. She was absorbed and overlooked Paul's interest in his female students, which continued when she was no longer one of them.

Kate opened a yoga studio in San Diego, enrolled in Middle Eastern history classes and at night went to see belly dancing. Sometimes Paul accompanied her. One evening at a San Diego club, the drummer of the performing Arab music troupe urged Kate, who was swaying in her seat, to get up on stage and dance. It did not take much coaxing.

Perched on a stool at the bar was Mustafa, the swarthy Palestinian with an infectious laugh who promoted San Diego's Middle Eastern dance festivals. A renowned solo dancer, he captivated audiences with a specialty from the south of Egypt known as the "cane dance." This specialty had once readied warriors for battle. It required concentration and skill when the dancer chose to wield the original long, heavy staffs.

As Kate began to dance, Mustafa sat bolt upright. Then the club's star male dancer jumped off the stool and bounded onstage to dance with the Irish lass. The crowd went wild. When the musicians laid down their instruments, Mustafa left the club without a word. He commented to friends whom he knew would circulate his words, "I could make her a star."

Word did get back and Mustafa became Kate's teacher—and lover.

One morning, Kate went home to the apartment she still shared with Paul. Their marriage had cooled as his roving eye found new girlfriends. When he was home, they slept in separate rooms, barely speaking.

Now she wore the long white garment of Arab Gulf men, called a *thobe,* which Mustafa had received as a gift from a Saudi prince. She also wore a Middle Eastern engagement ring and bracelet that Mustafa had given her.

"What is this get-up?" Paul demanded.

"I'm leaving you," said Kate. She went off to shower, got ready for the yoga studio, and left the apartment.

After teaching class, she sat at her desk. Through a window, she saw Paul drive up, slam his car door and wipe a white cloth over her own parked vehicle. He flung the cloth down, stamping and smearing it on the street with his feet. Kate waited until he drove away before she went outside.

The white cloth was the thobe she had worn home.

When she moved out, Mustafa arrived to help transport furniture. Paul stood in their path. "I want everyone to know you're stealing my wife!" he screamed.h

"I'm not stealing her—you abandoned her! She wants to be with me."

"Damn you!" cried Paul, "You just wait. Pretty soon she'll be talking to you about your home, your land, your people . . . about going back to your roots!"

"I can't go back there," retorted Mustafa. "Your people took our land."

Kate understood she had crossed a political border.

*   *   *   *

At San Diego State University, I read the writings of Ibn Battuta and Ibn Khaldun, ancient writers from North Africa. Malik and I wanted to visit North Africa, to see its beauties and import goods to help ourselves and our Muslim friends who were struggling financially. Malik didn't have money, but I knew someone who did.

My mother was estranged from me, yet she allowed me to convince her, in a single phone call, to let me have enough money to try out this project.

On my first morning in Casablanca, the haunting call to prayer drew me out of bed before daybreak. The words of the chant had been indiscernible the day before in the rush of traffic. Now in the predawn stillness, when discothèques had long closed and the number of cars passing under street balconies in a half hour could be counted on one hand, the words were chiseled with a craftsman's precision into the cool darkness. "Allahu Akbar" or "God is great" sounded like a song of love by the human being for his Creator.

The *souks*, or open air marketplaces, of Morocco were scenes from a tale by Scheherazade. A heady distillation of smells assailed my nose. Scents of natural dyes, perfume oils, and spices at open-air markets mixed with wafts of sweat from pack-carrying donkeys. The rank rot of whatever filth collected in puddles along the winding, narrow streets was relieved by the delightful mustiness of tiny bookstores lined with publications in Arabic and French.

In between all these smells, mouth-watering odors of lamb kebobs sizzling over street grills beckoned clients to tiny street stands where diners hazarded the well-being of their stomachs.

On the train between towns, I practiced pronunciation of Qur'anic verses under Malik's tutelage. Burnoose-clad passengers nodded in approval. In the mosques, Malik listened to Moroccans chant the tale of the Prophet Muhammad's life, a practice forbidden in Saudi Arabia, he said.

Morocco was so beautiful, I thought, that if Saudi Arabia were like it, I could be fine. I did worry, at times, about my marriage and my decision to embrace the Middle East. Was it like Morocco?

We met rug merchants who had groups of little girls, aged 7 through 12, weaving on looms in upstairs rooms.

"What about school?" I asked.

"Oh yes, they have classes here and then work on the looms to earn extra money for their families." I wondered if the merchants might be lying.

We signed contracts with a manufacturer of ornate hanging lamps, with a merchant selling round brass tables, and with a dealer in pointed leather slippers and woolen Berber hooded jackets. Everything was to be shipped to the USA. Starting a business was exciting and scary. I wanted my mother to be proud of me.

One evening, while awaiting the train to Marrakech, Malik and I chose to sleep on benches at the station instead of spending the night in a hotel, in order to save money.

When I stepped into the women's restroom, a horde of mosquitoes rose off the walls to greet me. I pulled the long sleeves of my Indian cotton tunic over my hands and the elasticized cuffs of my thin cotton pants down over my feet, hoping to protect myself from bites. I rewound my headscarf so that my whole head was covered. I held my arms over my face, thinking that if the mosquitoes could penetrate cloth, better they should get my arms than my face.

Next morning, a red, a puffy red mass ran from either shoulder all the way down to the wrists. My legs were likewise swollen with bites.

"Look, Malik!"

Mosquitoes find my blood an inebriating cocktail, and the hundreds that lived at the train station got through the flimsy weave of my garment without a problem.

Rubbing ice on my arms and legs helped a little, but the train ride was an endless demand for cold drinks to hold on my skin. By the time we got to Marrakesh and had left our suitcases at a cheap hotel to walk along the streets of the city, the buildings were tilting and spinning.

Malik didn't know how feverish I was. "You act like I am a policeman!"

There may have been a certain woodenness in my march and a dullness to my eyes. Malik was excited to explore this historical city, so I was trying my best to act alive although every pause found me staggering towards a wall to lean against.

When I had nowhere to lean but on Malik, he put his hand on my forehead. "You're hot. Maybe you should go back to the hotel. I'll take you."

"No," I mumbled. "Go ahead and look around. I can return by myself."

"Are you sure?"

I forced a smile.

We separated. My leaden feet dragged me back to the place we had left our bags. The streets floated, but the little hotel at last

49

materialized through the haze. I got inside and then stood, appalled, in front of a staircase. How was I to climb it?

I put one foot on the first step and strained to pull with my hands on the rail up the blue tile-covered staircase. Climbing took forever. I was limp and dizzy. It was too bad the woven rugs and tasseled camel bags displayed on the walls were the last things I might ever see.

Up in the room, fear took hold. High fevers can result in death. I had no aspirin or Tylenol. I would not be able to descend those steps to the street again, not if it meant climbing back up.

I ran a cool bath and got in somehow without breaking my neck. My fever warmed up the cool water in no time. At some point I felt Malik's hand upon my brow.

"Malik?"

The room was empty. I blinked and he was back, laying cool, wet cloths upon my forehead. I was on the bed, with no recollection of moving there. A local doctor knocked on the door and came in with a creased leather bag. He gave me shots, handed Malik a prescription, and left. Malik held my hand.

"I don't like being hot," I whimpered. "Will it be so hot in Saudi Arabia?"

"When we live in Jeddah, you'll have air conditioning. I'll build you a courtyard with a fountain like the ones we've seen in the Kasbahs. We'll cover it with blue clay tiles. We'll plant fragrant flowers like Jasmine and Queen of the Night."

His words were comforting. Secretly he worried I would die and he would have to send my body back to my mother. Thank God, I got better.

In Marrakesh, we saw a troupe of young acrobats climb onto each other's shoulders and form pyramids structures. A snake-charmer played his pipe. A handful of blind devotees chanted the Qur'an.

But Morocco had poverty and ignorance to wrench the heart. The river-bathing children of Rabat used the dirt under a bridge near the beach as a toilet. Garbage was flung over the sides of cliffs facing the Atlantic Ocean.

Women and children begged for money in the streets, swearing by Allah we had never seen them before, though we recognized them as people to whom we had given charity the same day. Some pleaded, "Give us money so that we can believe in God!" Worse, officials in thread-worn uniforms sought money as often as beggars did, often averting their eyes for shame.

We struck up passing friendships. In Rabat, a young man invited us to meet his wife and take tea. Upon leaving, we watched him lock a padlock upon the door. This meant he valued his wife's virtue over her life.

"What if there's a fire? How will she escape?"

Malik shook his head and said, "It's wrong. Yet he would think I am butting into his private life if I say so."

We visited the aunt of an Algerian friend. This lady lived with three co-wives in an ancient sanctuary of Tangiers. The common husband of these women was long dead. The dilapidated stone house, looking narrow from the street, expanded into endless cool and shadowy rooms on the inside, with unscreened windows looking out over the twinkling Mediterranean Sea. Cushions were set against the walls of the rooms in traditional Arab seating.

The co-wives spent their days feeding and teaching poor women to read and memorize the Qur'an. However, it was not so much their saintly duties or the sun sparkling over the waters of the Mediterranean that lit up the lives of these old women as a small, beautiful boy who came tumbling out to meet us. He was four years old and an aspiring gymnast.

The blond child laughed between somersaults and cartwheels executed over the heavy Berber rugs. The old women clapped, cheered and clanked their spoons against their glasses of tea, demanding an encore.

"Who is he?" I asked.

Malik relayed the question. This handsome boy was the offspring of a Western woman and a North African father. He was being raised in hiding from his mother.

I stared at Malik in horror. "His poor mother!"

"Don't judge. We don't know the full story."

Looking back, these trips blur together. Malik and I lived four years as a married couple before going to Saudi Arabia, but I was not allowed to enter Saudi Arabia until he had permission from the Saudi government. I remember spending a cold month in Tunisia while Malik visited his family.

On that trip, we took the train to Sousse, a town on the Mediterranean Sea. The conductor of the train joined us in the street and asked us what we were doing in his city.

"I am going to find a hotel room for my wife to stay in while I visit my family in Jeddah," said Malik.

"No!" yelled the conductor, coming to an appalled halt. "Men will think she is a whore and knock on her door all night! You'll never see her again."

Really? The thrill would be that intoxicating?

Malik wrangled a bit, mainly because we had no plan B. The conductor, a sturdy, middle-aged man with a thick neck and graying hair, provided an alternative. "She can stay with my family while you are gone."

His name was Mr. Ali and he had made pilgrimage to Mecca several times. He loved talking to me in Arabic, and to Malik in French.

"Mr. Ali, Malik does not speak French."

"Oh no?"

Then he forgot and did it again.

Until my husband left, we stayed in an apartment in Mr. Ali's building just downstairs from his own. Mrs. Ali sent down three meals a day on trays unless we told her we were going to eat in a restaurant. We tried to pay them more than once. We felt like moochers, but they refused payment.

Except for breakfast, which was very strong *café au lait* with French bread, often accompanied by olives or cheese, all the meals were seasoned with explosive amounts of ground red hot pepper.

The hot pepper that is the primary ingredient for cooking is the reason people of Sousse had iced water within reach when they ate.

Mrs. Ali sent a full pitcher of iced water with every tray, lunch or dinner. After a single bite, we grabbed the glasses of water. It was either that or die from spontaneous combustion.

I witnessed Mrs. Ali spoon five to six large portions of ground red pepper into the lamb stew she cooked on her stovetop for about five people—one tablespoon per person. The local restaurants seemed to use the same amount. Malik and I ordered spaghetti at one place, thinking it might be gently Italian, but we were perspiring by the third bite. Mr. Ali claimed that hot pepper kept Tunisians warm.

People needed something. We had neither gas nor electrical heating in our apartment. Upstairs, Mrs. Ali burned coals on her balcony in a brazier. When the coals were red, she brought the brazier inside and roasted peanuts over it. That warmed the room a little, and she occupied herself by boiling water and then brewing dark tea with lots of sugar. Roasted peanuts were tossed in to float on top of each serving.

I had brought a beaver and muskrat fur coat that my mother had given me, but I did not wear it in the street. It made me look rich even though we weren't. We used it to sleep under.

We too bought charcoals and a burner. Our mistake was bringing the charcoals inside the icy apartment before the coals were completely red. Still we didn't know what we were doing, maybe because headaches and sore throats stopped us from thinking. My headache disappeared as I walked through the street to a pharmacy for aspirin. Memories of reading about carbon monoxide poisoning made me hasten to buy the medicine, rush back, and pull the brazier back out onto the balcony, leaving the doors open.

A local Tunisian doctor took care of our chills and sore throats by sending us to a pharmacy where we were told to drop our pants (behind a curtain) and given vitamin shots in the butt with a hypodermic needle.

Malik left and I moved upstairs to the Ali flat. During the afternoons Laila and I met her friends and stood on the balcony for long stretches, watching Sousse life.

Shopping and cooking were interesting. I went with Leila and brought home as much milk, butter and meat as might be needed for a single day. The Ali family had no refrigerator.

53

In town, butchers hung the heads of a cow or sheep above their windows and the fresh blood dribbled down the wall. Dried blood patterned the wall and attracted flies. The suspended cow heads demonstrated to shoppers that the meat was fresh. If the butchers sold out of beef or mutton, we moved to the covered marketplace where chickens swung from strings tied around their feet, hanging upside down so that the blood would drain from their slit throats.

The chicken man never ran out of chickens. It was an easy matter to slit another feathered throat if a customer did not mind waiting for the blood to drain. For that matter, a housewife could take the chicken home and drain the blood herself. The Ali family seemed to prefer meat to fish although Sousse had a fish market as well.

The strong odors of meat and blood from the chicken, beef and fish markets hung heavily in the air despite Sousse's seaside location. I held the ends of my headscarf against my nose, trying not to feel sick. Layla did not wear a scarf, but then she never felt sick from the market odors either!

My Tunisian friend did wear a scarf when we prayed the five daily prayers together. In contrast, Mrs. Ali wore a huge white sheet pulled around her head and body whenever she walked into the street. When she needed her arms free to carry things, she bit the two edges of the cloth between her teeth, like other married women of Sousse.

I asked Leila why I never saw her mother pray.

"She says she hasn't committed any sins in her life."

"But you pray!"

Leila wrinkled her nose. "I don't see things the way my mom does. It's okay."

Mr. Ali was sure right about one thing—I must have looked like a prostitute to the young men cramming the cafes of Sousse, even with my head scarf and long skirts. While I was walking to the market with Leila, a young man ran up to me and shoved his face so close to mine I thought he was going to kiss me. I pushed him away on reflex.

That made him mad. He came running up behind us and kicked me, hard, in the thigh. Leila caught me and started yelling at him.

"Come on, let's get out of here," she said, urging me to limp away.

A bed had been made up for me on a couch in the guest salon. As in other Middle Eastern countries, the Ali's guest salon had chairs and couches protected by dust covers to keep it in readiness for guests. My weeks of residency there must have been an imposition on Mrs Ali, who could not receive anyone elsed.

One day Mr. Ali made a shocking announcement to me.

"You have to go home."

"What do you mean? I'm waiting for Malik. You know that, Mr. Ali."

"He's not coming back."

Had Mr. Ali received a message from Malik? No. Mr. Ali had a gut feeling, based on Malik's being Saudi. Malik would never return, because other Saudi men were famous for abandoning young women.

"Saudis don't come to North Africa to visit historical sites. They came to find nightclubs and prostitutes."

"Yes, but Mr. Ali, we are married! He will be back in two weeks!"

My host stubbornly shook his head. "Send a telegram to your husband. If you don't get an answer in three days, I will take you by train to Tunis and put you on a plane back to your mother in California. She must be worried."

"My mother said she doesn't want to see me again." I was close to tears.

"Every mother wants to see her daughter again. You come with me now."

He took me to a telegraph office, and I sent Malik the message. Its arrival came to the attention of his mother. In that manner, Mama Johara learned of my existence.

Looking back, I realize there could not have been a more honorable soul than this man who worried that I was someone's abandoned child—even if Malik suffered by reputation for a few days.

In California, the Moroccan import business failed. Our friends took the goods and sold them, but the reinvestment of funds never happened because everyone absorbed the profit. I tried to forget about that huge loss of money and keep studying.

My mother never asked. Perhaps with time and a certain amount of success on my part, Mom might love me again.

I kept in touch with her but she was still very cold. She just didn't like me being Muslim, and said so in her letters.

Yet I made a lot of new friends, Kate remaining my best buddy. There were, surprisingly, a lot of American girls in San Diego marrying Muslim guys from the Middle East. There were so many of us that the men at the mosque wanted to make rules to govern us.

Malik told me "the mosque" had decoded we female converts must speak only in Arabic.

I suppressed laughter. "Sure! Teach me!"

Not having realized the new "rule" gave him more work, Malik grumbled something about others minding their own business. He didn't like teaching, and it showed. I was disappointed, wanting to learn.

After Mustafa married Kate, the Gulf Arab guys at the mosque insisted that if the Palestinian continued promoting dance, his brains would boil in hellfire.

It is a pity the poor man did not ignore them. On one occasion, when Mustafa and Kate came to our house for dinner, Kate showed her husband one of my kittens. Mustafa ignored the animal and groaned, "Don't you know you're going to die?"

All this focus on hell was depressing people. It certainly didn't make it easy to stay married. I couldn't help but wonder how Kate and Mustafa's marriage could hold up under the pressure.

Mustafa's temper flared during fasting in Ramadan. Since unprovoked fits of male anger have long been common in Middle Eastern marriages, no one understood why Kate kept asking for someone to "talk" to her husband.

The mosque preferred to find fault with Kate. When she asked for an Islamic divorce, the imam refused to grant it to her. She tried to make the marriage work for two more years though I would see her sob to break my heart.

We had our own problems. I never met Malik's dad because in my husband's last year in college, his dad died of a heart attack. That was the second time I ever saw my husband cry.

After Malik got his degree, he flew off to Jeddah to face the ordeal of getting permission to bring me into the country. His friend Abdullateef assisted us, through a family contact. Malik had to submit to cross-examination in order to convince authorities that I would not be a blemish upon Saudi society.

On February 13th of my own last year in college, I received a phone call from my father. I was making a lemon meringue pie at the time. Dad and I had not spoken since sending a harsh letter to me telling me what a colossal disappointment I was.

"Sylvia," he said. "Your mother is dying."

I didn't believe him. Mom was only 45 years old.

"What?"

"She collapsed at a spa in San Francisco. The doctors say it is an aneurysm of the brain."

I had to lean on the kitchen table and try to breathe. His words were a blow. I sat down, numb and shocked, and begging God to let it not be so. This was not part of the plan. The plan was to achieve my master's degree, teach at a university in Jeddah, and lavish my mother with gifts and love. I had sent her a blue Moroccan dress. The rift between my mother and me was supposed to heal.

"Can they save her?" I begged.

"She is in a coma," he said. "A blood vessel in her brain exploded. If she lives, she will be no more than a vegetable."

Dad didn't have to convey this news. He could have asked someone else to do it.

I called Malik, long distance.

"My mother is dying. She's in San Francisco. I want to take a flight there with Katherine."

"Yes," agreed Malik, "Go to her."

I decided to fly to my mother's hospital bedside that night. I almost didn't make it. Mischievous teenagers standing on the hood of a car had been looking over our fence that day and I had reported their actions to the police.

Our landlady, training herself to shoot a pistol, prowled around the house with her gun, looking for these derelicts. "Stay indoors!" she barked at me.

"I can't! My mother is dying and I have to catch a plane!"

She didn't seem to hear. Katherine beckoned me into the car. Then a police vehicle arrived and a female officer got out. She leaned against the car with a hand, looking at us. Katherine rolled her window down.

"Did you file a report of people spying on your house?"

"Yes."

"You can't go anywhere until you answer some questions."

"My mother is dying!" I cried, " I--" Kate's hand fell on my knee.

"Just answer her questions," she said gently.

We made it to the airport on time. Then we got to the hospital, and I sat by my mother's bed, alone.

Half of Mom's face had fallen. I picked up her hand. It was chilled. I spoke to her and the numbers on the vital statistics monitor steadily went up. Every word I uttered was love. She was the center of my heart.

An hour and a half passed. After walking away for a sip of water, I came back, held her hand again, and spoke some more. A doctor appeared behind me.

"Your mother's vital signs have improved," she said, touching my shoulder. "She could last for weeks or months. You need to get some rest."

My beautiful mother passed away in the wee hours of the morning. I wish I had stayed.

Kate and I were put up overnight at Hisham's apartment in San Francisco. He had left his landlady and married a pretty Saudi cousin. Both he and his wife were kind to me, but I will never forget Najah told me *not* to cry for my mother. I overlooked the discriminatory absurdity of her counsel. All I could do was cry, all the night long, and all the days that followed.

My monthly periods stopped. "You are going through shock," my doctor explained. Jolting pains zapped, unexpectedly, through my arms, at any given moment, night and day. I forgot about eating and sleeping, unaware of the hour of day or night.

Friends brought food to the house. One of these, a young woman from a Lebanese family, stayed with me for a week or so. God bless those kind people.

My mother had sometimes longingly spoken of grandchildren, but one evening at the dinner table before I went to Paris, she had said sadly, "I'll never see my grandchildren."

The day came when Malik, finished with his Bachelor of Science in Engineering, and I, with my Master of Arts in English, began our journey to Jeddah with my newly acquired visa. We took our gray cat, Ramadi.

The simple act of bringing my cat was a consolation. In mourning for my mother, I realized how severely I had cut myself off from friends, family and culture. This small gray cat was a balm. Malik loved her too. His Saudi friends thought he was crazy for taking Ramadi to a veterinary hospital when she was sick on the night before his big exam. They said I had too much influence over him with my American ways.

Malik tried to get me ready for Jeddah. He described how it would feel to arrive off the plane: how the hot, balmy air hits one in the face, getting off the airplane.

"The government calls the King Abdulaziz International Airport the largest international airport in the world. It's new. It just opened in 1981. But it's mainly a huge fence around a desert. Most of it is empty."

"Then they shouldn't call it the largest airport in the world."

59

"You'll have to get used to hearing things like that."

For nighttime travelers, the first glimpse of Jeddah from the air reveals a vast number of street lights twinkling in a flat desert city. On the ground, the impact of three times as many street lamps as needed is startling. When I first arrived, most of these lamps were on roads that ran through wide patches of empty desert.

When we boarded the plane, only a handful of women wore headscarves. Other female passengers were dressed elegantly in stylish clothes. I wore a long Indian dress of light cotton because I knew that Jeddah was hot. I had a scarf over my hair.

When the plane landed and taxied to a halt on the runway, I looked around in astonishment. All of the Middle Eastern female passengers I had seen showing their hair were now unrecognizable under long, black *abayas* that trailed the ground, long black scarves called *turhas* wrapped around their heads, and in many cases, black veils covering their faces. Some eyes peered out of slits while other faces were totally covered. I had been one of the most modestly attired of the women getting on the plane. Now I looked like I was screaming for attention in my thin blue dress.

*   *   *   *

A man came to the Prophet and said, 'O Messenger of God! Who among the people is the most worthy of my good companionship? The Prophet said: Your mother. The man said, 'Then who?' The Prophet said: Then your mother. The man further asked, 'Then who?' The Prophet said: Then your mother. The man asked again, 'Then who?' The Prophet said: Then your father. (Bukhari, Muslim).

Chapter 4

A Baby in the Desert

In Jeddah, the first contraction of childbirth tore me from sleep before dawn. My groans jarred Malik.

"Do you want me to take you to the hospital?" he mumbled.

"I'm sorry I woke you. Go back to sleep."

I arose in the dark and felt my way, carefully, into our second room, holding my extended belly and wishing with all my heart my mother were alive. Taking some Tylenol and leaning back upon the Arabic-style couches Malik had built, to wonder when my baby would come and if life would be happier thereafter, seemed the only thing to do while waiting.

Ten months earlier, Malik had dropped me off one morning at King Abdul Aziz University for Girls. A *haris*, or gate keeper—in this case, a poor, middle-aged man with a scratchy, loud voice and ragged clothes—sat in a fold-out chair at the entry, sweating profusely. I stepped past him, zigzagging between walls to enter. Once inside, I found gardens. Birds sang in trees. Girls walked around without headscarves, which Saudis called *turhas* or the silky black body coverings called *abayas*. It was a hidden sanctuary.

Presenting myself as a post graduate with a Bachelor's and a Master's degree and as the legal wife of a Saudi national, I was interviewed not for a teaching job as I desired, but on my conversion to Islam, what my parents thought, who my husband was, where he worked, whether I was going to have children, what their names would be, whether I had made pilgrimage, the name of my city of origin in California, and if I knew someone's cousin who was studying in another Californian city. Tea was offered by each one of my interviewers. Delicate glasses with lipstick marks on their rims and containing soggy mint stems littered desk tops. Every time I asked for the dean of Humanities, I was pulled into another office and interviewed by someone who was, at the end of the interview, not the right person.

Eventually I met the dean of Humanities, an Egyptian Ph.D. She decided I might teach classes. The problem of my nonworking visa was airily waved aside. Her assistant gave me a schedule of classes and answered a few of my questions.

The duty of the man in the foldout chair was to keep other men from entering campus grounds. At the end of each school day, this "gatekeeper" shouted family names given to him by arriving drivers. Then the girls, covered up in black from head to foot, exited the campus. They knew how lucky they were to be getting an education. Their grandmothers had probably told them how a military guard had been posted around the first girls' school in Saudi Arabia to protect it from attack by angry males.

When news of my teaching "job"—though still not official and hence unpaid—got around the Al Shamsi family, my sister-in-law Soraya brought me a gift: six pairs of thick nylon stockings in a variety of Popsicle shades. I left them in the bottom of my underwear drawer. At the university, many assumed me to be Christian because I wore sandals without socks or stockings.

One day at the beginning of that semester, when I sat in someone's office sipping tea, cool hands slipped over my eyes, covering them. A voice demanded, "Guess who!"

"I honestly don't know." I said. The hands flew away, and a face peered over my shoulder. "Oh!" I laughed delightedly. Kareema was a young Saudi woman I had made friends with in California. Now I had a real friend in Jeddah. Once I became pregnant, (to my great surprise and joy!), Kareema took me to see a gentle Egyptian female doctor on campus. The doctor sympathized with my unending nausea, of feeling faint and ill from heat, and being able to tolerate only apples. "Apples will be just fine!" she promised. "As long as you promise to eat them."

The extreme heat and humidity of Jeddah was a challenge to people unused to it. I learned to avoid walking in front of air conditioners when my clothes were wet with perspiration and to keep my chest covered throughout the summer, even when alone in my room. Something about sweat on the chest, when passing under a cold blast of air, invites instant bronchitis.

If pregnancy was daunting, my working status proved even more so. I taught classes, but no one brought up the subject of payment. The other American or English teachers on campus received salaries. Like me, they had Master degrees in English literature. Unlike me, they had working visas, acquired while they were in the USA or England, their countries of origin. Given the relaxed pace of paperwork procedures in Saudi Arabia, Malik and I believed if we were patient, I would also be granted a working visa sooner or later.

A letter "inviting" me to teach at last materialized. Kareema translated it. We hugged in excitement. There was an offer for a foreigner's beginning salary: 3400 Saudi riyals (about $900 dollars) a month. While this was less than the salary of 6000 riyals about $1500) per month for a Saudi graduate with a Master's degree, Kareema said foreign teachers were also given a basic housing allowance and round-trip plane tickets for themselves and their spouses.

Saudi teachers were given housing in the new university apartment compound. The apartments were lovely. Hope swelled in my heart, made me giddy. Malik and I might have our own apartment!

"My letter didn't mention the housing salary or the apartment. Which one do you think I'll get? Will they get me a working visa?"

"I am sure they will offer you what everyone else gets!" said Kareema. "Let's ask."

"There is no foreigner's housing allowance being offered to you," an administrator explained in a flat voice, "because your husband is Saudi."

"What about plane tickets?"

"No. You live in Jeddah and your husband is Saudi. No plane tickets for you."

"Will I get the salary a Saudi salary, then?"

The administrator looked at me like people look at dogs who barf up the carpeting just eaten. "Of course not!" she said. "You are American."

"What about an apartment at the university compound?"

"That is only for *Saudi* teachers," she said slowly, so that my feeble mind could grasp her words. "You are not Saudi, are you?"

"No. But my husband doesn't get a housing allowance from his job."

"That's not our problem."

I tried smiling brightly. "I would be a foreign employee. I'll just go back to California and you can hire me from there."

"No!" the woman shook her head. "Don't try to cheat. We know you are here now."

"Excuse me," I said, my stomach twisting uncomfortably, "but the most important thing is a working visa. The letter doesn't mention that."

"Oh that," she said, raising her eyebrows. "You will need a *wastah*—a contact. You must teach *without* a salary, naturally, until you have a legal working visa. Your husband needs to find a *wastah.* In the meantime, you can start teaching your classes or we won't hire you at all."

"He doesn't know anyone to ask."

She folded her arms. "Then you shouldn't have come to this country."

Her response staggered me. "Look," I said, "If I go back to California, then you *could* hire me and obtain a working visa for me, just as you have done for the other American teachers."

"No we *can't* because we *know* you are *here* now!" She waved for me to leave, losing patience with the American imbecile.

I fought back tears. Nothing made sense.

That night, Malik said, "Everyone I ask to help get a working visa for you says he is powerless, but I know that isn't true."

Malik was relearning something he had forgotten during his years in the USA and reaping the benefit of his scholarship and the freedom and ease of life in the USA: everything in Saudi Arabia is based on a contact. Scholarships, permission to marry non-Saudis, attainment of jobs, maids, drivers and telephones all require knowing an influential person.

Malik and his friends had marveled at how easily students could enroll in school or get a telephone in America. I openly wondered if his boss couldn't help.

"You can't ask someone to help unless you can provide something in return," explained Malik.

My husband was right. When I asked friendly ladies at the university if they knew anyone who could help me, their faces fell. "I am sorry," each one said mournfully.

Malik's boss was a rich man named Jawwad whose income had mysterious sources given the low salary of all government employees. Malik finally did ask him for help anyway. It was no use. Jawwad was about helping himself, not others.

I was teaching at King Abdul Aziz University without a salary. Malik had translated the sting of the words on my visa to me: "May not work, with or without money."

"They can't be serious. What have I done to merit permanent nonworking status? I thought your country adored Muslim converts!"

Despite the Saudi desire to convert the entire world to Islam, for business, they preferred non-Muslims.

We needed the salary I should have been making. Every penny of the liquid cash I had inherited after my mother's death had been sunk into a piece of land far out in the desert, but it was not enough. (Buying land was Malik's idea.) To pay for that land, Malik had needed to ask his mother for a loan.

Malik's idea was to build a house for us and her, with ample land, so that eventually we could put in a swimming pool. If not for this expensive venture, I expect Malik would have considered returning to America, where anyone could get a telephone and we both could get jobs.

Instead we ran out of money a week before the end of every month. I hunted for coins at the back of drawers to buy cucumbers, lentils, rice and apples. Someday, I told myself, we would be able to afford things like cookies, strawberries and steaks. At work, I presented a face of hope, but when I got home and had put lunch out for Malik, I lay on my bed and cried. I was an employed but unpaid convert to Islam with two university degrees as well as an Alliance Francaise. Surely this could not be happening.

Pregnant and penniless, I refused to bring up the subject of a private hospital to my husband even if I felt terrified of the public hospitals due to the stories I had heard about them.

The newspapers were and still are full of horror stories taking place at the public hospitals. Patients died of neglectful hospital practices every day. No one was made accountable.

Malik did not have the money to put me in a private hospital. I determined to go to a nearby public hospital and be brave. He never knew how petrified I was, how much courage I needed to walk into that horrible hospital all alone. I knew he suffered at work from being unappreciated, and I did not want to make his burden heavier.

During the day, strolling through the inner gardens of King Abdul Aziz was calming. Colonies of birds warbled. Street cats were the birds' main assailants. The felines were suffered to exist on the university grounds—just barely. Homeless marauders, the poor cats sprinted from shadow to shadow in the corridors of the university's hallways. Girls yelped when the mangy creatures knocked into their legs. One day as I stood with chalk in hand at the front of my class, the girls in the back two rows shrieked and shot out of their seats as if electrocuted.

"What's wrong?" I cried. The girls stared at the back of the empty room as if transfixed by jinn. I saw nothing and moved closer to investigate. Was there a scorpion? A snake?

My students were standing pressed against each other along the walls. At the back of the room, hidden by desks, I found a litter of newborn kittens.

Completely puzzled, I looked at the girls, trying to understand why some were trembling and others pressed scarves to their wrinkled noses and puckered mouths, seemingly ready to retch.

"Those are *kittens*," I said, thinking they didn't understand. "*Hurairah.*"

They nodded. They knew.

"Are you scared of kittens?"

They nodded. They were scared of kittens and I was scared of their damn public hospitals. What a strange world!

Removal of the litter was essential in order to carry on class. I found a rag at the maids' station and carried the little creatures out to a shady place behind the stairs. Moving the kittens prevented them, temporarily at least, from being killed as vermin. The girls elbowed each other and whispered behind their scarves about the foul work I could bring myself to do, handling these baby cats.

Sometimes I could understand the culture gap between my students and me. At other times it was too wide to see across.

When the school year was about half over, my need for money had grown desperate. I pursued endless circles to talk to women on campus, hoping they could help me. I had only one pair of sandals and I wore them every day, scared they would break. Malik could not afford to buy me new shoes.

Every single day, the university officials assured me things would be sorted out—by someone else. "You are our sister in Islam," each said, smiling.

The female president of the women's university suggested I go to Dr. Wafah, dean of the Home Economics and Medical English Department. Dr. Wafah's power came not from her position but through marriage to the *male* president of the women's university. In an incomprehensible triangle, the female president (Dr.) was subordinate to this male president, who was subordinate to the male president of the male university. King Abdul Aziz University had three presidents, but none of them were responsible for getting me permission to work— I needed a royal family member for that.

When Kareema and I first ran into Dr. Wafah on campus, the older woman announced, "I've been arguing for women's rights! Feel my head; it's hot!" She bowed forward, neck bent to proffer her cranium. "Go on, touch it," she commanded.

I laid my palm unwillingly upon the sweaty parting of her hair, and agreed, "Yes, it's hot," wiping my hand dry with a little stealth, afterwards, upon my skirt.

Dr. Wafah abruptly launched into a diatribe on women's rights in Saudi Arabia like we could see them being won all around us. She kept her argument in the abstract until I asked for an example.

"What *kind* of rights?" she echoed, lapsing into silence to think. It took a few moments.

Finally, she crossed her arms and said, "I'll tell you what rights: I drive a car!"

Surely she was joking. Maybe she drove a car in her dreams at night.

Dr. Wafah laughed at our expressions. "On campus!" she said, as if it were a greater victory than driving on the streets.

One female dean driving a car around inside a small, walled space was not the same as Saudi females winning the right to drive in public. King Abdul Aziz University for Girls had a pretty small campus; there were not any paved roads. Did she drive on the walkways after the students went home?

Never before had I felt like a complete hypocrite, smiling politely at this woman who might help me get a working visa. Part of me wanted to believe her, believe that things were opening up for women, and that it just would take dedication and patience. When she had exhausted her topics, Kareema and I brought up the subject of my employment situation.

"Ahhhh!" Dr. Wafah cried in sympathetic tones.

"You have come to the right person. I am the best person to help you get a working visa and a contract. I will hire you through my department!"

If this hiring was approved, which of course it would be (given her social status, repute and royal contacts), I would earn four thousand Saudi riyals per month (just over $1000).

That sounded amazing, and so much better than zero.

"You come to my office tomorrow. You will like working for the Home Economics department, teaching medical English to prospective doctors," she said.

My bruised heart embraced the woman, sweaty head and all. Here, I thought, was a sincere, dynamic and educated Muslim lady, one whom I would be proud to know better despite her delusions about female driving progress.

That evening, I told Malik the news. We were both so relieved and hopeful, we laughed and joked for hours.

Over the course of the next couple of months, whenever I came to Dr. Wafah's office, she grinned and bellowed, "Assalaaaaaaaaaam Alaaaaiiiikum wa Rahmatullaaaaaah wa Barakaaaaaaaaatuhu" while rising from her seat to pump my hand. Her greeting meant "Peace be upon you and God's Mercy and Blessings." She was happy I was Muslim. "Your reward with your Lord will be great!" she promised.

I knew she referred to a reward in the Hereafter. As time passed, I couldn't help yearning for news of a reward with the university in my present life, at least enough of a reward to buy groceries.

Ultimately, Dr. Wafah was more hospitable than helpful. I could always find a glass of tea in her office. Progress on my employment status was another matter. If I tried to get her to discuss the topic my getting paid actual money, she shifted topics until someone else walked into her office.

Her door was always open, literally. With each newcomer, she cried out her greeting, pumped the newcomer's hand, and ordered a maid to serve more tea. Conversation in Arabic ensued, most of which I barely understood. Then it was time for me to teach another class.

On the day I brought Kareema with me to push the lady for discussion of my employment, Dr. Wafah started talking, in loud English, about the honor of working for one's country.

"I helped plant the very first trees here," she shouted, her cheeks flaring red. "The other ladies and I brought shovels and dug all the holes! We were determined to have a university for women in Jeddah!"

"That's wonderful," said Kareema and I, exchanging glances.

69

"I taught classes for *free* during a whole year," shouted Dr. Wafah. "Understand that Saudi Arabia is a new country! Sometimes we have to make sacrifices for change."

Dr. Wafah came from a wealthy family. The only other teacher at the university not being paid (like me) was an American Muslim woman named Shareefa. We were the only two converts and we both needed to buy groceries.

"All the other American and English teachers are paid regularly," I said.

"Ah," said Dr. Wafah, shaking her head and wagging her finger at me as at a naughty little girl. "But *they* all have working visas."

* * * *

Malik tried to make me forget the week's struggle through outings to the beach on weekends (Thursdays and Fridays). One glorious day was spent dabbling in the bathtub-temperature, turquoise waters of the Red Sea, alone when we could manage avoiding the woebegone faces of his little brother Ziyad and his teenage nephew Ashraf, son of Malik's eldest sister, Nafeesah.

To get to a deserted coastal area, we drove one hour north of Jeddah. I loved taking a picnic lunch and reading books in a tent or wading while Malik went fishing. Whatever he caught—a *luteh* or a parrot fish, for instance—he barbecued, making rice pilaf on the side. Malik was good at cooking and taught me to make rice by sight measurements.

The rest of my free time I spent reading 19th century English novels found in corners of Arabic bookstores, sewing, writing homesick letters to friends in California, and trying to figure out how to spend a few more hours alone with Malik.

Five-year-old Ziyad lived in the family villa on the floor below us, which belonged to his "second" mother, Madame Leena, and her unmarried children. Ziyad was cute, but I had not asked to adopt him. He was in our rooms at mealtimes, nap times and evenings. Madame Leena didn't worry about his whereabouts.

Ziyad waited on the staircase every day for Malik to come home from work. When I started working at the university and Malik picked me up on his way home from the office, we both found Ziyad on the staircase. There was never any chance of not letting the child into our portion of the apartment. He dogged our heels like a puppy. We would have had to physically push him out. By Saudi definition, Ziyad was an orphan. In Arabia, an orphan is a child who has lost his father. Losing a mother doesn't count.

Ziyad's presence prompted Arabic conversations, a language I had studied for only one year. When I asked Malik to translate, he said, "Ziyad isn't really making sense. He's just a little kid. It's gibberish."

So the gibberish went on, day after day. Since Ziyad was a guest, Malik had to pay attention to him. I would have liked using Ziyad's presence to learn more Arabic. If I said, "I feel excluded," Malik scoffed at me for being silly.

I wanted to be kind to the little boy but felt despair at the unending competition for my husband's attention. Malik did not *ever* ask Ziyad to leave. In fact, he responded to the child's conversation before responding to mine. I had to wait my turn, which was when Ziyad might run out of questions. Since Ziyad was a bubbly kid and didn't understand English, he would cut me off if I tried to talk to my husband. Even waiting for Ziyad to gasp for breath didn't work.

It was as if I didn't exist.

I sometimes wondered if I had made a colossal mistake in following Malik to Jeddah. Apart from poverty, there were so many problems I had not envisioned, most of which I had to face entirely alone. The foremost among these was resentment from Saudi women.

Western wives are viewed as thieves by Saudi girls. I cannot say I blame them. Foreign wives drain the stock of marriageable men from Saudi society. If and when Saudi girls become aware of suitable bachelor candidates of non-Saudi origin, they have to overcome the prejudice of their families and obtain the necessary "*wastah.*"

Saudi women who succeed in taking non-Saudi husbands endure a level of prejudice that often drives the couples to divorce or leave the country. I met a Saudi medical teacher at King Abdul Aziz University who had married a Pakistani. Former Saudi girlfriends dropped her like a dirty diaper upon her marriage. When she went into labor with her first child and rushed to the hospital, she could hear remarks of contempt and disgust from various Saudi female staff who thought she was appalling for having married a foreigner.

There was an American man, reputedly a genius, who had met and married to a Saudi woman. Living in Jeddah, he had been pushed to bouts of insanity through the prejudice he encountered. He began walking on the rims of the roof of his building, three stories up, and scaring his Saudi wife to death. Finally he had to be placed under psychiatric care.

I reflected Patti would have found that story interesting, about a genius gone mad, but correspondence through the Saudi mail system was so heavily censured, I mainly sent away for magazines and catalogues. If I started complaining to old friends, they would ask why I stayed.

What every foreign wife of a Saudi seeks out is someone else like herself—when I met such women, we discussed what we had observed. In the case of prejudice faced by non-Saudi husbands married to Saudi women, I could learn through Kareema that it was a prejudice strengthened through legislation. Kareema's children were never granted Saudi citizenship. Her husband, though a distance relative, could never become a Saudi national.

A foreign wife of a Saudi man, however, used to be able to apply for and receive Saudi nationality after many years have passed, (provided she was Muslim). This permission has been rescinded.

Today foreign wives are given a permanent residence visa. That way they cannot inherit anything. Nor, for that matter, can the children of Saudi women married to non-Saudis, even if they are born and raised in Saudi Arabia.

It made me uncomfortable to know my presence, in a general way, was not welcome by Saudi women, whose situation I now appreciated. I had taken one of the eligible bachelors out of the pool .My pregnancy made it clear that I would not be leaving anytime soon.

Ziyad remained a constant visitor to our rooms, even when my belly stuck out in front of his face during the last months of pregnancy. I couldn't tell him to stay in his own quarters without offending the entire family. Of course I cared about the little boy and tried to amuse him. Yet he wanted Malik's attention more than he wanted mine.

72

        *   *   *   *

As the school year came to an end, I was cornered by a representative of the university. "We've been looking for you," she cried in exasperation, like I was a fugitive on the run.

"I'm always on campus," I said. "You know which classes I teach. I just don't have an office."

She frowned. "We wanted to tell you," she said, arching a brow and sidling closer, "that you are strongly advised not to hold grades back."

I raised my eyebrows.

"Foreign women who have done that before have been blacklisted, you see," she warned, with a narrowing of her eyes. "They were never able to find work anywhere in Jeddah, not even in private schools."

An iron hand squeezed my stomach. I had been considering exactly that move.

"So it has happened to other women before me?" I asked. "Other Western wives of Saudis? I was told there have *never* been foreign teachers without a working visa teaching classes here before. Why have all of you allowed me to work for free?"

"It's not the students' fault your husband won't find a contact," flung back the administrator coolly. This retort had become an administrative refrain. The "fault" for my lack of a working visa was always shifted to Malik, who was, according to them, a bum.

I decided to ask help of a new friend, So'ad. She frequently traveled with her husband to Europe because of his need for healthcare. At the time I met her, she wanted private English lessons, and I was recommended by the female president of the college.

So'ad spent her time running a charitable sewing business. Sometimes I visited her house to give her lessons; other times she met me on campus. So'ad treated me with kindness and sent me little gifts:

73

an embroidered scarf, dried fruits in a Syrian boxes of inlaid wood, a new Qur'an. Because she was loveable, I refused to accept payment.

She agreed to talk to Dr. Wafah about my situation.

Dr. Wafah's hospitality came to an end on the day I brought So'ad to that office. So'ad came from a prestigious family. Doctor Wafah's manipulation of me might be gossiped about in social circles.

Dr. Wafah trumpeted "Peace be upon you and God's blessings and mercy!" for the last time. When she learned the purpose of So'ad's visit, a vein on her forehead visibly throbbed.

"This girl," she erupted, leaping out of her seat and sweeping her arm in the air to point at me, "always comes in here crying her eyes out!"

This was basic Arabic. I understood. My pulse raced. How dare she! I had never once lost my calm in this office. It was true I wept at home, but how could she know?

"She has no patience," shouted Dr. Wafah. "She came to Saudi Arabia on a nonworking visa. This is government business. It does not concern me! Who does she think she is?"

So'ad tried to protest, but futility had cast its pall.

"Never mind," I said, furious but quiet. "Let's go."

So'ad refused to shake hands with Dr. Wafah.

"That woman is a liar," I said to my friend once we were outside.

So'ad squeezed my arm. "Come to my house for lunch," she said.

Concerned for my financial constraints and worried about my upcoming childbirth, she recommended I go to the public Children's Hospital of Jeddah, *Al Mustashfa Al Waleed Wa Atfal.*

"I have a friend there who can be with you during your delivery. You'll like her." So'ad's friend was an English-speaking Egyptian G.P. named Dr. Kulthum.

"I wish I could be with you during your delivery," So'ad told me. "I would do that with any of my daughters, and you are like a daughter to me. Unfortunately, hospital rules forbid it. But they'll let Doctor

Kulthum stay with you because she works at that hospital. Just meet her; you'll like her!"

I did like Dr. Kulthum; she was a friendly, warm-hearted woman who spoke good English. And I *loved* So'ad for arranging for someone to hold my hand.

*   *   *   *

When the morning contractions began, I knew it was labor. The contractions were not close, but the pain was intense. My moans jarred Malik.

"Shall I take you to the hospital?" he asked.

"You are not dilated enough," said the receiving doctor at the Children's Hospital. "You must go home. It will take hours."

Malik drove me home and went back to bed. I waited alone, trying to breathe and not shake. My pain and ignorance were remarkable. I knew nothing. I had taken no breathing classes.

I wanted my mother. Two of my sisters-in-law had just had babies. Malik's mother, Mama Johara, was exhausted looking after her daughters and their infants, all of whom were staying with her in our building. She bleakly described them as "zay moot," meaning "as if dead."

If my sisters-in-law were "as if dead," it would be unfair of me to take attention away from them. Besides, I didn't want to annoy anyone.

I endured the contractions until I had to clap my hand over my mouth to keep from screaming. Holding my huge belly, I walked carefully back into the dark bedroom and woke Malik up once more.

"Take me back to the hospital. Please! I don't care what they say. I can't stand it."

When Malik walked me through the hospital entry corridor, I clung to his *thobe*, wrinkling that long white men's garment in the grip of my sweating hands.

75

"Your husband cannot come in here," commanded a male staff member. He blocked the way to the delivery rooms. The only men allowed into the women's delivery section were doctors. It was creeping past 7 a.m., so Malik went to his government office. I wished he could have stayed.

A male physician examined me and then left the room, saying, "Wait right here." Ten minutes later, an old Arab woman shuffled in, cloaked in a faded black *abaya* and *turha* and wearing grimy rubber sandals. She needed deodorant and a bath, in the reverse order. She picked my file off the desk in her gnarled fingers like it was a piece of filth that she did not want to soil her skin.

"*Goom!* (Get up!)" she barked.

"Don't talk to me like that," I retorted, in Arabic. "I'm not a dog."

Her eyes widened. She snorted loudly, threw the file back on the desktop, and shuffled out, leaving the room smelling like her armpits.

The male physician came back in. "What happened?"

"That woman has bad manners," I said. "And she needs deodorant."

Some minutes later, another dour but this time nonverbal woman shuffled in. She led me in sign language to a room where pregnant women lined up in front of a gurney. The woman on the gurney was having her private parts shaved. Soap and water were slopped all around the room. A woman in a hospital staff jacket whisked a razor across the pregnant woman's pelvis with a brisk pull of her arm. My stomach turned. Blood dribbled over the pregnant woman's thigh and I averted my eyes. The scene reminded me of a butcher's block.

"I won't do it," I said when it was my turn.

"You have to," the shaver said.

"No, I don't."

"Yes, you do."

We had a staring contest.

"Let me do it myself," I finally said. With a bit more pleading, and maybe because of my American accent, I was given a bar of soap and a razor and led to a bathroom. I think by rebelling, I had established a psychological profile in their minds: The uncooperative American. I would play that role many times over the years.

Finally, I was conducted to a plain, long room where skinny metal beds were lined up against the wall, beds in which women were awaiting their final agonies of labor. The women were all poor Arabs, some from neighboring countries. There were a couple of Pakistanis too. The nurses were English-speaking Filipinos.

"Get on this bed. There isn't a pillow," one nurse told me. I looked around and saw pillows under the heads of all the other women, none of whom were moaning. How I managed to stand and walk upright, I'll never know.

"They have pillows," I gasped between sobs. "M . . . m . . . may I have one?"

"No. I told you, there isn't one. You have to wait."

Five minutes later, another nurse marched up to my bed. "Stop crying!" she scolded. "Why are you crying? Stop it."

I couldn't. I was scared and alone and very far away from California. It had suddenly come upon me with crushing weight I was having my first baby in a public hospital in Saudi Arabia where no one except Malik gave a damn whether I survived or not.

An hour later, Dr. Kulthum came and finally the delivery doctor. Things got a little better. I asked Dr. Kulthum to recite the Qur'anic surah "Ya Sin" for me. She held my hand. I remembered to pray for my mother, family and all my friends during the labor because I had read that prayer during such a time is powerful.

When they put little Yousef in a bassinet near me, I was in a stupor.

"See? That's your baby," said both the delivery doctor and Dr. Kulthum.

"Uh-huh," I whispered. They didn't place my newborn on me, as medical practice does in the West, so I remained stunned. *Just put him anywhere close by me.* I was amazed to be alive.

Malik told me later how he had been in a daze of worry that morning. He kept calling the hospital. There was no word of my progress, nor, indeed, record of my existence.

"There is **no** Sylvia Fowler here," the male receptionist had insisted over the telephone.

"She's my wife! I just left her there!" Malik exploded. He couldn't understand why the receptionist wasn't listening. What had they done with me? He had left me at the hospital barely able to walk. It was unlikely I could have left on my own two feet. His worry escalated. He knew as well as I did, though neither of us said it aloud, that for the hospital, I as an American counted for very little. Perhaps I had died and they had been told to hush it up.

"You are mistaken, Sir," retaliated the man with ill-concealed impatience. "There is absolutely **no** Sylvia Fowler here. You are wrong!"

Silence hung on the line between my husband and this person. Malik said he felt he was sliding down a deep, dark hole.

Then the clerk added, as a glib almost meaningless afterthought that surely Malik would find of no use at all: "But we *do* have a Cindy Fuller. *She* just gave birth to a boy."

To this day, my name is misspelled on documents from Jeddah. When Malik sends me a ticket to come to Jeddah, it is invariably made out to Cindy Fuller, Cynthia Foster, or some other variation. The misspellings irritate airline clerks, and I have to plead for the alternate identity. Yet when I fly any British airline—for they have had the most dealings with the kingdom of Saudi Arabia--the British nationals who have lived in "Saudi," as they call the country, don't even blink. They nod and pass me through.

They know. They've shimmied to the same wild drumbeat. They've seen the glint off a sword in the desert moonlight and have braved the souk—open air marketplace—in 113 degree heat (Farenheit).

They've had their names permanently misspelled.

Only mad dogs, Englishmen and Cindy Follers go out in the midday sun.

*   *   *   *

78

'A'isha said, "I never saw anyone more like God's messenger in gravity, calm deportment, and pleasant disposition than Fatima. When she came in to visit him, he got up to welcome her, took her by the hand, kissed her, and made her sit where he was sitting; and when he went in to visit her she got up to welcome him, took him by the hand, kissed him, and made him sit where she was sitting." *(Abu Dawud transmitted it.)*

Chapter 5

The Most Beautiful of her Daughters

I met Grandmother Zainab in the second month after my arrival to Jeddah. Malik's description of this vibrant, strong-willed maternal grandmother had contradicted the stereotypical image of the submissive, reclusive Muslim female. No Saudi woman I had ever heard of impressed me in her independence, piety, intelligence or kindness as much as Zainab.

Zainab's lifetime spanned the last part of the Ottoman Empire, the Arab Revolt of 1916-1918, and the rise of the Saudi dynasty. During the tumultuous dynastic takeover, many inhabitants of Jeddah fled to Suakin (a city on the African side of the Red Sea that resembled old Jeddah) while others sought refuge in Yemen. Zainab's parents insisted that she leave the country until it was safe to re-enter Jeddah. When she returned, she saved her new king's life.

Her service to her king was rendered during a visit to Mecca. She was circumambulating—walking around—the holy Ka'aba at the same time as King Abdul Aziz ibn Saud, who always engaged in such activities with the common people. Shoulders bumped and bare feet trod upon trailing *burkahs*, snagging women backwards. Cautious female hands grabbed onto husbands' pilgrim waist wraps or tunics. Pungent body odors wafted up in the heat, stinging nostrils, turning heads. Toddlers on their fathers' shoulders bounced and swayed like camel riders.

Among this swarm of humanity, Zainab spied a man entering the crowd with a dagger half-concealed in his robes. Most men wore daggers in those days, but they did not make their devotions gripping one at the hilt, nor while approaching the worshipping king at quickened pace.

Zainab drew a sharp breath and pushed through the supplicating crowd to the king's entourage. She gave the alarm, describing and pointing out the man. The king's men laid their hands on the would-be assassin. Afterwards, they turned to reward the courageous lady, only to discover she had melted back into the throng.

By the time I met Grandmother Zainab, she was incalculably ancient and no longer able to walk. Her son, Siddik, regularly carried her to our building, up the four flights of stairs, and placed her on a thin floor mattress in Johara's rooms. (Zainab refused to be laid on Western beds. She had never slept so far off the ground in her life.)

Salha, the Indonesian maid who looked after the elderly woman, was the one who fed Zainab, washed her, combed her hair, and changed her diapers. That was Salha's entire job, and she went with Zainab whenever she changed houses. Each of Zainab's three surviving daughters—Johara, Khadija, and Fatima—kept their mother at their homes for a month at a time. However, the ladies were themselves prone to ailments and could not bend and carry like the young woman hired from Indonesia.

Siddik transported his mother between houses and stayed for tea with his sisters on those occasions. He lived in the house still under Zainab's name but did not insist his mother spend a month there. Apart from those four offspring, there was no one else to care for Grandmother Zainab. Other children, born of earlier marriages, had lived their full lives and died.

Something about Zainab's diminishing sight and accumulation of years, Mama Johara said, enhanced a sporadic gift Zainab had possessed since childhood. Having reached the other end of her life, she was once again seeing jinn—creatures made of smokeless fire, whose existence is acknowledged in the Qur'an. Sometimes Zainab would admonish an invisible presence before her. Those who overheard knew by what she said that she spoke to a jinni. She had been harassed by jinn as a child. In vast old age, when they accosted her again, she was ready for them.

When Grandmother Zainab didn't address herself to the unseen, she blessed her family members and remembered her manners. The hallmark of Arabian etiquette is hospitality and Grandmother Zainab was, even prone and feeble, an example for all younger generations.

I was introduced to her as the new wife of one of her youngest grandsons.

"This is Malik's wife," Mama Johara told her mother in a raised voice, repeating and emphasizing our names, hoping her mother heard and understood. "*Malik*. He married a girl from America, and now she is here. This is Malik's *wife*; her name is *Sylvia*."

Zainab's lips slowly stretched over her wasted face into a beautiful smile. The withered facial structure had pleasing lines of symmetry.

"*Ahlan, Ahlan!*" she said, extending her hand blindly into the air to grasp mine, like a flag of acceptance pitched slightly askew. Then in simple Arabic, she added: "You are most welcome here. We are so happy to have you with us. May Allah bless you!"

I pulled the gnarled fingers into my palm and held them there long enough to say, "*Shukran*--Thank You."

I could see that she had been a handsome woman. In these last years of her life, when she had to be carried everywhere, even Zainab recognized she had been remarkable. Once she was asked, "Of all your daughters, who was the most beautiful?"

Zainab thought long and then replied solemnly, "Of all my daughters, *I* was the most beautiful."

Girls are said to mature early in subtropical climates. For that reason, and because Muslim families used to think (before the need for university educations) that daughters were best off "safely" married,

Zainab took her first husband when she was 12 or 13. On the morning of her first wedding, Zainab was sent by her mother to buy coal at the market. When the girl returned home, she found decorations strung upon the house, delicious smells wafting from the kitchen, and relatives arriving. The females had put on their ceremonial white dresses trimmed with gold buttons. Zainab's wedding attire had been laid out for her, and her bath was being drawn. It was a surprise wedding party. Her husband had met her, but not she him, because by tradition when he had come to ask for her hand, she had been led in front of her suitor with her eyes squeezed shut. (She could have peeked had she wished.)

Zainab's six marriages all ended in the husband's death or divorce, and she outlived every spouse. She was a long-distance walker who ended up having families descended from several husbands. To visit them all, she traversed Jeddah on foot, sometimes walking from one end to the other twice a day.

Malik remembered seeing Zainab carry her own mother—his great grandmother—on her back when visiting them. When that forebear died, Zainab had her arms free to carry other valuables, like boxes of fruits. It did not matter to her that the fruits were cheaply bought because of being partly spoiled. She found the good in everything. A fruit half spoiled, she taught her grandchildren, was also half good. The spoiled part could be cut off and the good part eaten.

Such thrift came before the oil boom, before wealth changed the face of the city. It was a time when camels were tethered in stalls in the downtown marketplace and when boats with lateen sails came and left at the port. The rich were few in those days. Their families could be named and their houses counted on two hands. Jeddah had barely begun to depart from the description given to it by the medieval Spanish Muslim traveler, Ibn Jubayr, who wrote of its inhabitants, "They lead a life so wretched as to break the hardest stone in compassion. They employ themselves in all manner of trades, such as hiring camels should they possess any, and selling milk or water and other things like dates which they might find, or wood they might collect."

Throughout her 6 marriages and after, Zainab bought and sold real estate in her own name. She used her wits to gain a livelihood and her high spirits to inspire others. She was an entertainer to her grandchildren, singing and dancing for their merriment in the days before television. She told them stories, much like the street story tellers from earlier centuries in Arabia.

One day in her walk home from the marketplace, not wishing to be trampled by a merchant's caravan of camels coming into the market square, Zainab took to a narrower street shadowed by tall buildings on either side and only wide enough for two people, or at best a human and a donkey, to pass each other. A dark-skinned woman wearing a scarf over her head (but no all-concealing *burqah)* lay curled in the door well of a fine house. A tin cup of water rested near her head. Zainab guessed she was a slave.

"Peace be upon you, "said Zainab, leaning over the woman. "Why do you lie here? This is not a place to sleep!"

The woman lifted her head and the scarf fell away, revealing damaged, lesion-covered skin.

"Go away," warned the girl in a mix of Swahili and broken Arabic. "I make you sick. My mistress burns sleeping mat. She throws me out so she not be sick. I have no place."

Zainab appraised the slave girl's skin and bloodshot, ravaged eyes. "Are you free, then, to go? Can you walk?"

"They do not want me. You must not want me."

"I am not afraid of you," said Zainab. "You will not make me sick."

Zainab put her hand under the woman's arm, helping her up.

"Why you want sick slave?" mumbled the woman, stumbling a little.

Zainab steadied her. "I do not want a slave. I do not own slaves. But you need a friend and I have a place for you. You will be comfortable. Come now."

Zainab possessed a formidable knowledge of natural medicine—for instance, of the Neem tree, the steeped leaves of which she used for bathing, drinking and when dried and burned slowly, for fumigating the rooms of her house. Most Jeddah people only knew the tree for its shade.

The outcast slave girl lived with the lady who fed and tended her until the sick slave died. Zainab buried the woman and prayed over her. Zainab herself did not contract any illness.

Whenever I simmered and decocted herbs for my own health purposes, buying indigenous gums like myrrh from the *souk*, the aromas gave Malik pause in his walk through the house.

"You remind me of my grandmother Zainab," he told me. "She used to make strange teas, which she made us drink. She told us they were therapeutic."

As my first year of residence in Jeddah went by, I grew accustomed to seeing Grandmother Zainab in Mama Johara's quarters whenever it was my mother-in-law's turn to care for her. Mama Johara chuckled to recount whatever amusing things her mother had said that day. It pained Mama Johara when her mother would ask, "When will I be at Fatima's?" Fatima (who died not long after Zainab) was the daughter who sprang from Zainab's marriage with Kizmet, the Turkish man. Of all her husbands, Zainab had been most in love with Kizmet.

For Mama Johara, whose own father had died when she was very small and who had been taken away from Zainab, hearing her mother ask when she would be at Fatima's was painful. To Malik and me, Mama Johara commented sadly, "Love is not a controllable thing." She believed her mother loved Fatima more, because Zainab had loved Fatima's father, Kizmet, more.

As we became closer over the years, Mama Johara recounted to me what she and her mother had experienced in being pulled apart while Mama Johara was a little child. She also confided to me the affinity she and her mother shared for the supernatural.

Zainab's age at death was calculated at somewhere between 120 and 150 years. Only one sister lived as long, but the family will never know their ages for sure. Calendars were not used in her lifetime. Recording dates became mandatory only under the Saudi government.

On the day of her funeral, I saw Zainab's corpse set upon a crude wooden platform in the marbled entryway of the apartment building we inhabited. Professional funeral women had been hired to chant prayers and ritually wash the body. Their loud, beseeching prayers ricocheted against the walls.

Water splashed out of metal ewers, over the corpse, and onto the tiled floor, drenching the cloth that the women had modestly arranged to cover Zainab's private parts. A maid took turns with a female relative in pushing the water out under the closed main door with long-poled squeegees. The water streamed down the outside marble stairs, into the street. We were all females inside. The men had left. They waited to be summoned by phone to take Zainab's corpse to the cemetery, a desert place of weeds enclosed by a wall, with no marking stones.

I did not have four-month-old Yousef in my arms when I tiptoed down from the third floor to watch the funeral preparations. This was not something I wanted him to be in the middle of, even if he couldn't understand. Loitering in the airless sauna of the stairwell was a feat for adults only.

Sobs echoed up the staircase. I descended into the solemnity, the chants and the moans, to find Zainab's three daughters as well as another Fatima, wife of Siddik, standing about the corpse as the mourning women did their paid duties.

Khadija, Mama Johara, and Fatima (daughter of Kizmet) took turns in tenderly kissing Zainab's forever-stilled feet. I watched in a tired, sleep-deprived state because of my new baby. I thought about how much a mother's feet pace the floor, or walk swiftly everywhere for the sake of a child. Kissing them made sense. Siddik's wife Fatima leaned against the wall and sobbed brokenly.

They called the corpse lovely. It was fit and trim, like the body of a twenty-five-year old. The facial features were symmetrical with few lines. After washing, the funeral women dried Zainab's body with fresh towels and plaited her hair into long braids. Herbs and dried flowers were sprinkled over the corpse. Then it was wrapped in long stretches of clean, white cloth.

The men of the family, including Malik, transported Zainab's corpse to the graveyard by car. The women did not follow, for in Arabia, women do not go to graveyards. There are religious rules prohibiting it; and truly, Arab women have a strong tendency to become hysterical in grief.

The male relatives took turns carrying the body at the graveyard. God bestows blessings for this action. While men will eagerly volunteer to carry a bier, few wish to descend into the pit itself. That takes nerves.

Despite all the wide desert gaping as far as the eye can see around Jeddah, its graveyards are ancient and in continual re-use. About six months after burials, graves are opened and the bones pushed aside to make room for another corpse. No one knows where in a graveyard a relative is buried unless he remembers from the funeral. The desuetude of Muslim graveyards is meant to remind believers of the finality of death. They are to hasten to do good and be kind in this life, for once dead, earthly works are a thing of the past. Graveyards are only visited by men, who come on holy days to pray for their deceased. Saudi graveyards have no flowers, only weeds.

Malik volunteered to descend into the pit. He positioned his grandmother's corpse with her face turned towards Mecca, the direction in which Muslims turn when they pray. I will never forget the stricken look on his face when he returned home.

"The grave had a horrible odor," he said, "and its walls were oily."

I shuddered. "Why were they oily?"

"What do you think happens when a human body decomposes? I saw oil and grease streaked on the earth walls."

I didn't want to picture it, but he had already created an image. In Jeddah's soaring heat that bakes the ground, Malik's description seemed logical.

"What a place to leave my grandmother!" Malik said, shaking his head. Once more I admired this woman whom I had barely met, so beloved that her grandchildren grieved to leave her in the grave, even after a long life by anyone's standards.

Chapter 6

Breaking Tradition

Sa'adiya was a burly woman from Egypt with an irrepressible grin that stretched over her whole face despite a grueling workload as maid for my husband's second mother, Leena. I met Sa'adiya downstairs in Leena's apartment. I got to know her much better upstairs on the roof when we found each other with laundry bins of freshly washed clothes to hang. Depending on the day, the clothes baked in the airless heat or flapped in a balmy breeze off the Red Sea.

Jeddah, like many other Arab cities, is a world of flat roofs. Women don't have to wrap themselves so carefully there. The roof offers more freedom to be a person, feel the air, and look across at other people on the tops of houses. Women and children can stretch their limbs, walking, or in the case of children, roller skating. It is a place to go to feel the sky. For women who miss freedom, that's a big thing. Some of us didn't leave the house at times for days; for others, it was weeks.

I probably tried Sa'adiya's patience by calling her *sayadiya*, a delicious Jeddah fish meal made with blackened rice. She didn't seem to mind. It took practice getting my tongue around Arabic words, and she encouraged my efforts. We hung clothes together and chatted over the clothesline.

"Do you have children, *Sayadiya*?" I asked.

"Yes!" She told me how many and their ages. Sa'adiya was with Leena's family from the moment I arrived in 1983 until 2004. Her children grew up and married without seeing their mother more than once every two years during her contract-permitted vacations. They attended school, bought clothes and ate, all thanks to her ongoing bank transfers.

Sa'adiya's exuberance could be overwhelming. About seven days after my son Yousef was born, the family arranged the party known in Jeddah as *Al Rahmani*. It coincides with the traditional Muslim celebration for a baby's birth.

On that evening, most of the extended family showed up. Strangers I had never met knocked on the doorframe of my bedroom and traipsed in to sit on my bed. They had come to see the American woman.

When Mama Johara entered my bedroom to tell me it was time, I put on a Moroccan caftan and crossed through the stairwell into her apartment with my baby bound up in his swaddling cloth. Yousef looked like a newborn kitten with his long eyes and eyelashes. Sa'adiya sucked in a deep breath as soon as she saw me and belted out what sounded to me like a high-pitched Native American war cry, her tongue flicking against her upper lip and her flattened hand positioned over her mouth.

I like that sound, known as "ululating," when it's on the soundtrack of a movie, or when—in a film—I see village women from Jordan or Morocco making the cry while standing under palm trees. I don't mind it in real life at a distance—across the street, say. Right in one's ear, it has the appeal of a police siren.

Sa'adiya could have been an opera singer. The other women joined her, yet the ringing in my ears was the echo of that powerful Egyptian voice. Seeing me knocked off balance—maybe that was the point--Sa'adiya scooped Yousef out of my arms and carried him into the center of a crowded room of children, ululating all the way.

My heart pounded and blood rushed to my head. My baby! I watched Sa'adiya, wildly trilling her tongue, set Yousef on a pillow upon the ground. Little children crowded in on him like cats around a snack.

The tiny girls were dressed in frilly, lacy new dresses. Small boys under six moved stiffly in tuxedos. They thronged around Yousef while unsteadily holding their dripping, burning candles.

It was all I could do not to cry out, "Move back a little; give him room to breathe!" Some of the urchins knelt down close to my baby, forgetting they had a candle and not hearing Sa'adiya warn them to stay back. They were intrigued by his tininess. More than one runny little nose needed a tissue.

Every time I was ready to leap over all and grab my newborn, Sa'adiya managed to get the children to back up. I reflected that people in Jeddah had been holding this tradition for generations. Deep breaths steadied me. I didn't want the children (or their watching mothers) to decide that I was not willing to be a part of their culture. Gifts for baby Yousef were piling up in my bedroom.

A solid brass mortar and pestle sat two inches from the ornate pillow upon which Yousef lay. I did not question what it was for until Sa'adiya picked up the pestle. My heart pinched. No. . . .

Cardamom, cloves and stick cinnamon were in the receptacle. Like a female elf, Sa'adiya raised her twinkling eyes briefly to meet mine. Still I did not want to believe what she would do next, so close to Yousef.

She brought the pestle down into the mortar with all the force that her impressive biceps and triceps could muster and banged the daylights out of that mortar. Yousef's little head bounced like a tennis ball with every clash five inches from his tiny right ear. He didn't let out a peep. His eyes were big, shocked. . . .

This are moments when new mothers think of all that can go wrong. My heart was beating erratically as I stared at Sa'adiya. Might she have a seizure mid-pound and miss her mark? Could I grab him this instant, leave, and endure the hatred that a black X on my door would occasion for the next twenty years?

Much later it occurred to me that Saudi babies learn to sleep through din because they become hearing impaired from the first week of life.

The children who had come to the party were led in the song:

Ya Rab, Ya Rahmani;   *O Lord, O Merciful,*

91

Barik lana fil alwolani	*Bless our baby.*
Allah sa'adna	*God made us happy*
wa ada'anu	*And gave us*
ma wulud jedeed	*a newborn child.*
Min ferh'gulubena ghaneana	*From the happiness of*
	our hearts we have sung.

Blessed, happy celebration!

I counted the seconds until I could flee with my baby back to our bedroom. Perhaps Sa'adiya had added the mortar and pestle entertainment to *Al-Rahmani;* how could I know? This party was not going the way Malik had described.

In the old days, he had told me, up until the first few decades of Ibn Saud's reign, it was the *daiyah* or midwife who officiated at *Al Rahmani.* The *daiyah* visited the house on the seventh day after the birth, bringing sesame oil to massage into the mother's skin, especially in parts that had stretched during pregnancy. After thoroughly massaging the mother, the *daiyah* bound the mother's waist in a wrapper to counteract any tendency towards sagging.

Then came the turn of the children who had been invited. They were handed candles, much as they are today. In those days, the candles were huge and fat. Today they are skinny dinner table candles. The midwife used to hold the baby and apply kohl to his or her eyes. Now the mother or grandmother does that. According to tradition, the children's candles are lit and they walk slowly around the baby, who may or may not be held aloft by someone, depending on whether anyone cares about hot wax dripping on the baby.

The children sing and are sometimes led up to the roof. The mortar and pestle comes next. While smashing sweet spices, the *daiyah* or a female relative calls out prayers for blessings upon the baby, its mother and father. The guests chorus "Ameen" and may clap their hands.

Not all families let children light their candles. Times have changed. Now maids to watch over the children. The maids are

92

generally uneducated girls from the Indian archipelago or Sri Lanka. Their employers do not give them the authority to ensure discipline and order. (Or maybe it is the employers who are uneducated, in which case the problem is even worse.) At any rate, *Al Rahmani* was gaining the reputation of a pyromaniac's fiesta when children ended up setting the curtains, the furnishings, or each other on fire.

If the candles have been lit for even a minute of pyromaniac joy, the children's clothes are covered with drops of wax. They take home their candles and little gifts from the baby's family, usually a pretty container filled with candy-covered almonds. No one leaves before the traditional Muslim feast of a lamb (or two, or three) roasted in underground pits and accompanied by rice into which the same slow-cooking lamb has dripped its delectable juices and fats.

Sa'adiya may have made *Al-Rahmani* terrifyingly memorable for me, but when the dangers receded, I was strangely touched. She had been moved by my comradeship. We were two non-Saudis caught in a world where we didn't feel at home. She tried to initiate me into Arab culture with every ounce of fervor she could muster. It was a staggering performance.

*   *   *   *

For the first four months of Yousef's life, I coped against what every young mother copes with, the only difference being that there was no internet to consult and no books on motherhood available in English at the local bookstores.

My sister-in-law Husna, who had given birth to three children, sternly instructed me not to lie on my side when I breastfed. "Sit upright!" she commanded. "That is the way it is done." Doing as she said tore out two stitches. People who act like they know everything generally don't.

"You should have nursed on your side," my doctor told me after the damage was done. An ongoing low-grade fever hurt my efforts to breastfeed in the first eight weeks after Yousef's birth. Mama Johara insisted I feed Yousef bottled milk, "or he will starve!" Once or twice, she took Yousef into her quarters.

"Sleep!" she cautioned. "I cannot do this often."

Knowing I had only one day in which to get better, panic brought insomnia.

"If not for my back, I would have him in here every day," she told Malik.

I was fatigued and homesick. Yousef cried a lot. I had no idea what to do and no one to consult except Mama Johara. I was afraid he was, as she said, *starving*. I gave him more and more bottled milk.

Sometimes I knew better than to take advice. Every culture, for instance, feeds off superstition (one doesn't think about it so much in one's own culture as in a foreign one). There was a day my mother-in-law came into my bedroom with a baby's bracelet of black beads with red dots painted on them.

"What's this for?" I asked, fingering the small necklace.

"That's to counteract the evil eye," explained Mama Johara. "Put it on the baby."

"This stuff doesn't work." I dangled it over the wastebasket. "To protect ourselves from evil, we seek refuge in God."

She looked disturbed and left. I told Malik about the beads, and he said, "Don't forget my mother never had the chance to go to school. Sometimes she thinks superstitions are religious beliefs. She will probably realize you are right after she thinks about it a little."

*   *   *   *

In Arabia, the first son of a new generation is commonly named after his paternal grandfather. Malik would have been remiss not to have named our son after his father. He asked his family if they agreed. No one objected. I was pleased because "Yousef" translates to "Joseph." I wanted my son to be at ease in the USA as well as in Arabia.

A few months after my son's birth, a boy baby was born to Leena's son Tarek and his wife/cousin, Soraya. He was duly named Yousef. Malik and I wondered if Leena had been altogether honest when she had said she didn't mind our using that name.

On the day Tarek's newborn baby "Yousef" was brought over to the family house for inspection, Soraya sent her sister upstairs to get my little Yousef. I was told that this was tradition too: the two Yousefs needed to meet each other.

"You didn't tell me about that tradition," I said to Malik that evening.

"What tradition?"

"Introducing babies with the same name to each other," I answered.

Malik frowned. "There isn't any tradition like that. But I think I know what they were doing," he added, slowly. "They were probably deciding which baby was more 'Yousef.'"

"Huh?"

"Which baby is more handsome."

According to scripture, the prophet Yousef (peace be upon him) was so handsome that a room full of women carving their meat with knives and lying on their sides, Roman style, accidentally cut their hands when Yousef walked into their midst. He was so handsome he made all of them forget what they were doing.

The following year, Leena's son Muhammad and his Turkish wife also had a boy. That child was named Yousef. Then followed Leena's sons Abdur Rahman and Ghassan; upon having sons, both were ordered by their mother to name their boys "Yousef." During his teens, my son Yousef Al-Shamsi had four first cousins by the same first and last name. At large family gatherings, when someone called out "Yousef Al-Shamsi," five boys answered. That's not tradition. That's confusion!

95

96

Chapter 7

The Red Stroller

I asked Malik to buy a stroller for our baby. He went to the local *souk*—open air market—and bought one that took me from one to ten minutes to open or shut depending on how adept I was feeling that day. When I was in a rush and couldn't get it to close, Ramadi, our longhaired gray cat from California, took naps in it.

We used the stroller for the big event of the week: going to *Al Fao*, the local supermarket. We also pushed it through the air conditioned malls with shining interiors of marble tiles and brass trim that were just going up on streets like Tahlia, Sitteen and Medina Road. For deals—underwear made in China, cheap kitchenware or fabric— we pushed the stroller through the open air souks of Bawadi or Bab Mecca where vendors boomed out *"Ashara, Ashara, Ashara!"* in raspy voices. With this cry, the sellers meant all their little trinkets cost *ashara riyal*—ten riyals, roughly $2.75.[4]

The clothes vendors of the souks hung layers of quasi-Western or Middle Eastern and Indian garments over the sides of their stalls. I

---

[4] The Saudi government has traditionally kept the rate of exchange stable, so that 1 dollar equals 3.75 riyals, and 10 riyals equals 2.66 dollars.

looked at everything, my neck twisting like a swivel. Sometimes whiffs of rose, amber or Oud perfume oils assailed our noses (the better qualities were to be had downtown or at the malls); at other times, it was the sweat of passing *abaya*-clad women who hadn't yet come to trust deodorant as a good Western experience.

I was stuck in my rooms too much. They were like two boxes I could bounce between. I thought I would lose my mind. There was little to do except hunt the yellow lizards I did not then recognize as geckos, and the cockroaches, large and small, that found their way into my kitchen cabinets.

Prior to Yousef's birth, I walked the grounds of the women's university, where I imagined I was starting a real profession as a college teacher. The girls had called me "Lady Diana." While I enjoyed the thrill of teaching, Dr. Wafah had failed to inspire in me the noble dream of working for the Saudi government for free. With a baby to care for, I could not go back to teaching—not without receiving a salary.

That meant I was housebound and bored. I needed to get out a little. Malik did his best. Sometimes he took me to the beach, where we liked to set up a blue-and-white-striped tent for the day. We had to drive an hour south or north of Jeddah because swimming off the local beach had become forbidden ever since a Bedouin government official's son drowned there. It didn't matter that the youth did not know how to swim. His father was important, so the fish swimming there should have lifted his body to shore.

Before Yousef was born, and before my pregnancy was advanced, I swam a lot. Malik, always a daring man, took me out with him by inflated raft to the place where waves broke and the bottom of the sea floor fell off. There sharks swam and larger fish could be caught. An island was attainable. It took about twenty minutes of rowing to get to the island from the shore area where first Malik and I could walk, submerged to the necks.

On one occasion, coming back, Malik became rough with me.

"Row!" he cried. "Row! Put your back into it!"

I was rowing as hard as I could and I thought to myself that being pregnant, I should not have to row so hard. And he certainly could be nicer.

Instead, he became angrier, yelling. "What's wrong with you? Row, I told you. Can't you hear me? Row!"

Men become angry and women get hurt. Maybe marriages would not be torn apart at the seams if men would kindly communicate. Malik was typical of every male on earth in that way.

Years later, I discovered that sharks circled underneath us as the air raft slowly deflated from a rip that Malik did not want to alert me to.

I think he should have told me.

The Saudi beach is hot. The heat made my son's cheeks turn as red as tomatoes. When Malik waded two or three football field lengths out in the shimmering turquoise waters to fish where the waves broke and the shark pups darted, I waded into the shallow regions, holding my baby and wearing a big straw hat over my head.

The Red Sea is shallow for a great distance. Sand dunes shimmer under the clear turquoise water. Other patches are rocky or full of seaweed, sea slugs and conch shell creatures. I stayed with Yousef in the clear, sandy spots about a hundred meters from our vehicle.

When he got tired, I rocked him in my arms and the sea lapped over our legs and laps. Shaded by the hat, my baby fell asleep to my lullabies and the sound of water moving gently around us. Then I daydreamed, watching seabirds hunt the silvery fish that leapt above water.

After Malik sloshed back with his catch hidden in a burlap bag that he pulled through the sea with him, he cooked the fish over a fire, making rice in a pot. We feasted like royalty. The Red Sea could be heaven.

But heaven is a place devils want in. Cars with men and no women passed along the beach, stopping if only I but not Malik could be seen. To avoid stalkers, Malik and I tried to choose deserted spots.

One day, when Malik went far out into the water, three fellows parked as close to me and the water as they dared. Malik was no more than a speck in the distance. Yousef was asleep on my lap in the shallow water.

I calculated my chances of escape or self-defense should the men decide to visit me. All I would be able to do, I realized, was move around in waist-deep water, holding a baby. They could probably catch me if they tried.

My fingers dug into the sand. The grains sifted through my tensed fingers until I found a good-sized piece of broken coral. I dug it out, trying not to let Yousef awaken. It was big enough and sharp enough to use as a dagger. Holding it made me feel better. The men stayed parked for at least half an hour, watching us. I really wanted some cold water, waiting in our car, but I dared not leave the water.

Finally they got sick of waiting and left.

It was not the first time men bothered me, nor would it be the last. Before Yousef was born, I was alone in a tent while Malik fished. A car's engine grew louder and I thought it would pass, but the vehicle stopped. The door opened and slammed shut.

Why oh why would anyone want to stop right here? There were miles of deserted shoreline.

I held my breath. The sound of footsteps trudging through the sand got louder and neared the tent. I looked around but there was nothing to hold up in defense. The book I was reading? A soft drink? The lid of the cooler?

A man's legs appeared. Then I saw his face. He was a stranger, squatting, peering at me. A small red crab skittered behind him and gulls called overhead.

I glared back with every ounce of outrage in my eyes I could muster. We stared at each other, this stranger and I.

Then, the man made a decision. He stood and walked around the tent.

The sound of his steps receded. Only when I heard his car start and drive away did I realize I was shaking.

Was any woman who ventured out of doors fair game?

Malik came home one day from work to tell me that he was being sent on a seminar to Cardington, England. His government department was paying expenses.

"Oh my God, that is great!" I exclaimed, thinking of Dickens and Shakespeare. I jumped up in happiness.

I had stayed in London with my grandfather during the Christmas of my 16th year, "crawling" from the Cheshire Cheese to the Sherlock Holmes and many another touristy pub.

Even if Cardington was not London and I no longer did ye olde bottoms up, I could see myself and Yousef bundled up for a wintry walk while Daddy was at a lecture. We would watch interesting TV shows in English and strike up conversations. We would be *free*.

"It's only me going," Malik added. "They don't send family."

I looked at my husband blankly and wondered what being left alone in Arabia could possibly feel like.

There was no hope of mustering the extra money for tickets. We didn't have it. We couldn't afford the strawberries flown in from the West that were at the grocery story.

I pretended not to see such things. At the end of every month, when we were down to coins, we lived on lentil soup, eggs, bread, cucumbers, rice and tomatoes. Now my friend, lover, companion and entertainment package was leaving me in his hot, sluggish, foreign-language-speaking desert homeland.

"For how long?"

"Five weeks."

My heart sank. I felt nauseated, but I commanded the edges of my lips to lift.

"Oh well."

It was my second winter in Jeddah, and the first time Malik was leaving me alone there.

"Don't worry, my family won't let you feel lonely," promised Malik gently, as if he could read my thoughts. "They'll take care of you. You can go to the store with them or ask them to get you whatever you want. They'll come sit with you and invite you into their salons for tea. They'll take you out visiting relatives. You'll learn more Arabic."

His voice was earnest. I believed him. He believed himself. He had once described to me an Arabia where men dropped whatever they

101

were doing in order to drive women to shop or visit friends. While women were (and are) forbidden by Saudi law from driving (until this 21century, as incredible as that seems) the men made up for that, he had insisted, by existing to do their will.

So according to Malik, the men of the house would be at pains to chauffeur me around in a spirit of compassion and chivalry.

At that time, Malik had plenty of driving-age brothers living at home. (The age of driving is whenever a boy can see over the dashboard.) They were always borrowing his car.

I figured he was right although I knew that no one in the house would make up for Malik's absence even if Ghassan, a half-brother, or Haroun, Malik's eldest brother, did speak English. My in-laws were pleasant to me although so far, I hadn't really been embraced by the females as one of their own.

Whenever I came into Mama Johara's apartment on the weekends and Malik's two married sisters, Nafeesah and Husna, were there to visit their mother and three younger unmarried sisters, Shahida, Mahasen and Amahl, I always found the girls in a tight circle with their backs to me. They might throw a "Peace be upon you," or a "Welcome" over their shoulders, but the circle didn't break. After a few minutes, I went back to my own rooms.

I psyched myself for an interlude alone. Communication with the few outside women I had met depended on my borrowing Mama Johara's telephone. Malik and I did not have a phone, nor would we have one for another nine years. For such luxury, Malik would have to work his way up into career prominence and powerful business associations.

Malik left for England, which made his little brother Ziyad weep copious tears. The child stopped coming upstairs. I was almost regretful. Conversely, the rooster downstairs, which roamed around the two cement-covered meters enclosed by a wall around the family house, stoically kept on crowing at odd hours throughout the day. Malik's brothers had the keys to his jeep so no one knocked on the apartment door to borrow the car.

The family children no longer paraded into our two rooms because without Malik to chatter at, there was nothing better to do than play with a half-American baby.

I won't say it got quieter. The rooster saw to that. It was one of the animals belonging to the ever-shifting menagerie of half-brother Mohammad, who lived on the second floor. The creatures were all cooped up in the airless cemented jail downstairs. Not long after, Mohammad stashed a living horse down there.

The rooster crowed at endless hours of the day and night, praising God as birds are said to do when they crow or sing. This one was very devout. It was winter and I heard the crowing vividly. The outside temperature was not warm enough to warrant turning on the air conditioners, so the windows were open.

In summer, the mechanical drone of the single unit air conditioners muffled outside noises. Somehow Yousef had gotten so used to the rooster he managed to nap through its worship unless the rooster worked itself into a sort of pious frenzy, like a vocalizing whirling dervish.

I had books to read but I couldn't really read them unless Yousef was sleeping. No one besides me ever played with our baby while Malik was gone, though there were at least twenty people and a couple of maids in the house.

Yet I was utterly alone.

Yousef was too tiny to be interested in TV, all talking heads, daily documentaries in Arabic on Saudi Arabia's amazing technological strides. In the morning, Saudi ladies covered in black scarves demonstrated how to spray paint gold a basket or a fake flower.

Who on earth would want to know such things?

The only good thing on TV was ten minutes of Tom and Jerry cartoons.

In truth, Mommy was entertainment center. Somehow, despite that, I had started doing a little writing, publishing essays in *The Saudi Gazette*, a local English language newspaper. I wrote about the experiences of my life as a Westerner married to a Saudi: trying to learn Arabic, the principles behind the Saudi wedding, and what it was like living with an extended family.

Writing and selling articles was not against the law. That was a strange but welcome fact. The money brought the joy of toys to our home.

103

After Malik's departure, I visited my in-laws in the same building. The American mother and baby did not generate much notice. No one talked to me except to say "how are you?" and ignore me. I decided to stay in my quarters and see who visited. Groceries were in the kitchen; there was no need to purchase anything.

The red stroller stood uselessly in the corner of our living room. It occurred to me it could be pushed up on the roof. I took it upstairs on one of those first lonely afternoons when the sun had started to drop into the Western horizon. I ran downstairs and pulled Yousef out of his crib. On the rooftop, the stroller went around in the largest circle possible, accompanied by the singing of songs and the fantasy of walking along the Corniche, a boulevard bordering the Red Sea. When that got old, the Corniche turned into 17th Street in Costa Mesa, and then the peninsula in Newport Beach, California; morphing soon into the major streets remembered from Lausanne, Switzerland, and Paris, followed by any place at all locked in memory. This is what prisoners do.

It worked for a day or two.

Eventually, I dragged the stroller back downstairs and left it in the corner of the living room, bouncing my son around in baby games between two rooms. Our only visitor, my pretty sister-in-law Amahl, came in about three times a week in the evenings to say hello and coo at her infant nephew. Little did she know how meaningful her visits were! She cared.

A week after Malik left, Yousef took his nap as usual under the air of the overhead fan. I had been yearning for this half hour of siesta time to lose myself in a book. When the baby slept, my nerves relaxed with the solace of literature. I put on the kettle and came quietly back in with my mug of English Breakfast Tea.

As in all subtropical countries, there was a tradition of siesta time in Arabia. Saudi government offices closed at 2:30 pm. Employees went home, ate lunch and slept until the time of the 'Asr prayer. Schools let out in conformity with this schedule. Families took their main meal together at midday, just before the nap. All small shops and doctors' offices shut down at this time and reopened right after the sunset prayer.

While the neighborhood slept, the amplified notes of an electric piano screeched out from under our bedroom window. The player was Malik's younger half-brother, Sameer.

I turned my head. Yousef was awake and blinking expectantly at Mommy. There would be no reading or quietly sipped tea.

No young, exhausted, forlorn mother should be abandoned in a foreign country. Humans tend to block bad memories, but this one has held. I was not mad at my baby. I was stunned at the lack of consideration from others and at my absolute isolation and loneliness.

"Just a minute, Darling." I closed the book. A march into the bathroom brought me to a plastic bucket kept there for various jobs. I stuck it under the bathtub spigot to fill with water. It was so heavy I needed two hands. I wobbled back with it into the bedroom to the beat and screech of Sameer's electric piano, all the way up to the window through which noise flooded in.

"Flood" was the operative word. The window screen opened easily.

"Here you go, Buddy," I said, pouring the contents of my bucket out the window.

I didn't realize Sameer had placed his electric piano precisely against the wall so he could look outside while playing. Not that it would have mattered. I would have poured, no matter what.

A shriek pierced the air.

This was followed by a tirade of verbal outrage in Arabic. Sameer didn't take a breath. He kept screaming. Well gosh, that meant he was alright, didn't it. If electrocution had occurred, it hadn't been lethal.

Nonetheless, Malik's younger half-brother Sameer sounded crazed.

Was he going to stop screaming? Didn't he understand he had started the problem? His music was a message; my water was a reply message. Screaming, screaming, screaming.

My stomach started hurting. I breathed faster and my heart pounded so hard it hurt too. I sat down on the edge of the bed, grabbing the side to hold on. Yousef stared at me, and I wondered how bad a thing

I had done. I was not in my own country. I was not really in what I could call my own house.

Screeched *curses* rolled out of that downstairs window. My limbs trembled under my eyes. *Take deep breaths,* I told myself.

Minutes rolled by. God, he was still screaming. What would the neighbors think? Where could I hide with the baby? Sameer was going to kill somebody. It wasn't hard to imagine who that might be. I needed help. I needed mercy. I needed a mother. I knew one, though not mine, but she was my best shot at protection.

Sameer's mother, Leena.

I was now going to collect on all those promises of hospitality and being "like a daughter" to her. I threw on a scarf and tore down the stairs with Yousef in my arms. Sameer was shrieking holy hell in his room and probably wiping the water off his piano, which is why he hadn't come to kill me yet.

Whoever got to Madame Leena first had the best chance of her sponsorship. Arabian tradition gave me a chance--if I could make my pitch first. The law of the desert states a stranger from a tribe has the right to three nights of hospitality. Here I was a stranger in a strange land, the mother of a (half) Saudi child and at the mercy of my husband's family while he was gone. Who would stop Sameer?

My hope was that Leena would keep her son from hurting me or seeking revenge.

First I had to rouse her from her nap. She was in her bedroom, far off on the other side of the building, where Sameer's piano playing hadn't bothered her. It had affected no one but lucky me and my baby.

Most of my vocabulary had been picked up in an Arabic course taken at Monterey Peninsula College. It involved useless words like "the secretary," "museum" and "the employee." Dire circumstances can sometimes help trigger ability. Even so, my torrent of speech came out in a truly frenzied pigeon Arabic:

"I am sorry; I am sorry, Madame Leena!" This apology was launched into Leena's curtain-darkened bedroom where an air conditioner droned full blast.

"No, no, never mind," she said in a groggy voice, swinging her feet off onto the floor. Maybe she thought I was sorry for waking her up. "Sa'adiya, make tea!" she called out. Then she turned the single unit bedroom air conditioner off.

Now I *could* hear Sameer's screaming, albeit muffled, from the recesses of the other apartment. Man, didn't the guy stop to breathe? Madame Leena frowned.

It was now or never. "I am very tired, Madame Leena," I blurted. "Yousef does not sleep much. He sleeps little. Malik is not here. I am tired. There is only me. Yousef was sleeping and I wanted to sleep, like you, but Sameer made big music, a very loud music under my bedroom window after the 'Asr prayer when everyone sleeps. After one minute, Yousef is awake. I pour water out my window. Sameer is angry and I am sorry. I don't think good. I am very tired. I want my mother."

I held tight, bracing for what might come. Malik had told me interesting stories of Madame Leena's disciplinary methods. While Mama Johara had clear ideas of conduct conducive to peace between neighbors and co-wives, Madame Leena liked to go with the flow.

When Leena's children stole into Malik's room in days gone by, breaking the tape recorder or telescope that he had bought after a summer job slapping labels on canned goods, or uprooting his vegetable garden, she excused her kids for just "being children." If Mama Johara demanded an apology, Madame Leena might beat the child with a shoe so relentlessly it made one wonder if the beating was meant to trigger shame in the complaining party. Or create a new culprit.

Such beatings were timed to take place in front of the father. *Now see what she's made me do! Your first wife doesn't like the children we have produced together, my love.*

Personally, I didn't mind if Leena beat Sameer with a shoe. That would have been okay with me.

Sameer's screams were getting louder and closer. Even I could understand what he was saying. "I AM A MAN!" he roared. "I AM A MAN!"

Some part of my brain found this amusing. I thought he would cry, "That damned bitch!" or "Wait till I get my hands on her!" but no, he kept screaming out that he was a man. Like we didn't know that already, *duh!*

The snorting bull arrived with loud bangs from intervening doors. His face was suffused red. Sameer saw me cowering behind his mother. He launched into an angry spiel that seemed to take forever. His mother allowed him to vent.

"She's sorry," Madame Leena finally tossed out, adding something else I couldn't understand except "baby," "Westerner," and "American." She put her arm around me.

My gaze stayed lowered and my lips moved to form the customary "*Ma'aleysh*" for personal faults which, curiously, means "It doesn't matter." I rather liked that meaning at present.

I had once seen a man at Mecca, inches in front of Malik fling his wraparound white body towel over his shoulder. The fringes stung Malik's right eye. Tears ran down my huband's cheek and his eye got very bloodshot. The man who had caused the injury glanced backwards with a muttered "It doesn't matter" that I had found lacking in brotherly contrition.

Now, however, I appreciated the wide interpretation.

"Forgive me," I added because I was a woman intent on survival. Then I repeated, with relief and a sense of catharsis, "It doesn't matter. It doesn't matter. . . ." Gazing at the floor, I made my way out of Madame Leena's apartment.

Not surprisingly, Sameer didn't offer to drive me anywhere while Malik was gone. Mohammad did once, probably because there were no hand grenades around for me to drop on his rooster. By then I was a bit scared of going out with that side of the family, at least for the moment. Yet I was grateful to Madame Leena. She had saved my life. May Allah reward her!

Now it was up to me to protect my sanity until Malik got back. Little do Saudi men know to what mental agony they subject their Western wives by abandoning them alone in that country! Perhaps Saudi women handle it because they have been cooped up all their lives and are used to having no freedom. They also have their families around to distract them.

When I returned to my rooms with Yousef, I knew I would have to use my wits or lose them. I couldn't have Malik coming home to a basket case.

The first thing I saw, back in the apartment, was that red stroller. It teased me with its wheels. If only I could get to a mall on my own! After having stirred up the family, I didn't need the humiliation of begging to be taken out. Why couldn't I go somewhere by myself?

The stroller teased the periphery of my vision. It looked like a magic carpet. When Malik called by phone from England, he could tell we were lonely and bored. He promised to take us out as soon as he got back. But that was three weeks away. I tried to assess the situation.

What was different about my life? God, where should I start? I had driven a car in California. I had to cover up now whenever I went out although I had dressed modestly, as a new Muslim, in California after marrying Malik. In Saudi Arabia, I had a visa that said I wasn't allowed to work ("may not work with or without money" were the exact words). That was why King Abdul Aziz University had refused to break the law by paying me for my year of loitering on campus, teaching classes. Naturally I had been and was still barred from attending classes since I was not a Saudi.

The government had neglected to send me a maid, so I was still breaking the law by doing housework without money. I didn't have any social life to speak of although I had met a girl who spoke English, whom I found wandering around the university grounds. She was from Curacao, an island in the southwestern Caribbean. She had no phone number to give me, so I had lost track of her.

That was normal. I would have no phone number of my own for ten years.

When Malik took me out, I had approached women who looked Western at the grocery store or souk and introduced myself. A good number of fair-complexioned Syrian women who backed away when I stuck my hand out and said "hello" in English.

I was caving in, jailing myself. Why didn't I just take a damn *walk* out on the street? The stroller was right here. Who cared if Saudi women didn't do that?

"Oh you fool!" I cried happily, jumping to my feet. Yousef, nearby, toppled over. I grabbed him and danced around, singing, "Baby! Baby! Yes!" What a great idea! What was wrong with me not to have thought of this before?"

My son was delighted with my elation. He tried to fly with his chubby little arms and laughed along with me. He approved of *whatever* Mommy had up her sleeve. (Babies are so supportive.)

"My beautiful little boy, we are going for a walk!"

There was, of course, no need to broadcast my decision. It was all a matter of timing my exit from the building before everyone got up from naps and started drinking tea and wandering out on the balconies. I didn't care if anyone saw me once I was pushing that stroller down the street. I just didn't want to be caught setting it up near the front door. That could get sticky. I might be stopped.

I tiptoed downstairs with the folded stroller, trying not to look sneaky. I set it up and whipped back upstairs. Yousef looked at me with big eyes.

I picked him up out of his bed with a warning "Shoosh!" and started back down those three flights, my heart beating fast. Mama Johara's door was closed. Madame Leena's door wasn't. The form of Sa'adiya, her maid, suddenly filled the doorway.

Sa'adiya took me in, swathed in my black robe and scarf. She gave the barest of nods. In Egypt, the *fellaheen* (countryside) women move around as they pleased. Sa'adiya understood, bless her heart. I exhaled and kept descending.

Yousef's eyes were as big as possible. He was noticeably alert, but his little lips were pressed tight. He let me strap him into the stroller without a peep. How did he know to be so still?

To get the stroller down the stairs leading onto the street, I had to pull it backwards, one step at a time. I felt like a bird escaping a cage. It didn't matter that there was nowhere to go. It was a neighborhood of apartment buildings, villas, and one compound across the street from our building. There was only a single *dokkan* within walking distance—a little store where locals could buy bare essentials like lettuce, milk, ice cream or potato chips.

"This is a walk, Pretty Boy," I crooned. "The kind of thing your wife is going to do when you get married. But you won't abandon her, will you?"

Babies always agree with their mothers.

"Daddy didn't really *abandon* me," I corrected, feeling magnanimous. "He just doesn't know how lonely we are. Right? We'll try to have our own fun, won't we?"

Yousef chortled, eyes twinkling.

A sports car came alongside. I pushed the stroller a little faster. The car went ahead, made a U-turn, and came back, stopping a few meters in front of my path. The driver leaned over and opened the passenger side door. He waited, engine running.

The intent was clear. This idiot assumed I was going to abandon my baby and get in his car. "Ahlan," he smirked. "Welcome."

"Get away from me, you Pig," I retorted in English. A volley of curses did nothing to move him. Looking for a rock did. He saw the stone in my hand and stepped on his accelerator.

That experience took some of the joy out of the walk, but I tried very hard not to let it get me down. What was the point of being covered head to toe in black? We women had to get used to this behavior from unknown young Saudi drivers. They were always doing that.

As I was coming back to the family building, I saw one of my sisters-in-law on Mama Johara's balcony. Good manners made me wave. She gave a hesitant wave back.

The next day, when I had just got out the door with Yousef and the stroller, I heard a call from Mama Johara's balcony, in Arabic:

"Wait just a minute! I'm coming with you!"

I didn't know which sister's voice it was. The girl disappeared from the balcony. I stood in the street speculating. Maybe I was going to inspire new freedoms among Saudi females. "Who do you think wants to go on a walk with us, Yousef?"

Yousef was impatiently kicking his feet against his stroller for me to start walking.

To my surprise, Mahasen came out of the door. In a family of beautiful people, she was the one who reminded me of Greta Garbo. She was a little breathless, yet accompanied me with grace—that is, until some other jerk pulled up beside us in his car.

Then Mahasen let fly with a stream of abuse in Arabic that included the words "donkey" and "dog." The day before, when I had cursed in English, "pig" had been the nicest thing I had called the driver. The rest of my curses had involved four-letter words with analysis of mental capacity and threats of spiritual damnation.

Her curses worked better than mine did. That Arabic lesson was almost worth the irritation.

That evening, Mama Johara came over.

"Why do you have to go out on the street?"

"I need to walk," I answered. "In America, I walk."

"In Jeddah, there are problems in the street."

"That's not my fault," I said.

"Why don't you wait until Malik gets home?"

"He won't be home for weeks. Yousef likes to go out too. We are bored."

"Patience," she said.

I had an answer for that: "Your mother used to walk alone all over Jeddah."

Mama Johara sighed. "Times have changed."

"Maybe times have changed because women don't try to take walks."

She ran out of replies. I was invited over for tea, and that was nice although the conversation died out and I got bored of listening to orders given to maids and the talking heads on Arabic TV.

As the days passed, I realized the sisters who accompanied me on walks were not thrilled. The revolution I had hoped to spark was all in my mind. No one argued about my right to go outside in the street, but they seemed to think it a chore. Mahasen, Amahl and Shahidah took reluctant turns accompanying me. It was not long before I was back to tiptoeing downstairs before anyone could see or stop us.

*   *   *   *

"Ode to the Red Sea"

O, you colors from the nomad's loom:
Scarlets, oranges and ambers
Seeping into the gloom;
Rock-a-bye, rock-a-bye,
Breeze me, brush of a plume—
I'll wait here until the sun drops completely
into the sea's watery womb.

Sleep gone, mist upon the morning star;
Beach creepers scuffling past,
All wakeful at the Fajr prayer.
A gull's cry breaks above a crest,
back and forth: a sandy bar
lapped on all sides by waves
like a cradle rocking afar.

Red Sea, gather me,
Gently to that place ahead.
Soothe me, sing to me.
Rock-a-bye, rock-a-bye,
My life in my arms: baby

breathes peacefully; back and forth,
the only place we feel free.

Periwinkle sky, beguile my eye,
and flash-dazzle of jewels upon the water;
Veils abandoned, joy in a sigh,
Last refuge of a Muslim woman.
Rock-a-bye, rock-a-bye,
Young, blessed sea, shelter baby and me
by Allah's will from the heat on high.

1985, Jeddah

Chapter 8

The Last Traditional Doctor of Jeddah

When I met Mama Johara and Madame Leena, they were both in mourning for their mutual husband, as strange as that sounds. The one who openly grieved most was Mama Johara.

Noting a degree of lingering childhood resentment in my husband against his second mother, I asked him to explain how his father had come to have more than one wife.

It was not uncommon in the Middle East for an older man to take a very young bride and it still is not. Because Johara had been a child bride, her mother, Zainab, and mother-in-law, Shahidah, took care of her first baby, a girl named Nafeesah, while Johara played outside. When the infant cried with hunger, one of the grandmothers leaned out the door and cried, "Johara, come nurse your baby!"

Likewise, because she was so young, her husband did not encounter any great objections when he thought of marrying again. Approximately four years after their marriage, Yousef announced to Johara that he was taking his cousin, Leena, as a second wife. Leena was Johara's age. An injury to Leena's eye had attracted his attention and compassion. A male cousin had thrown a rock and hit her in the face when she was a child. The eye never recovered, losing sight and appearing forever murky.

Leena was an outgoing, cheerful person who commenced a written correspondence with Yousef when she was a teen. She asked him if her eye would ever regain sight. Yousef, the most medical of her cousins (and by far the handsomest), was exactly the person to consult. Leena kept the correspondence going. She was a resourceful young woman and proved that one tiny facial flaw would not keep her unmarried.

Yousef loved Johara enough to try to get her blessing. Before marrying Leena, he asked Johara's permission to marry again, kissing her head and feet. Being a sad and lonely teenager, with no living father to stand up for her, she gave in.

Yousef's mother, Shahidah, was another matter. "Why do you have to marry a second wife?" she asked her son. "If you do, I will not forgive you in this life or the Hereafter."

Apparently he didn't care.

18 years old and already the mother of three, Johara felt the blow to her heart heaviest on the day Yousef requested she help in the wedding preparations.

"It is the wealth," explained Zainab to her sad daughter. "It makes men think of taking other wives. It has nothing to do with your beauty, goodness, or lack thereof."

Zainab was referring to Yousef's financially successful enterprises. He had invested in a string of taxis. These were doing well. He had also opened up a dairy shop in town. By day, he worked for a government ministry.

By nightfall, his expertise with camera projectors earned him extra income with princesses who needed a camera operator for screenings of Egyptian movies. For many decades, Egypt was Arabia's Hollywood.

Some teenage brides are adept at manipulating their middle-aged husbands. Johara was not. On the eve of Leena's wedding, Yousef made a final request that plunged into her like a knife.

A year earlier, Yousef had presented Johara with an expensive Arabian perfume given to him by a Saudi princess as thanks for running a movie projector. Johara prized the dark woody 'Oud oil. It had a sweetly subtle woody scent. The merest drop lingered on her clothes for weeks, sometimes even after washing. The bottle was kept in a heavy safe with other valuables.

Yousef pulled a small empty bottle out of his pocket in front of his first wife. Johara tried not to look at his face. She had not spoken to him (save in monosyllables) for several days. Her heart was broken.

He led her to the heavy safe in her room. "Open it. I want you to divide your perfume oil in half. It is only fair that Leena have half."

Johara turned the dial to the numbers—right, left, right—that she had already opened once that day, to anoint herself.

Her hand pulled the crystal bottle out of the safe. The heavy liquid trembled in the cylinder. This was a gift from a princess to Yousef, and then from him to Johara, his wife. The day she had received it had felt like a honeymoon. He had called her *his* princess.

She pulled out the stopper with a trembling hand, not able to see from the tears filling her eyes.

"You will drop it, your hands are shaking!" cried Yousef, taking the bottle from her. She fled the room.

"Mother, he gave it to *me*!" she wept later to Zainab.

"Men control this world, my daughter," said Zainab. "It gives them the illusion of being masters. Trust me, nothing of material stays with humans long. It is all fleeting illusion."

Zainab caressed her daughter and the grandchild who slept in Johara's lap. "You will safeguard your sanity and survive if you can accept these truths. You will always have your children who put you first, so long as you can stay near them. And don't forget," Zainab added, pulling away to look into her daughter's tear-streaked, beautiful face, "You already share your husband with every woman in Jeddah suffering from a bone complaint."

"I wish I had been born a man."

"I used to wish that too. Being a woman is harder than being a man. Your husband will get over today's fascination for his new wife.

You are the beauty of the two. She caught him through his pity, her laughter, and their blood relationship. Be yourself, Johara. There is much to love in you and your husband knows it. God knows it too."

*   *   *   *

Yousef Al Shamsi and his wife-cousin Leena came from a seafaring family. Leena's father and grandfathers had been, like Yousef's, sea captains.

In the days when the only oil that boats spilled was olive oil gushing from broken casks, and when ships rounding the tip of Yemen brought musk, ambergris, camphor and sandalwood as well as silks from India and China to be sold in the markets of Jeddah, Arab sea captains had been adept at the art of setting bones. Yousef Al Shamsi, land practitioner of this maritime medicine, gained an ever-growing repute for skill.

From youth, he was renowned for beauty. Yousef was tall, muscular, lean and as handsome as his name could have prophesized.

Females peeked out at him from the openings in their wooden window latticework, a practice of the cloistered women of Jeddah. They saw a wide forehead, a chiseled bone structure, an aquiline nose and beautiful, large brown sparkling eyes.

When Yousef was young, he wore his hair in long braids that swung from under his white turban. In the era of Egyptian film stars, he cut his hair short and donned Western clothes to travel in. He had a mustache, but not a beard but always maintained a mustache.

He made his female patients' hearts flutter.

With time, he became known as "Uncle Yousef." He read every published medical article on bones and bone setting that he could find in Arabic. Local chemists (pharmacists) brought him samples of modern medicine to evaluate. He also relied upon the ancient Arabian natural medicines. One such was *Baylassan*, named for a tree that grew abundantly in Taif, a mountain town. Its sap was used instead of sutures or stitches to close a wound and promote healing.

118

Uncle Yousef did not use plaster casts. He made splints and bound them to broken limbs with clean cloth. His method allowed him to monitor the healing.

He was not a certified doctor. He was not affiliated with a hospital and he did not advertise. Dozens of people came to his house every day, sometimes from distant countries. No one was turned away. Patients knocked at his door at two or three a.m. in the morning. Sometimes they appeared at his government office, where he dealt in paperwork.

A broken bone is at all times an emergency. Yousef went whenever called. Patients came and went at the back door all day. Many a *shisha*, the large, brass water pipe that Saudis smoke, was left to burn out, untouched, in Uncle Yousef's house. Just as the lighted coals were laid by one of his wives over the tin foil-covered *jirak* (an oily fruit substance smoked in the *shisha* instead of tobacco) a patient would knock, and Uncle Yousef rose without hesitation.

He treated soccer players from the Saudi national team. These were the hardest patients to deal with: they would not follow orders to lie still for indicated periods of time.

Uncle Yousef knew how long it took bones to heal in various conditions. If he told a patient to stay off a leg or to rest in bed for two weeks or two months without putting pressure upon that limb, he *meant* it. Rebellious patients who ignored his advice paid for it with troubles that broke out afresh.

Dignitaries and high officials sought him out, in preference to hospitals. Western expatriates often came to him as well.

Besides healing, he was remembered for a disinterest in money. He accepted payment only when offered, and only if patients had the means. Yet, save for a brief period of his life, Yousef Al Shamsi was not a rich man. He spent the better part of his life struggling to support the many children born to three women.

*   *   *   *   *

After Yousef's second marriage, Leena and Johara became pregnant at the same times. Their children were born in pairs, weeks or even days apart: Malik and Tarek, Hisham and Rihab, Shahidah and Ghassan, Mahassen and Mohammad, Amahl and Sameer.

During the four years she had Yousef all to herself, Johara gave birth to a girl, a boy, and another girl: Nafeesah, Haroun and Husna. Hard work resulted in back problems. After ten years of pregnancies, she had her last baby, a girl she named Amahl ("Hope").

As soon as her first son and daughter entered school, Johara began studying the books they brought home. In this way, she taught herself to read and write.

Her husband Yousef had no objection to his daughters' schooling. Things went much harder for Johara's half-sister, Fatima, daughter of Kizmet. Fatima had married a Turk like her father. Turkish attitudes stemming from the Ottoman era prevailed in their household. (Turks and Bedouins, in those days, did not support educating girls.) Fatima had to sneak her daughters out of the house every day, after her husband had gone to work. She snuck them in again when school let out.

Meanwhile, Yousef's second wife, Leena, continued to bear children after Johara stopped. In the end, Leena gave birth to seven boys and two girls. Johara had three boys and five girls. A third wife had a single child.

Yousef bought a parcel of land in the desert, where he set up a dairy farm. Once or twice a week, Yousef piled his growing number of children and their cousins into the back of a truck to visit the farm. Sometimes Leena and Johara went too, turning the excursion into a picnic.

The keeper of the farm, who daily milked the cows and fed the chickens, hated a monkey who had made the farm his home. Yousef thought the monkey was a nice distraction for the children. They played with the monkey, who loved them. It allowed the girls to dress him like a baby, burp him and feed him.

For all the children, the monkey danced and rode the donkey.

When the children left, the monkey showed its hatred of the farm attendant. If the keeper milked a cow, the monkey drank the milk, spilled it, or urinated into it. If the keeper brought out tools, the monkey stole and hid them. If the keeper sang, the monkey screamed.

At first Yousef laughed at the stories. "If you don't like animals, you shouldn't be working on a farm!" The keeper tried to endure his life, but when the monkey broke into his room and defecated on his clean clothes, as well as upon his bed, he could take it no longer.

The next time Yousef came to the farm, the keeper shook with rage. "That monkey hates me! He destroys everything I own."

"The children love him!"

"But the monkey does *not* love me, and *I* work for *you*. You will have to choose." Remembering Yousef's fondness for the little ones, the keeper added, "The monkey doesn't feed or milk your cows."

Without explaining why, Yousef asked the children to lure the monkey into the truck. They were delighted, hoping the monkey was coming home with them. They did not notice their father drove several miles into the barren desert, not far off from the low mountain range separating Jeddah from Mecca.

Stopping near the mountain foothills, Yousef carried the monkey away from the truck, set it on the ground with a bunch of bananas, and drove back in the direction of home.

"Baba, Stop!" wailed Malik, Tarek, Mahasen, Shahidah and all the rest. In protest, some stood in the back of the truck, clutching its side and lurching every time wheels hit a bump or rock. "Stop!"

Finally Yousef stopped and got out of the truck. He peered into the desert but saw no freakish brown creature madly scampering towards them.

"What have you done?" cried the children who dared reproach his somber face. All had tears in their eyes. Yousef ordered, "Sit down or you will fall out and get hurt. I will explain later."

At the farm, Yousef could not bring himself to say the truth. "The keeper told me that the monkey's mother and father have been discovered living in a cave near that very spot," he fibbed. "I was taking the poor monkey back to its parents so it can be happy."

"He was happy with us!"

"But the monkey cried at night for missing his parents," countered Yousef, feeling ashamed. "You would not want him to miss his parents?"

"No."

Malik told me that his father later said he hoped the monkey would find a cave, berry-sprouting shrubs, or some other farm where it might be tolerated.

Because Yousef could never say "no" to little ones, the back of his truck brimmed over with cousins on excursions to the farm or the Red Sea, where the bone doctor from Jeddah taught the children how to fish and catch crabs.

One day Yousef stopped at a town of sea Bedouins to buy gas. The children poured out of the truck to investigate the sandy pathways winding between the thatched huts and run after the freely roaming goats. The Bedouin women did not hide in these villages. Their braids hung down from under their scarves.

Yousef called the children to get back in the truck. He got all the way home without realizing that five-year-old Malik had been left behind.

Malik said a kind man found him, wandering around, crying. The shanty town had no telephones, so a messenger was sent into Jeddah to inform the doctor he had forgotten an offspring.

Those moments do something to a child, I think.

As his situation prospered, Yousef met among his patients a woman who emanated a sizzling sensuality like an alluring Egyptian female movie star. The lady, Hayam, whose name meant "deliriously in love," was a widow. Her son (from a first marriage) had been taken to be raised by her deceased husband's brother.

She lived alone, a condition she hoped to change.

She had creamy skin and an opulent figure. She spoke in a soft, melting voice. Her pearly teeth were perfectly even, her lips full and pouting. When she moved, she swayed like a reed in the wind.

Yousef felt that this poor young widow should not be left alone in the world to fend for herself.

For once, Johara and Leena beat and bled as a single, if broken, heart. Their service at home lost precision. Meals were not on time. Faces once touched with lipstick and rouge looked blotched and tear-streaked. Two sets of eyes had dark circles under them.

Yousef felt irritated and guilty. He did his best to ignore those feelings. Hayam, who had a hard-to-find complaint of the hip joints that didn't prevent her from undulating in a most hypnotic fashion, came to his office. She clearly needed a protector.

She was the most persevering of patients until the day of their engagement. It was not a happy time for Johara and Leena, nor for the children. Hayam's realm became the off-limit zone that the more daring of the boys challenged each other to trespass. They never forgot how their aloof "third mother" hung red embroidered silks, burned incense, played music and set out fruits for them to steal.

While a man with one wife can follow nature in his intimate relations, an Arab with two or more wives feels obliged to physically prove himself. Yousef decided to try out an herbal therapy to enhance his virility despite knowing that too much could have dangerous side effects.

The herbal supplement worked for a while, and he was able to satisfy two, and then three, wives at a time. However, the herb he used contained unsafe levels of arsenic and mercury. Nausea, vomiting and cramping brought him to bed. Kidney damage sent him to the hospital.

Johara was alarmed at the unsure nature of his ailment, for doctors gave conflicting reports.

She was further suspicious that her husband had taken ill due to studying white magic. This too was not unheard of in Jeddah society. A massive book on magic had found a place in Yousef's study.

One day, young Malik entered that study. It was empty. The book lay open in full view. He began reading until he came to the words:

"Only the strongest of souls should attempt repeating these words to invoke the presence of jinn. The weak will lose their health and their minds." Malik dared not read further. He ran out from his father's office.

Yousef eventually recovered. During his illness, his fortunes crashed. Drivers embezzled and the taxi cars were sold off.

Hayam, meantime, gave birth to a girl whom she named Farida. Without Yousef nearby, Hayam felt her solitary position for what it was. She had never bothered to make friends with Johara or Leena. Without Yousef's presence, Hayam left, later asking for a divorce.

At this point, Yousef had to work harder in order to provide enough food to feed his family. At the wharf, he bought spilled rice and grains that were swept up with dirt and filth from merchant ship floorboards. This was sold in sacks at the port at reduced prices. At home, the grains were sorted through and cleaned by the Al Shamsi women.

The land that had been the farm was expropriated by the government, which claimed the right of eminent domain. Yousef was offered a nominal fee unreflective of the booming value of real estate. He sought recourse to the courts, an unsuccessful project occupying the remainder of his years.

Even when struggling with finances, Yousef served as a doctor to the community. He treated many cases that seemed hopeless.

A neighbor's family took called him to see a patient being treated without success at a local hospital. Yousef advocated a complete change in treatment and the patient was cured. This story repeated itself many times.

Jeddah hospital directors collectively filed a complaint against Yousef, but Saudi officials refused to take action. Who knew when one might need him? Relatives of two famous Arab singers, Fairuz of Lebanon and Um Kulthum of Egypt, had already come to Jeddah for treatment by the Hejazi doctor.

A pregnant woman broke her pelvic bone. Uncle Yousef cared for her. She was cured and safely delivered her infant. A teenage girl suffered a crushed hip bone. Uncle Yousef oversaw her care until she walked again.

A man with legs crushed to seeming pulp by a car accident was carried into the doctor's house. Malik and Tarek helped their dad and narrated their stories. Within a year the patient walked again.

The Hejazi doctor insisted on one basic thing: that the patient not use the injured limb. Pressures had to stay off the broken bones in order for them to heal. He repositioned his patients during his daily

124

visits to their homes, keeping his instructions clear on how to imitate him.

A decade after Hayyam left the Al Shamsi household, she resurfaced, newly divorced. Yousef decided to remarry her.

Leena battled with vigor to discharge the usurper from Yousef's mind. Johara became withdrawn. Shehe fell upon a staircase and needed surgery for her back. Haroun, Johara's eldest son, begged that she come to Boston, where he was a university student.

"You will have the best care in the world," Haroun assured his mother. Haroun flew back to Jeddah and accompanied his mother to Boston.

In Boston, Haroun lived with his girlfriend, a sweet and brilliant young American woman named Diana. Diana had learned rudimentary Arabic. She used it to welcome the woman who might become her mother-in-law.

"Think of me as your daughter," said Diana, at the airport. She kissed Johara's hand in Arab tradition. When they arrived at the apartment, Diana told her, "This is your home." Haroun nodded.

Johara wiped her eyes. She had never thought that she might have a home in a place where women drove automobiles.

After Johara's surgery, Diana coaxed Johara, every day, into a therapeutic ice bath. "It is for the pain. Think of how much better you feel afterwards," Diana put one arm around the convalescent's waist and helped her walk.

"It is cold; it is so cold," moaned Johara.

"It is what the doctors ordered. May Allah bless you and cure you." Diana had learned the words Johara needed to hear. "God willing, you will get better and live long." She eased Johara into the bathtub and placed ice on the key points to the low groans of the patient.

Diana cooked, taught Johara to play checkers, and helped her wash for prayers when she lay prostrate in bed. Johara thought America was nice; here she did not have to be harassed by a husband's polygamous desires.

"Why should I leave?" Johara said to Haroun. "Your father is in love again with *that* woman. I am nothing but the first wife who bore

125

him some children. He has no more use for me. Leena is glad I am gone. I will stay here with you."

"You always have a home with us, my mother," said Haroun, knowing Diana agreed. His mother's heartache caused him grief. He discussed it with his girlfriend.

When Haroun brought up their own future, she said, "Darling, why can't we stay in Boston where there are career opportunities for us both?"

"The terms of my scholarship force me to return."

Diana was not sure she wanted to throw caution to the winds to be a modern American woman in an oil rich medieval society.

Three of Haroun's younger siblings came to Boston when one—Mahasen—needed specialized medical care. A blow to the back of her head had caused blindness. No one knew if the condition was permanent or temporary.

Mahasen and two "escort" brothers stayed with Haroun, Diana and Johara. The Saudi boys kept vacation hours and left strong memories for their neighbors of loud music and frying fish at 3 a.m.

Months slipped by. Whenever Yousef called by phone, Johara told Haroun to say she was sleeping. One day, seeing Haroun much distressed in speech to his father, Johara agreed to talk.

"I will *not* remarry Hayam," announced Yousef over the phone, without preamble. He was afraid—though he would have been appalled to admit it—that Johara would hang up.

"It doesn't matter to me one way or the other," Johara answered. "Why do you think I care?"

Six months passed, and Yousef was beside himself. His threat of divorce by telephone had brought an apathetic response. "Do whatever you want," Johara told him.

"I am coming to Boston," Yousef announced. He was a man who had taken a second wife, and then a third, only to choke on words to the first via transatlantic phone calls. "I miss you, Johara. Every day I want you next to me."

"Peace be on you," Johara said coolly, hanging up.

Yousef arrived alone in Boston, shivering at its brisk icy air, and glad of the wool coat he had bought from an Egyptian tailor. He knew enough words of English (with the help of an address written on an envelope) to ask a taxi to take him to his eldest son's apartment.

"If you love me so much, why did you marry two other women?" Johara asked, her face turned away.

Yousef had no reply. Saudi men often took more than one wife. He had been married to Leena almost as long as he had been to Johara.

"Johara, when I die, I want my head to be here." He touched the place on her shoulder, where so many of their children had laid their heads for comfort and sleep. "On *your* shoulder. Please." He waited for her to look at him. He was in his 60s, and she in her 40s. A man, he thought, must know with what woman he will die.

Far from the Arab desert, in this modern hubbub of progress where his eldest son studied towards a second degree at M.I.T., the chance of losing a wife by her own decision was very real.

Yousef took off his coat and accepted tea. Then came dinner and sleep on makeshift bed on the ground. It took a humbling eternity and examination of his own human choices to win her agreement to return.

After Johara softened towards him, Yousef enjoyed his stay in Boston more than he could have imagined. His favorite TV show was *Sanford and Son*. Haroun translated.

Johara was by his side on the plane back to Jeddah, knowing Leena was part of her life, waiting like a sister with children who called Johara their "second mother."

Hayam remarried a man twenty-five years her junior and was content.

Diana lived with and loved Haroun until they graduated. She declined his invitation to accompany him to Jeddah.

Not one of Yousef's nine sons followed in his footsteps as healer. The oil boom had ushered in a new era of young men who dreamed of becoming pilots, engineers and architects.

Yousef developed a heart condition. Leena knew he missed a high-cholesterol, fatty soup she made with minced organ meats such as liver and kidneys. She made it for him as a treat. "Surely you can have it once in a while," she said.

Yousef could not resist.

The next day Yousef was on his way to the mosque when a small niece came to him with a fractured bone. While tending her, an excruciating pain shot up his left arm. He collapsed to the ground.

"Johara!" he gasped.

The niece found Johara, who came running. Seeing Yousef ashen and unable to rise, Johara got on her knees, pulled his head against her shoulder.

He looked up at her with luminous dark eyes. "I witness that there is no god but God and I witness that Muhammad is His messenger," he whispered. This is the declaration every Muslim attempts to make before passing into the Hereafter.

Eyes full of tears, Johara kissed his forehead. Yousef had fulfilled his promise.

Moments later, a female patient arrived accompanied by her husband. She had received treatment a few days earlier. When told that the doctor had died, she broke down and wept as if he had been a close relative. And so he was, in spirit, to many of Jeddah's people.

The Al Shamsi family set out chairs in the street, following the local custom, to accommodate mourners. The streets filled for two blocks with Saudis and expatriates who came to pay their respects at the funeral ceremony.

Yousef's sons physically resembled him. For a while after their father's death, when any one of them went to the open air fish market adjacent to abandoned boats with broken lateen sails that lay side down in the brine, or to the sparsely shaded fruit and vegetable markets in the center of town, the sellers said, "You remind me of someone."

"Maybe it's my father. He did the shopping. But he died and I am shopping."

"May Allah have mercy on him. Your father was the one who never bargained. You remind me of him. A handsome man. But taller. Older. "

128

The son in question would blush, having fiercely haggled over price, and admit, "That was he."

"Here," the merchants said, adding a fish, or several fruits or vegetables to the recent purchase. "For the sake of your father."

Chapter 9

Cover Your Face

Malik got back into Jeddah on an evening flight from England. He leaned, late that night, over our baby's crib, which he had bought and assembled months earlier, and softly whispered, "Yousef!"

Our son was a deep sleeper, but Daddy's voice cut through the drone of the air conditioner like sun rays breaking through heavy clouds over the ocean. Yousef's eyelids opened and he caught his breath at the sight of Malik's face. His chubby arms flew up, small hands grasping Malik's neck. Before his father could lift him out of the crib, peals of delighted laughter filled the air. The darkened room shimmered with a child's bright joy.

Family love helped build a wall between my disappointment with life in Saudi Arabia and utter despair. This wall was strengthened by faith. However, the culture that claimed to embody Islam presented much that was troubling to me. The therapeutic aspects of prayer and fasting were undeniable, but huge discrepancies between tradition, culture and ideology were so blatant I wondered how no one else noticed.

I was sad to see that the position of women in Saudi society conformed more to Western stereotypes of Islamic culture than the ideology I had read about or that Malik had described during our first years together.

Fundamentalism, prejudice, and self-righteous preaching made me first uncomfortable, then angry. It grew tedious to hear the West condemned by my husband or other Saudis when no place had been allowed for me, as a convert, in this Muslim society except as a useless appendage of marriage. It hurt when Malik asked me to cover my face, which he did with increasing frequency.

Covering of the face has *nothing* to do with Islam. It is a made-up rule. Arab men invented it.

Never for a moment in the USA had I imagined Malik would force me to cover my face. I thought he would employ the courage of his own reasoning. If I had been able to tolerate taunts and yells in my country from people who didn't understand why I would wear a scarf and be covered with long sleeves and long hems, why couldn't he demonstrate similar conviction in his own country? Why couldn't he be as brave as I had been?

"Why do I have to cover my face?" I asked him, more than once.

"It's what people expect."

"Malik. I converted to the faith, not the culture. It's not *my* fault if Saudis decided to make up a bunch of new rules to oppress women."

"If you don't cover your face, people will stare at us," Malik argued. "And then we will have the religious police to contend with. Do you want them to take me to jail because I won't tell my wife to cover her face? Can't you make life easier?"

A woman in love wants to think her husband courageous and intelligent. Instead, Malik asked me to accept a double standard. My life would have been easier staying in the West and remaining Christian. Wasn't that obvious?

Covering my face was to accept as normal a scene I had witnessed in Mecca. During one of my first *umras* (the lesser pilgrimage), there had been a commotion at one of the two hills of al-Safa and al-Marwa (now leveled) between which pilgrims walk swiftly back and forth seven times. The walk commemorates the hardships undergone by the Prophet Abraham's concubine, Hajr, when Abraham left her in the desert by God's command. [5]

At one hill, I saw a man wildly jerk on the arm of a human form under layers of black fabric. The female so shrouded was dead weight, unconscious from heat and lack of air. Even though there were plenty of fans in the holy mosque, there is no way she could catch any breeze through the multiple layers of black that covered her face and body. The man's face flushed a dark red of fury. His jerking and shouting became frenzied. Not *once* did the man, who must have been a husband or some other relative, attempt to uncover the woman's face.

Malik watched the scene with me. "Poor lady," he murmured.

Yet my husband was asking *me* to accept the same standards that led to this abuse.

I loathed the face veil yet wore it, sometimes, to avoid arguments. Malik refused to take me anywhere if I did wear it over my face, although he admitted, when prodded, that the face cover was an innovation.

Covering the face was as unsafe as it was uncomfortable. Once I carried my sleeping son upstairs from the car and didn't have a free hand to pull the veil from my face. Yousef's head hit against the wall and he cried. (So too did I.) Another time, walking at night with my husband and child, I barely avoided stepping into an open manhole. I could have broken a leg or worse.

Western women who came with their Western husbands to Jeddah did not veil their faces, nor did Egyptian, Pakistani or Indian women who lived in Jeddah. Many Saudi women did not veil their faces in public. I pointed these ladies out to Malik.

He sighed, tired of the subject.

"They're rich. They have contacts. Why can't you just cover your face without arguing, like a good wife, and make life easier?" he complained.

---

[5] Hajr ran between the two low mountains looking for a sign of travelers. At her seventh crossing, she saw that a spring of water had miraculously erupted just where her son Ismail's foot had struck the sand. That spring is known as Zamzam.

One obedient American acquaintance came to my house with four veils over her face. Expatriate wives like her, who complied happily with oppressive traditions, made things worse for me. Sometimes Malik heard about them and held them up to me by way of example. I had no idea how this woman saw or breathed.

"Why do you wear four veils?" I asked.

"If I wear three, you can see my face. See?" She pulled down three, keeping one up over her head. I was about ten inches away from her face and the room was brightly lit by a chandelier with half a dozen bulbs.

"I can see that you *have* a face," I acknowledged. "That's about it."

She was deaf to my assertion that she was not required to cover her face even by the strictest of Islamic interpretations.

The subject of face-covering hung as a black cloud over my marriage through all my years in Saudi Arabia. Malik didn't mind my uncovering when we were in the car or sat in a restaurant. But if I was slow to pull the veil over my face in the marketplace, he would command me: "Cover your face!"

Arguments often veered into a comparison of cultures. "We were supposed to be talking about why, as a Muslim woman, I am being asked to cover my face," I often objected, "Not about which culture is better! Respect for the head of the household is a good thing, but nowhere in the Qur'an does God say, 'O Women, stop using reason.' I have the right to voice my opinion about an innovation you are forcing me to observe."

"When my father asked my mother to do something she didn't like, she refrained from comment," argued Malik. "If he got really mad, he insulted her, her family and her tribe. My mother knew he didn't mean it. She always waited a few days before she gave her point of view. Why can't you be more like that? Why do you have to argue?"

"Malik, if I were the submissive type, I would never have considered leaving the religion of my family," I said. "Your father was a nice man, may God have mercy on him, but he shouldn't have been insulting your mother's tribe or her family. The prophet Muhammad didn't insult people's families!"

Sometimes, I challenged Malik: "Why don't you try wearing a face veil? See how hot and stuffy your breath gets behind it. Put an *abaya* on too. Then it can get caught in the wheels of the cart at the supermarket. If you're really lucky, it might get caught in an escalator."

By that time, the conversation was over. My husband felt my belligerence without understanding my sense of being tormented. He believed if his mother and sisters could cover their faces, then a female convert should be able to get used to it without complaint. When we went to dine at the house of our old friend, Essam, Malik asked me to "cover my face" before I passed in front of our host. The latter had seen my face fifty times in the States. I had typed his engineering paper as a favor. Essam had seen me before I was Muslim. Now I had to act like he was a crazed lunatic and hide from him.

Covering my face made me feel like some sort of leper. It made me feel hated. Many Muslims will say I wouldn't feel that way if I had faith. I disagree. Covering the face is about brain washing, and the message it sends to either sex is a powerful one. What I found more revealing than anything else is that the struggle for moral rectitude should always focus on and stigmatize the weaker sex.

Despite these struggles, there were spiritually inspiring moments that could be had nowhere else. On the 29th night of Yousef's first Ramadan, Malik and I took our toddler to Mecca on *umra*. Yousef wore a white *thope* that I sewed for the occasion. It was not my first visit to Mecca, but visiting the holy mosque always produces a unique feeling.

The magnificent pearly marble Grand Mosque emanates a spell in the dry desert heat. It shimmers. In physical proximity, there is a palpable radiance. Yousef and I fell under that spell. Malik carried our child on his shoulders. We circulated seven times in the misted-cool air around the Kaaba, the first house of worship ever erected on earth, built by the prophet Abraham and his son the prophet Ishmael, peace be upon them. The house they built is at the very center of the Grand Mosque. Drinking the Zumzum water made me think of how all divine messages are linked together, from a single source.

Malik and I separated to sit down in male and female sections to await the call to prayer. A lady next to me kissed my sleeping, golden-haired toddler twice. When Yousef awoke, he began to play with another elderly woman, a sweet lady from Algeria. In the Grand Mosque were people from every corner of the world, brothers and sisters in faith, come to worship God at His bidding. We all knew we would meet again in the next life, and we all prayed to God to pass the test on earth.

*   *   *   *

Among a few Saudis, there was friendly curiosity about Western converts, even a bit of compassion for our struggles. Not everyone despised us for not being them.

Shoaa Al-Rashed (one of the first female journalists in the kingdom) came to my house to interview me for *The Saudi Gazette*. She was a lovely woman who quickly grasped my frustration at being stuck at home with nothing to challenge me. She suggested I try writing for the English Service of the Saudi Broadcasting System.

I went to the Saudi Broadcasting System radio station. A Palestinian gentleman named Yousef Salah, director of the English division, was welcoming. Without hesitation, he assigned me a weekly radio show. Getting paid for written work gave me a little hope for the future. One article a week was published in the newspaper, and one essay a week was read aloud on the radio by an English-speaking broadcaster. The articles and essays brought in about $30.00 each, totaling almost $240.00 a month. Neither the newspapers nor the radio station ever brought up the issue of working visas.

Conversely, King Abdul Aziz University had not paid me a riyal for my year of teaching. Four months after I left, Shareefa, the sole other American convert who had also taught for a full year without being paid, told me how she finally extracted wages.

"Call this number," she said, giving me the phone number of the male president of the female university. "Keep calling and nagging. If this guy refuses to help—and believe me, he will find all kinds of excuses—threaten him with the Day of Judgment. It's the only thing that works with them. That's what I did, and he finally paid me."

The male president of the female university was initially polite when I dialed his number, but he blew off my request and hung up. I continued calling and his patience wore thin.

"You worked without a working visa," he burst out on my third call. "Your husband *should have* obtained a working status for you. *He* should have found a contact."

I had borrowed Mama Johara's phone, unraveling the extension cord to sit in the relative privacy of the building's stairwell. Anger made the stairs turn from grey marble to a red blur, right under my eyes.

"You think you are talking to an ignorant Westerner who doesn't know how your society works," I said. "I *know* you have the power to pay me. How cowardly of you to attack my husband!"

"Wait a minute."

"No, you wait," I said. "Saudi men claim they are kinder to women than men anywhere in the world, don't they? I promise to never bother you again, but hear what I have to say. It will be hard for you to change your phone number."

"Go on," he agreed coldly.

"Here it is: Pay me what you owe me or I will ask God to pay me from your rewards on the Day of Judgment."

He grunted and hung up.

A week later, I received a call from King Abdul Aziz University. A reasonable sum of money was waiting for me—about SR 10,000, which was roughly $2,600. Dr. Wafah handed the envelope of money to me with an expression of grim death. The money probably came from a personal account.

I took the envelope and beat a hasty retreat.

Now I had a little money but I was still lonely. Kareema lived forty-five minutes to the south side of the city and worked fulltime as a teacher. She was also a busy mother and wife. I wanted a friend who could my experiences and point of view, another Western wife of a Saudi.

Looking for Western women at the marketplace, I had run into a good many Syrians and Palestinians who backed away when I tried introducing myself in English. Finally I met two young English women: Ghazala, who had given herself an Arabic nickname meaning "female gazelle," and her friend Ursula. We three shook hands, broadly smiling.

"We always suspected there were others like us, but we don't know how to meet them!" exclaimed Ghazala.

Ursula was a tall blonde and Ghazala, a fair brunette. In addition to stunning looks, Ghazala had so much charm, grace and intelligence she seemed more beautiful every time I saw her.

Ghazala's husband came from a well-to-do family that ran a tile business. She had a car and driver she sent to my house to get me. Her two little boys, just a bit older than Yousef, made our relationship close to perfect.

It was Ghazala who inspired me to write a fable about a young desert Arab who journeys on camelback to the green lands of scholars in quest of knowledge. In the green lands, the Arab finds a cherry tree whose beauty inspires him. Her shade shelters him as he studies. He takes the tree back with him to the desert.

"The cherry tree represents *us!*" exclaimed Ghazala, when I read the story to her.

I nodded.

Sometimes Ghazala visited me. I made tea and we sat in one of the two connecting rooms Mama Johara let me use for guests. The Saudis called these rooms, where guests were received, the salon.

The larger salon room was filled with Western furniture. It was separated by an accordion door from a smaller room, no bigger than a small bedroom, filled with Arabian-style cushions. The narrow, rectangular cushions lined up against the walls. A round brass table that Malik and I had given to Mama Johara stood in the center of the room. The Arabian salon was the room Ghazala and I preferred.

Conversely, Arab mothers of suitors for Mama Johara's three daughters were always shown into the Western-style salon. If the boy's mothers liked the girl, then the young man was allowed to come on a different day to take a look at his potential wife without a scarf on her head.

When I arrived in Jeddah, Shahidah was the eldest of Mama Johara's unmarried daughters. By tradition, she had to be married before the other two. She received several proposals and finally accepted a young man we came to know as "Abdu."

138

Abdu couldn't have been more gentlemanly with the girl who was the shyest of Malik's sisters. His family provided all the expected bridal gifts for a girl of Shahidah's class—the 18 to 24-carat gold necklace, earrings, bracelet and ring; the set of new clothes (dresses, shoes, lingerie, abaya and turha, purses, belts, and black gloves); the set of new quasi-Western style (made in Turkey) furniture for the rented apartment they would share; perfume; and of course the sum of money she could place in the bank as her own, the equivalent of one thousand dollars. This was Shahidah's dowry. Some Saudi girls get much more.

In short order, Shahidah was married and installed in her new apartment. She kept her job as an elementary school teacher. It was not so much open-mindedness as the need for a second income that had young Saudi bridegrooms not just allowing but encouraging their wives to work. In due course, Shahidah became pregnant.

By her sixth month of pregnancy, the souring marital secrets that Shahidah had guarded burst open like rotten fruit. Abdu was arrested and jailed for possession of drugs. If he was a dealer, he would be beheaded. Shahidah came home and unburdened her soul to her mother.

Abdu, high or drunk, was apparently not much different than post-wedding Abdu when sober. Both forms of the young husband did mean things like flick cigarette stubs behind cushions without telling Shahidah, then punishing her when he searched for and found the stubs two days later. It was his little test to show she was a bad housekeeper. Shahidah had not wanted to reveal her deep misery to her family, hoping a baby would create a warmer home. Little did anyone know the depths to which this man could sink.

The Al Shamsi young men were furious at the way their sister had been treated. They refused to allow Shahidah to return to Abdu when he was sprung from jail. An influential uncle got Abdu's record wiped away as if he had never been to jail.

"I don't want a divorce!" cried Shahidah.

"It's too late," said Sameer. "Do you think we would let you return to a son of a bitch like that?"

"No way!" agreed Hisham and Abdur Rahman.

139

Her brothers did not want her to go back. Shahidah, however, was prepared to sacrifice herself to a life of misery. In Saudi Arabia, men do not want to marry divorced women.

Malik's family forced Shahidah to sue for divorce. They brought the papers, she signed. Three months later she gave birth to a little boy.

As soon as she had recovered from childbearing, a miracle occurred. Another suitor began visiting the Western-furnished salon. This was Jameel, a young man Shahidah had turned away earler. Now she looked upon him with the grateful eyes of the non-virgin divorcee reject.

Jameel had one condition to their marriage: the boy baby, Miyaz, should have no place in it.

Jameel's mother did not approve of what her son was doing. She was dead set against her son marrying a "used" woman. When Jameel married Shahidah anyway, the mother sobbed through the marriage ceremony and reception as if her feet had been cut off. If the situation had not been weird and cruel, it would have been funny.

When Shahidah moved into her new home with her second husband, baby Miyaz remained with his maternal grandmother, Mama Johara. Shahidah was not allowed to look at him when she visited her mother with her new husband. Miyaz might as well have been a cat or a cockroach. Any gifts she managed to purchase secretly for Miyaz had to be smuggled into her mother's house. So it went for a dozen years and more.

Meanwhile, Salha, the Indonesian girl who had been hired to look after Malik's grandmother, was without work after Zainab died. Mama Johara asked Malik and me to hire her. I didn't particularly want a maid, but Salha became something more critical. She became my friend. She slept at Mama Johara's apartment and when there were extra moments in her day, she played with Yousef when I wanted to do some writing.

After Miyaz was born, Mama Johara took Salha back to care for that child. We paid half her salary, but Salha was with Mama Johara all day long.

The young Indonesian woman came over for about an hour a day, carrying Miyaz. I babysat and played with Miyaz while Salha

140

mopped my kitchen floor or washed my dishes, if I hadn't done them already. Afterwards we chatted. I taught her how to embroider, something she wanted to learn.

By midmorning, Salha always ran back to prepare lunch for Malik's unmarried older brother, Haroun.

Sometimes I would be out visiting Ghazala. As Mama Johara felt that Miyaz was too constricted by diapers, the child played naked in my apartment when Salha brought him over to do something for me. When I came home and prostrated in prayer, my gaze often fell upon dried-up toddler droppings that I had not (yet) noticed in the carpet. I don't think I would have minded so much, given that I felt sorry for Miyaz having been torn from his mother, but competition made everything worse.

Family members tried to please my mother-in-law by showering love on Miyaz. That would have been fine with me if family goodwill towards Yousef did not diminish, but it did. It was like a basketball game: Arab team baby against American mother's baby.

Some people think love is shown best by a fierce demonstration of hate in another direction.

Yousef was barely six months older than Miyaz. They were both toddlers. Yet when Yousef was in his grandmother's quarters, at her invitation, taken there by Salha the maid in order to play with Miyaz (who needed entertaining), I heard my son being yelled at as if he were a demon by anyone who could yell.

I had to go rescue him, always!

Sometimes I peeked. It was understood that Miyaz could do no wrong; everything he wanted should be given to him. When a small tyrant is created, someone else needs to be scapegoat. In history, young princes could not be punished, so village "whipping boys" were beaten instead.

Yousef was handy for the role.

The situation worsened. Often I refused to let Yousef go, making up excuses. When I played with the two toddlers in my own quarters, there was no problem. They both got toys and enjoyed each other's company.

When someone insisted Yousef be taken over to entertain Miyaz, and I had work to do in my quarters, the yelling would recommence. How could this be?

A few times I crept into the hallway, close to the door, just to hear exactly what they were yelling at Yousef about. It usually worked out that the two toddlers wanted the same toy, and Yousef was expected to forebear like the mature grown-up he wasn't. If the toy was something I had purchased for my son, it didn't matter. If Mama Johara gave each child exactly the same cheap toy, and Miyaz wanted both, it was Yousef's fault for not sharing. Everything was supposed to be handed to Miyaz.

I heard the word "spoiled" screamed at my son. Female voices yelled that Yousef should be nice to his "brother."

No voice ever lifted to reprimand little Miyaz.

It is a trend in far too many Saudi families to give certain children everything their hearts desire. They are spoiled and not raised to share. Many Saudis believe spoiling is a sign of love.

The situation grew more trying with the years. Miyaz was both spoiled *and* abused, poor kid!

As a youngster, Miyaz was hated by two fathers: his biological one and his stepfather. Abdu, his true father, saw him as the spawn of a disloyal mother, a woman who had left him for another man. Shahidah's new husband, Jameel, saw Miyaz as living proof of another man having had sex with Shahidah.

Both men yearned to hurt the child, and they both did.

Mama Johara, damaged by a childhood in which she was ripped away from her beloved mother, loved Miyaz madly and sought to protect and coddle him. In many ways, she saw herself in him, the orphan. Yet who would have raised the child had it not been she?

God gives us struggles for a reason. We are all in this soup together.

One day there was pounding on my bathroom door. I was in the shower while Salha watched Yousef. I thought Salha was the one frantically knocking.

"Come in!" I called, peering around the shower curtain.

It was Mama Johara. She entered the steamy room with tears rolling down her cheeks. Miyaz was in her arms.

"Look!" wept Mama Johara, holding out first a small arm, and then a plump thigh of the toddler. "Look what he did!"

Miyaz's dark skin had much darker marks—black and purple—in strange, half circle shapes.

"What is that?" I asked.

"He bit him!"

Bite was not a verb I had learned to conjugate. I must have looked confused. I repeated the word without understanding. "Bit?"

"Eat," choked out Mama Johara, mimicking the biting motion with her teeth. She gasped and sobbed. The water ran down my back as I stood against the shower curtain, horrified.

"Who!?" I demanded.

"His father!" cried Mama Johara, now pointing to teeth marks on Miyaz's buttocks. "And look at these!" She held out Miyaz's arm at another angle and showed me the inside of his thighs. There were white blistered dots.

"What is that?"

"His cigarette. He put out his cigarette on his son! More than once." There were quite a few white blisters.

I grabbed the towel. Mama Johara was beside herself in grief and anger. I was mistakenly afraid she might drop Miyaz. The toddler didn't cry but he looked stunned. Still, he must have felt the fierce love emanating from the grandmother who held him. She could have the courage of a lion.

I dressed and followed Mama Johara to her apartment. After she showed everyone the marks, she took pictures and presented both the snapshots and the damaged baby at the local police department. That bleak event helped her obtain full custody of Miyaz, freeing him, for a time, from his father's abuse.

My friend Salha was "freed" at almost the same time, for her contract ran out. The young Indonesian woman asked me whether she should renew it. I didn't think so. Salha's life was too hard, and I encouraged her to leave, even if it meant missing her. "If you want to come back to Saudi Arabia later, come to another family. Maybe there will be less work there."

She took with her an Afghani-style dress embroidered, in my own hand, in hues of blue and turquoise. On the day she left, we cried like friends who knew they would never see each other again. Little Yousef adored her too, and we all three threw our arms around each other, hugging for the last time.

Chapter 10

Two Women in the World of the Unseen

It took me years to understand how Mama Johara saw *herself* in little Miyaz and attempted to give him the love she had lost when both parents were ripped out of her life by a single tragedy.

In the early 1940s, Johara's father died from the yearly fever contagion brought by pilgrims. Every year millions of pilgrims poured in and out through the port city of Jeddah, often staying in the homes of the town's residents by invitation.

Johara was four years old and very attached to her mother, Zainab. Seeing her mother cry at her father's death made the little girl worry. She kissed her mother repeatedly and wiped away the tears on her mother's cheeks. "May God make you better, Mama."

In a way, Zainab was losing everyone. Khadija, Johara's older sister, had recently become engaged to be married. This pending change helped distract her from the blow of losing her father.

Siddik, Johara's 11-year-old brother, marauder of the beaches and bustling port, was already addicted to the freedom that girls only dreamed of. Even before his father's death, Siddik had shown, with his quick temper and rebellious nature, how much he hated school.

When his father died, Siddik ran away for a time, to sleep on empty boats or a patch of sandy shore at the port. When the boy returned at intervals, a distraught Zainab tried to reason with her son. "Who feeds you?"

"I do jobs and the captains give me money or a meal," Siddik replied.

The loss of another husband had tipped Zainab's world. Late night tears wet her hair and pillow, and the ache of grief reopened the old wound for Kizmet, the proud Turkish husband who had died before Hamza wooed her. Kizmet had fallen head over heels for Zainab, choosing an Arab port city as permanent home.

Zainab now saw her new family unit dissolving. Hamza's older brother, Yahya, took Johara away from Zainab by court order. It was a standard practice, demonstrative of the negligible legal weight women have wielded in this male-dominated society.

Granting a paternal family the right to rip children away from mothers when a father has died is not supported by all perspectives of Islam. The prophet Muhammad, peace be upon him, said, "He who separates a mother from her children will be separated from his friends by God on the Day of Judgment." [6]

Yahya was called "*Sidi*" (*seedee*)--a term of respect given to elder males in Arab households—and particularly to the affluent. Sidi Yahya was a rich trader. He had a barren Yemeni wife, Aunt El Ham. El Ham would take over raising Johara.

Panicked, Zainab pleaded for a waiting period during which she could stall and keep her youngest near her. The courts denied her request.

On the designated morning, Zainab woke Johara, fed, bathed and dressed her, and led her by the hand to her new three-story home

---

[6] Al Tirmidhi

146

in downtown Jeddah. Breezes off the Red Sea stirred their clothes on the walk to Yahya's house. It was coolest to stay close to the shade cast by the sun-bleached sea limestone dwellings that pressed against one another. Sometimes mother and daughter had to cross directly under the sun, and then Johara, who had a simple scarf tied around her head, lifted the cloth doll her mother had recently made over her head to keep the bright rays out of her eyes.

Standing in the cool crevice of shade offered by Sidi Yayha's door well and wearing a *burqah* that covered her entire body save for the webbed patch she looked through, Zainab knocked at the heavy, carved wooden door. It creaked open.

"*Ahlan*—welcome!" said Sidi Yahya, smiling down at the little girl. He reached out his hand to shake hers. One of Johara's hands held the doll and the other was planted in her mama's, so Yahya found nothing to grasp. He contented himself with kissing Johara's creamy cheeks and patting her on the shoulder.

"*Assalam alaikum*," Yahya said more somberly. He lifted his eyes to the shrouded widow who shared his loss though he would make hers the heavier.

"*Wa alaikum salam*," said Zainab in a muffled voice. "And upon you be peace." That morning, the words felt empty to her. She felt no solace of peace in her heart. If only Allah had created her a man!

Johara clutched her doll tightly to her chest. Her mother held the removed burqah slung over one arm. The air was tense.

"Mama?" Johara repeated, pulling on her mother's skirt. "Mama?" Something was not right.

"Do you like cookies?" asked Aunt El Ham.

The woman's harsh accent distracted Johara. The child looked cautiously up at the Yemeni woman. Mama had told her yesterday that Baba had gone to visit Allah. Johara couldn't wait for him to come back so she could ask what Allah looked like. In the meantime she had been offered more cookies than usual. Johara liked cookies.

Zainab saw the small head turn and leaned down promptly to kiss her daughter goodbye. "I'll be back, Habibatee," she said, her voice quaking. Yahya frowned in warning. He could make life more difficult if

147

he chose. Zainab pressed her lips tight and left with steps that got her outside the front door and no further.

There she sank into a heap. She was half in, half out of the shade, as the devil himself was said to rest. Her face was wet with tears under the airless *burqah*. She had steeled herself to show no emotion, but what did anything in life matter now?

Repressed sobs tore from her chest. She felt powerless to arise and so she lay, crying, on the hard steps in the heat. It broke her heart to think all her baby had of her mother to touch was the hair Zainab had donated to the doll's head.

In one of those spasms of silence when a weeper stops breathing, Zainab could hear Johara wailing against the door inside. The child did not know this new house or the woman with the strange accent. Mother and daughter cried for each other on either side of the heavy door.

All the neighbors knew the story. The mother's grief drew two sympathetic neighbor ladies, also attired in *burqahs*. In pointed-toe slippers, they met over the collapsed woman. Each one took an arm. They pulled Zainab up and helped her walk to the house of the closest house.

Zainab was coaxed to recline upon cushions in the *roshan*, or window balcony. Turkish coffee was served by the hostess on a brass tray. It was sweet, steaming, and spiced with cardamom. Gasses of cool water accompanied the coffee, along with biscuits and figs from the mountains of Taif. The hostess placed a pack of cigarettes near the widow.

"For your nerves. Be patient. Allah gives great reward for enduring afflictions."

"Our neighbor is a decent man," consoled the other lady. "No one speaks ill of him. You will have the visitation rights of every mother."

"I have nursed Johara through illness. And I have buried three others of my babies," moaned Zainab. "Stillbirths. My youngest lived only to be taken from my arms."

A sea breeze blew through the balcony's slates, stirring flower buds in clay pots. Their movement caught Zainab's bleary eyes.

"Better to have children die and taken away than not have children at all," said the hostess. She and the neighbor nodded at each other. A barren wife was soon made to welcome a co-wife. How to keep a husband from taking co-wives was forever a burning topic of female conversation in Jeddah.

"God Willing, you will remarry and have more children."

Zainab was not thinking of more children. She had a growing sense of indignation. She resolved to increase her involvement in business affairs. Money had favorable bargaining power. The fathers who died left so little for their offspring. If she had wealth, not only could she leave it for her children, but Yayha would respect her. Rich men and legal courts reserved their favorable rulings for those with money.

It was in the nature of being female to be left solitary. Children were taken away by in-laws after a husband died or divorced his wife. Zainab navigated her marriages like a vessel through the seven seas. Some waters were calm, but all voyages met rough weather. This was the society into which she had been born, and she had no choice but to consider how to empower herself.

In the opinion of Sidi Yahya, the little girl was not safe except under his supervision. That was an anticipated male attitude, yet it was true Johara possessed beauty. There was also no doubt in Yahya's mind Zainab would remarry. Men were inquiring after his brother's widow although the dirt over Hamza's grave was so freshly shoveled one could point it out from the gates of the cemetery.

Yahya wanted to protect his niece at close proximity. Men who sought out little girls as "brides" needed to know they would have to reckon with him. Let her enjoy the innocence of childhood while it lasted.

In the kindness of her new household, Johara learned to live without her mother. She saw Zainab two to three times a week and was allowed a full day with her once a week. The little girl eventually got used to this arrangement. She learned to play by herself, for Sidi and El Ham had no children.

One day Johara was alone, playing with her doll on the floor of a third-story room. She felt her skin prickle. She lifted her eyes to the window.

A man peered in from the street. She caught her breath. His face and neck were huge and close, yet enveloped in a mist. Her eyes locked in his gaze. The oddity of a man looking into a third floor bedroom did not dawn upon her because she was so young, but no one could be so tall, not even on stilts.

After many moments, the man's face dissolved. The little girl watched for it to reappear, but it did not. She went back to her play.

At suppertime, Aunt El Ham called for Johara. There was no answer. Sidi Yahya called. Still no answer. The couple climbed the stairs. Johara lay unconscious on the floor of the room in which she had been playing. Elheam shook her, uttered her name. Sidi Yahya sprinkled water in her face. The little girl did not awaken. Sidi sent a young boy to fetch a doctor.

The doctor examined the little girl. There was no sign in her pupils, nor upon her body, of any trauma. Nonetheless the child remained unconscious. The same boy was sent to fetch Zainab.

Zainab saw her daughter's state and dashed back out into the street in quest of a holy man. He was not a mere Qur'an reader such as might be brought for weddings or funerals. She sought a renowned Sufi mystic, said to have knowledge of the 100th name of God.

The ninety-nine names of God were not secret. Any Muslim could find and memorize them. The 100th name was revealed by the Beloved only to those whose lives were devoted to His adoration. Perhaps once in a generation such a soul was born.

Sufi mystics were known for their gentleness and the fact that their prayers were answered. However, it was difficult to coax a devotee away from private devotion.

Zainab located the mystic. Perhaps it was the prayer in her voice that persuaded him to follow.

At the house he sat cross-legged on the floor by the afflicted child's sleeping mat. He restricted himself to small sips of water in the many hours that followed. He recited Qur'an and made supplications. He spoke to no one but God, remaining without sleep for two days.

Zainab stayed awake nearly as long, sitting in a corner of the room with a shawl wrapped around her head. She whispered "ameen" every time the Sufi's palms were raised to heaven in supplication.

Sometimes her head leaned against the wall and she slipped out of the present, then she came back to consciousness with a start, only to see Johara still unconscious.

"O Most Merciful," she prayed, "keep me awake so I may beg for acceptance of your lover's prayers! Forgive my daughter and me!"

Johara came back to consciousness on the third day after falling out of it.

"I'm hungry," she said.

Zainab covered the child's face with kisses. The Yemeni woman, who had been more often at the door to the room than not, rushed downstairs to the kitchen. Within minutes, El Ham carried up a tray of broth and bread.

As Johara ate, the mystic asked her, "Whom did you see?"

"I saw a man in a cloud."

"Where?"

"In my window. He looked at me."

"*Ya Allah*!" exclaimed Yahya. "It must have been a jinni."

"Who else would have vision to see from the bright street into a dark room?" said El Ham.

Aunt El Ham and Sidi Yahya nodded together, smiling in relief at Johara. The mystic looked for Zainab, though he had not looked at her once since responding to her request two days earlier. "It was probably the same one," he said, as if she could understand without further explanation.

From that holy man's eyes, another face rose up in memory to claim her: the face of the half man she had first beheld on the day she was sent into town as a young girl to buy coal.

That half human had pushed a cart of sweets like any seller. But he was not half a man as one who has survived a birth affliction or tragedy, with only a torso to be pushed upon wheels.

He was half a man from the top of his head possessing one eye, through his half of a nose with one nostril, down through his neck and torso to the single leg and foot. That he stood erect behind a cart had ignited her terror.

She was too young to remember that jinn can take any form they choose. (Even adults forget to seek refuge in God, foregoing protection.)

Zainab had fled home as fast as her legs would carry her.

"The same?" she whispered.

"The same, but a different human master calling him to perform a task." The mystic rolled his prayer rug. "Seek refuge in God."

Nodding, Zainab rose to fumble for the money pouch in her *burqah*. She wished to give all that it contained, down to the last *girsh*. When she turned with her hands full, he was gone. The Sufi had left with steps so quiet no one noticed.

Zainab touched Sidi Yahya's shoulder. "Reconsider," she implored. "I am the one with knowledge of such experiences; I have seen jinn. My daughter needs me. I can help her cope."

Yahya raised his eyebrows. "All she needs is God's protection. How could our little girl be safer with you, a solitary woman? And if you marry? Who will protect her from your new husband if his heart is not clean?"

In her heart, Zainab felt Johara had become more of a target than ever as the ward of a rich man. Johara had related to her mother how her uncle showed off to her chests of gold stored in the house. If a practitioner of magic hoped to snare Johara for the sake of marriage or blackmail, surely Sidi Yahya's wealth was part of the reason!

A year later, Johara was again visited by a supernatural presence. Once more Yahya was powerless to help. The visitation occurred during the intense summer months, when people of old Jeddah slept at nights on their flat rooftops. There they carried thin cotton mattresses and were cooled by breezes off the Red Sea.

One such night, young Johara waited on the roof upon her outspread bedding. Sidi Yahya and Aunt El Ham had not yet come up. Since the occasion of falling unconscious, Johara could not sleep easily until family members were around her.

Her eyes kept watch on the door from which Siddi and his wife would emerge. It was to the side of the deep opening in the middle of the house.

Like all Jeddah dwellings, Sidi's home was built around a narrow open space, an air well. The space acted as a vent to bring air to inner floor windows.

Sensing she was not alone, Johara opened her eyes. From the air well, an enormous pair of eyes stared, unblinking, at her. They were part of a huge, dark, masculine face. That head stretched up from the gap, ten times the size of a human's.

Johara's blood turned to lead. Her heart struggled to climb out from her rib cage. She wished to get up and run away. She could not. She could neither swallow nor move. Her arm refused to pull the sheet over her head.

She saw the door knob twist.

"Johara?" Uncle Yahya's muffled voice echoed.

Why was the door not opening? There was no lock on it. The doorknob twisted violently; Johara heard its rattle. Meanwhile the long, dark face remained suspended in the air like a pillar of thick fog.

"Johara!" shouted Sidi Yahya. His heavy knuckles rapped on wood.

Johara had no voice.

"What have you done to the door?"

The door quivered with the force of a human body slamming against it.

Then it burst open. At the same instant, the huge face dissolved.

Zainab began fasting two days a week, beseeching Allah's protection for her daughter. She spent more time on her visits helping Johara memorize lines from the Qur'an.

Say, 'I seek refuse in Allah from Satan the Rejected' as many times in a day as you can remember to do so, Johara."

"I know."

153

"Do you really? And do you know that women are hostage to men?" Zainab saw her daughter frown. "Women are prisoners to men even when we are happy. It is a man's world. There is not much we can do about that.

"But no smart woman will also allow herself, as well, to become a prisoner to jinn. Do you want to become a prisoner to jinn?"

Johara did not think she did.

"Then fear no one but Allah. He is the only One who can protect you from harm."

In her newest marriage, Zainab maintained her own residence. She lived alone. She prayed to God she wouldn't have more children, and she didn't. She invested in property. Within several years she owned the house she had been renting as well as the empty lot next to it.

Her husband visited her and returned to his first wife afterwards, when Zainab wished him to leave.

When Johara was twelve years old, Zainab agreed to her daughter's match with a handsome, older man named Yousef Al Shamsi, then in his early thirties. Sidi Yahya had not sent Johara to school to learn to read, so she was uneducated.

The main drawback to not being able to read was that Johara needed others to read to her. Zainab hoped that Yousef, being educated and kindly, would teach Johara things she had missed by not going to school.

Yousef had a job with the government and practiced medicine. His work and his compassion were steady. When she asked him if he kept slaves, he said, "I am the grandson of an African slave girl. When I was a child and my grandfather died, I saw my grandmother had never been lifted to the level of his two wives. I vowed then to never own slaves."

"Allah allows slavery," said Zainab, testing Yousef.

"Yes, but He commands the freeing of slaves to attain salvation," responded Yousef. "Slavery exists only to be undone. If God created good and evil, it was to try one by the presence of the other."

154

Yousef cared for the sick through his gift of curing. As a hard-working man, he would leave his wife with some money in case he died suddenly. He was kind to Zainab, who knew that a young bride would need her mother around.

Zainab's approval of the match was not needed in Jeddah society. Approval was in the hands of Sidi Yahya. But Yahya was in jail. A partner had charged him with financial misdeeds.

El Ham was waiting for Yahya to serve his time, but she had no legal say over Johara's marriage. In fact, Johara had no male relative to look after her at all, save her brother Siddik, who was useless.

Siddik could barely look after himself. His primary talents in life lay in fermenting raisin juice, butchering sheep, and arranging sailors' dances on the beach during holidays. He was not the kind of brother a young girl could rely on for support.

Worse, Siddik had a trigger temper that dismayed Zainab, and for good reason. When mischievous nephews needled Siddik while he butchered a sheep for a feast, he swung his axe down to threaten the boys. He could have maimed or killed them. Zainab worried for the poor woman who might be his bride one day.

Due to these considerations, Zainab allowed the suitor to court her daughter, for Johara needed a protector. (In that society and era, girls were allowed to marry as soon as they had their menses.)

She suggested to Yousef that a small gift of money to Siddik—technically Johara's guardian while Yahya was in jail—might sweeten Siddik's willingness to give away his sister. Yousef complied. Everything went smoothly.

*   *   *

It was not until my own marriage was swinging in and out of purgatory, that Mama Johara came to love me as one of her own daughters and began relating these stories. She knew I admired her mother's character. Mama Johara never sought pity for what she suffered as a child, but her protective devotion to Miyaz was her way of making amends to the little girl who had lost her father and been stalked by jinn.

Chapter 11:

Parlor Games

The Jeddah of Malik's description had his Grandmother Zainab walking back and forth across town, alone, in pursuit of shopping or visiting friends and family. "But," said Malik, after we had settled into our Jeddah lives, "everyone knew everyone there. It was much safer in those days."

In San Diego, Malik didn't want me to walk alone to the grocery store, two blocks away. "Wait until I can go with you," he had said. "It's safer."

The only disadvantage I saw to walking around with a scarf on my head in the USA was in being hooted or yelled at. Sometimes people asked what country I was from.

"I'm from here!"

They didn't believe me. In the late 70s and early 80s, there were not too many converts who had taken to the tradition of tightly winding a scarf around their heads.

I bristled at the idea I should not be walking around at all. I believed in Islam, not Malik's cultural ideas. The Quran does not forbid women walking, swimming or sky diving. I thought with time, my husband would mellow out.

157

I went to classes at San Diego State University on my own and he said not a word. For some reason, that was okay with him—maybe because he knew I needed a degree in order to bring in an income one day?

Cultural differences were at the heart of all our marital difficulties. Before I got to Saudi Arabia, I did not know how much those differences would grow.

In San Diego, I snuck off to the store one day and told him afterwards. "See? I am fine! No one will bother me. And if someone does, I can run or defend myself. Malik, this is my homeland. It's not unsafe as you make it sound."

I heard similar protests from him when we got to Jeddah. I could not stop walking outside. It was easier not to bring my walks up in conversation. When we lived in the Alhamra district in Jeddah, I took walks to the *dokkan* (small grocery store) while Malik was at work and did not talk about it.

Control of women and their freedom stems from misogyny. Societies that support misogyny are ruled by men. In a misogynist society, discrimination is justified with illogical arguments.

The tradition in Western education is to analyze, but that does not mean those in power even in the West always appreciate the freedom analyzing nurtures. In ancient Greece, authorities forced Socrates to commit suicide because he taught his students to analyze.

Misogyny, however, is not healthy. I waited for Malik to speak up against it.

During one Eid prayer at a big gathering (Eid is like Christmas or Hanukah), an imam's voice swelled over the loudspeaker. The imam sounded angry. I returned to the relative comfort of our car. Amplified yelling did not fit my idea of a festive day. Gifts waited at home to be unwrapped and delicious food, eaten.

Malik looked a little dazed when he joined me. "You won't believe what the imam said!"

"Tell me."

"He said, '*A new phenomenon is occurring in our country. Women are coming to the mosques. Now they are here at the Eid prayer. Oh you women, for shame--stay in your homes!*'"

My jaw dropped. "Aren't these sermons reviewed beforehand by anyone?" I asked. "Everyone knows women are *supposed* to go to the Eid prayer." As soon as I said it, I realized everyone didn't know. The guy at the loudspeaker didn't.

Malik nodded, turning the key in the ignition.

"Did you approach him and say something? That is what I would have done if I were a man."

"It would have turned into a fight."

A sermon like this, broadcast to a huge gathering of worshippers who rarely or never read books, did not portend well for the future. That was about fifteen years before the end of the 20th century.

There was more than one time when I wished I or my husband had spoken up.

One Ramadan evening, Malik had told me we were invited to dine at the house of one of the sons of a minister to the king. The family was very "religious," he assured me. The Al Shamsi boys and the minister's boys had attended school together.

I had just taken a shower. My hair was wet. If I said yes, I would not have time to blow dry and style my hair. We had to go instantly because it was almost sunset, when people eat in Ramadan. Malik assured me it was a casual affair and no one would mind if I kept my scarf on.

So I agreed, figuring I could either look messy or keep my scarf on. The lure of not having to cook was a big factor. Laziness won.

We arrived before sundown and I was ushered into marble-lined rooms with ceilings at least twenty feet high. Scores of electric bulbs lit up glittering crystal chandeliers.

Expensive marble columns made navigating the foyer a challenge. Shining gold door handles gleamed everywhere. A scent of burning cedar and sandalwood, with subtle notes of balsam, Jasmin and rose, made me sure that expensive 'ud incense had been wafting from burners before I arrived.

The hostess extended her hand for my *abaya*. I was embarrassed to hand it to her. My abaya fabric seemed so plain compared to the *abayas* I saw hanging on gold hooks or in the arms of maids   dressed   in beautiful new clothing.

The abayas I saw had intricate gold and silver thread stitching on their hems. The interesting trims screamed Nina Ricci or Alberta Ferretti. Some women in Saudi Arabia shelled out the equivalent to a thousand and more U.S. dollars for their *abayas*. Wow. And were those diamonds on the head scarves?

My abayas came from the open air market, where I haggled for the lowest price I could get. It was a garment I was forced to wear, not one I wanted. Why spend money on it?

"Your *turha*?" asked my hostess, her hand out my head scarf.

"I think I'll keep it on." Oh what a mistake to have come!

She beckoned me to follow. I saw maids scuttling in and out of a room, loading a long dining table in its center with *sambusak* (meat pies), salads, steaming soups, glazed cakes, fruit drinks and more. My stomach growled. At least dinner would be tasty.

My heart dropped in the main salon. Not a single one of the twenty or so young females, in-laws and sisters to my hostess, had a scarf on. Their dresses were gorgeous. They looked like models from a magazine.

More of these gorgeous, rich ladies arrived, taking off their *abayas* and *turha*. Each one seemed to wear the most magnificent gold and sparkling gems from her ears, around her neck and on her hands and arms.

I shrank into my chair, self-conscious about being underdressed and over-covered. The scarf on my head was my most embarrassing feature. Still, what it hid was worse: flattened hair, straight out of the shower.

When describing the invitation, Malik had told me the family was "very religious." I had been given two minutes to decide.

Did he not know what I would find? My less-than-glamorous dress and plain little necklace contrasted poorly.

"Are you blonde?" two women asked. "Let us see your hair."

"I'm sorry, bad hair day," I answered. "Next time."

"She is a good Muslim," said one of them, laughing. "Don't bother her."

They could call my embarrassment piety if they wanted. I thought of taking my scarf off in the bathroom and running damp fingers through the smash-dried locks. I could amaze them with my courage. I had almost decided to go that route and was appraising my head in the bathroom mirror when I heard ripples of laughter.

I threw my scarf back on and stuck my head out the bathroom door. Oh my! The young women were playing catch-the-jewelry.

Walking out of the bathroom to scare them with a troll imitation would have been bad manners. The scarf went back on my head. I applied new lipstick and went back out into the guest salon.

Here was a strange game. The young women were taking off their 18 and 21-carat earrings and necklaces, sapphire, ruby and diamond rings. Sculpted multi-jointed pieces shimmered, dangled and shook, catching light as they sailed through the air to be caught by another pair of beautiful hands.

Too bad they did not have a piñata full of gold and diamonds. I wondered about the rules of this throwing game. If someone dropped an earring, was it finders, keepers?

No one dropped anything. They were a *team*. What polite remark did one make during catch-the-jewelry? *Good throw?* I had no idea. I held onto my smile.

"Don't worry, another American woman is coming," said my hostess, leaning towards me, guessing I felt left out. She must have guessed there is a huge culture gap between national parlor games.

My worry had been about being an ugly duckling, not about being the only American!

All the women put scarves on their heads when it was time to pray, of course, but afterwards they shed them like butterflies do

161

cocoons. Then the hostess announced that dinner had been laid on the floor of the dining room, and there the ladies fluttered.

Although the platters had waited on a dining table, we had never been destined to eat there. I had expected that. It is traditional in Saudi Arabia to eat on the floor.

The doorbell played its resonant sonata and within moments the second American was ushered into the room. She had tights on, like all the other women although I had not really thought about the tights, so taken was I with their splendid garments.

The American's tights were black, however, while the other ladies wore flesh-colored nylons, or perhaps Danskins. Even the maids wore stockings on their feet.

It suddenly struck me I was the only one barefoot. When they sat, I saw all the tights-covered feet. The only bare toes were mine. By now it became clear that black tights were a symbol of wealthy piety.

The tights were meant to make up for crystal chandeliers. It's a compelling cycle: "We have crystal chandeliers, so you women wear tights to show humility, and then we men will give you tons of jewelry to throw around to cheer you up."

Women get the worst of the deal, even with jewelry. Saudi men don't wear tights under their white thobes although they really should. Modern men's tunics (*thopes*) are narrow and silky. Any man walking into a breeze looks like he is advertising his hardware.

I mentioned that once to Malik and he said, "Why are you looking down there?"

Double standards. Men love them.

The newest American guest at the party, renamed "Fatima" from whatever her birth name had been, was pleasant and pretty. She was a second or third wife, the hostess told me.

That revelation did not make the girl more fascinating. I studied her without trying to be obvious. When she sat, her skirt crept up to reveal a second pair of tights covering the first one. Good Lord! The second pair began at the ankle and ran up to regions I could not follow unless I lifted her skirt.

I do not lift the skirts of women I do not know.

162

Poor girl! If it had been me, I would have been begging for iced water and asking the maids to fan me as I lay dying. The mansion was air conditioned, but it was at least 110 degrees Fahrenheit outside. I could feel the heat between puffs of cooled air.

After dinner, tea was served and the party broke up swiftly. Women started to receive word their husbands were ready to go. They began putting on *abayas*, grabbing their Gucci purses and stepping into the two to three-inch heeled shoes waiting by the front door.

Not so the other American. Thick, thigh-high wool socks that she had *taken off* in the foyer were brought to her by maids. It was at this point I stared at her without caring what anyone thought. Fatima was handed a pair of huge, bulky shoes—the kind children used to wear to correct curved bones—shoes that must have weighed two pounds each. The maids also brought her some thick black gloves, two long black *turhas* (one to be wrapped over the other), and her multi-layer face veil.

I wanted to ask her why she didn't just tell her husband to shoot her.

The hostess asked the ladies in the foyer to step back. The mummy-woman's mate was on the other side of the door with his Superman X- ray vision. He might see us and abduct us from our husbands.

A male voice outside barked orders. Malik revealed what was happening later:

"There was a man there married to an American. . ."

"I know who you mean."

"Before he let his wife came out the door, he asked us—well, ordered us—to stand on the side of the house, by the garden wall, so we couldn't see her. She must be stunning."

"She's okay." I said. Did that sound jealous? "I mean, well, she was pretty. But I don't think that's why he had you stand on the side of the house, Malik."

"Why else?"

163

"You couldn't have seen her if she had tripped over you and fallen into your arms." I detailed all the covering the American had wrapped herself in, ending "Don't you think that's *sick*?"

I badly needed my husband to agree! It is amazing how alone a person can feel when she is cooped up, wrapped up, and cut off. When the person she's doing it *for* doesn't perceive things in the same light, she feels buried alive. That evening, Malik agreed that the American woman's husband was a weirdo.

I didn't see how women in Saudi Arabia would ever gain the right to exist normally unless people stood up for women's rights. This must sound very odd to anyone who has never been to Saudi Arabia, but freedom of movement is the number one problem women face in that country.

When I arrived, females who walked around alone were either poor or prostitutes. God bless the doctors who tried to wage a war against that attitude! They did so because unhealthy mothers were on the rise. Sick mothers and babies gave hospitals a horrible time. Whatever the doctors and nurses advised the ladies and their husbands to do was ignored in the name of religious propriety.

By the late 1980s, doctors—including the Saudis among them-- were *begging* pregnant Saudi women to walk. Expectant parents who had enough education to see some logic in the advice drove to abandoned stretches of road late at night. Malik and I drove past many a strapping husband idly waiting in an air-conditioned sedan while his pregnant wife traipsed back and forth on a street in the far north of Jeddah.

I never realized to what extent movement, nature, freedom, health and happiness were intertwined until I lived in Jeddah. I didn't blame Malik for the attitudes embedded in his society, but I had no coping system.

Malik could walk anywhere he chose. He walked at work, where there was a huge garden and a certain degree of wildlife, like ducks and other large birds, to admire. And he could drive. I was forbidden to drive by law, forbidden to walk by the culture.

I could only move to my heart's content when we left the country on vacation.

There were other culture gaps, some afflicting men like Malik who had experienced the West. When he went to work in Saudi Arabia after graduation, he wanted to wear the *thopes* I sewed for him, using patterns from different countries.

Saudi men may not do that. Malik's appalled friend Essam dragged him into an empty office and told to go home and change into Saudi clothes. "You could lose your job or be arrested!"

The individualist traits America had seeded in my husband died off, little by little. For instance, at first he dreamed of building a small submarine. Friends warned he would be seen as a radical.

In my culture, he had learned a person can be different and not go to jail. There was wiggle room. Most Saudis, I saw, embraced freedom when on vacation. Boredom was their biggest complaint at home, but they submitted.

Not me. I could not stop pining for freedom. It was freedom that allowed me to marry whom I wished in the first place. That was a lesson for me: freedoms are earned by societies. Freedoms are not transferable.

My dreams were pinned on travel.

In July of 1985, by the time Yousef was a year old (using the money I had been paid writing and teaching in addition to the small amount Malik could save), we went to Morocco and Spain. We stayed in cheap hostels. The rooms had openings over the doors to admit air and mosquitos. Bathrooms with dripping faucets and hole-in-the-floor toilets were shared by everyone. The lack of comfort was not so different than my life in Jeddah, but it was worth enduring to get out of Saudi Arabia and see things in the world.

We visited the historic garden of the Sultan Abi Yousef Al Mansour in Rabat, Morocco, and we ambled through rooms and gardens of many an ancient Moorish castle in Spain, like Al Hambra in Granada.

At Al Hamra, water sprang from dainty fountains and rippled through tiled canals where my little boy splashed his hands to play. We found beauty, comfort, inspiration and strangers who liked us and our son. No one called Yousef spoiled or a devil.

165

It made me feel a lot better to see Muslim women walking around without male chaperons. I pointed them out to Malik until he became weary of my noticing.

Little girls older than Yousef followed my cherubic toddler with the wild gold-brown tresses. He ran into the center of groups of people of all nationalities, smiled brightly, and pointed to the sky or to a tree. Adults snapped his picture. Some photographers took pictures of Yousef and me together because of the clothes I had sewn. We looked like we had stepped out of an Orientalist painting. People liked that.

I ran after Yousef and apologized with a smile for the intrusive toddler. Friends were made this way. Owners of a Moroccan dry cleaning business refused to let us leave when their little girls fell head over heels in love with my kid. They played with, combed the hair of and kissed our toddler. We were detained for a very long time by their pleas, tea and refreshments.

Malik and I looked at each other with astonishment. It felt very strange to have people find our child cute when Malik's family didn't seem to want him around.

We dashed off to eat lunch at a nearby eatery, refusing to impose on a family that was supposed to be making money from us. Other Moroccans (and on a different trip, Tunisians) likewise invited us into their homes for meals.

The world outside Saudi Arabia felt appreciative of history and accepting of visitors. In that world, Yousef and I existed, not just for Malik, but for everyone. People liked us and we liked them. I could walk where I pleased, my face uncovered.

Chapter 12

The Faraway Land

One day I heard Hisham, Malik's younger full brother, just back from the U.S.A. with his degree, bark, "Get out of here, Girl!" I peered from around the corner. There were no girls in the room, only my little son Yousef and Hisham. No one else.

"Don't call my son a girl. Malik won't like it."

I looked him straight in the face. He glared back, but there was no point in denying what he had said.

Mama Johara frequently interceded with Malik on behalf of Hisham. He was her youngest son, and she had spoiled him. "He's your brother," she told Malik, meaning he should overlook whatever rude thing Hisham had done.

I met Hisham when his mom sent him to the USA to live with Malik. Hisham resembled two famous male movies stars melded into one. Girls fell over themselves to get his attention. He came without any school records, so Malik had to beg and plead with counselors to give his brother a chance. They did and he was enrolled.

Hisham's female ESL teacher fell in love with him and invited him to live in her house. She was our landlady. That meant Hisham collected Malik's rent.

When Malik and I got married and moved to San Diego, Hisham came with us at first (to please his mother) but refused to talk. He was very gloomy.

Then I think he realized his parents were not there in the USA to tell him what to do, and besides, hadn't Malik secretly married an American?

He went back to Monterey until he could speak English well enough to finish community college. Then he returned to Saudi Arabia, where he married a cousin named Nadia. Nadia returned with him to California for him to complete his studies.

Malik's problems with his mother's preference for Hisham and with a secretive, plotting boss at work kept him, I think, from noticing my unhappiness, much of which sprang from the discrimination I saw levied against my own child for being the son of an American.

That is how I explained his indifference to my misery at the time. It may be I gave Malik far too much credit. People see what they want to see.

It wasn't just Hisham who picked on Yousef. Almost everyone had a turn, particularly a good portion of the little cousins who should have been my son's playmates. Certain parents didn't like me because I was from the West. I never completely understood that attitude until years and years of discrimination changed my life.

Like many Western wives, I had never felt discrimination for others. I did not anticipate my in-laws would dislike me. I was careful about bringing gifts for them. Kate had accompanied me on shopping excursions to purchase pretty fabric for my new mothers-in-law (I had two at once, widowed at exactly the same moment!) and their daughters.

The cotton print fabric from San Diego was not a big hit although the chintz was appreciated. I discovered that despite the heat, Saudi women preferred silky fabrics often made of polyester, even if it made them sweat.

Malik and I gave away many of the Moroccan tea trays and pots, brass platters and handcrafted jackets acquired from Morocco. To my eye, these were beautiful replicas of ancient artefacts. To my Saudi in-laws, it was all junk. In those days, Saudis thought anything old looking belonged in a trash can.

By the time I had Yousef, I could find no reason for him to be so unwanted by Malik's relatives. If I had spoiled him, making him unpleasant to be around, that would have made sense. However, I was good at disciplining.

Only Amahl, one of Malik's beautiful younger sisters was completely untainted. She liked everyone and she loved Yousef.

Far too many others created a competition between Yousef and Miyaz as children, turning the situation into some sort of soccer match. I guess they did not see what they were doing.

By the time Miyaz was eighteen months old, he had picked up the terrible habit of spitting on people. He spat on his great aunt Khadija, Mama Johara's sister. Aunt Khadija didn't say a word. He spat on me.

He did not spit when Mama Johara was in the room, so she must have rebuked him. As a toddler, Miyaz could be sneaky.

One day I heard Miyaz' name loudly chanted from Mama Johara's side of the house. I had been forced to leave Yousef there, upon request. In the stairwell, my toddler stood by himself, wide eyed and hypnotized, as 6 grown-up cousins and aunts paraded up and down the stairs clapping and singing Miyaz' name. Miyaz was perched on the shoulders of the eldest cousin. Miyaz beamed in joy and crooned along as best he could.

I took Yousef's hand and led him back into our two rooms, closing the main door behind us.

Between the ages of three and four, Yousef began to understand that the photos of my father, mother and brother meant he had another family.

"Your mommy?"

"Yes. Your grandmother. My mommy," I said.

"I want to see your mommy."

169

Of course Yousef didn't understand what it meant when I said my mother was dead.

"My daddy," I said pointing. "I will bring you to my daddy. He's nice. He's your grandfather."

"Bring him here!" said Yousef. "Where is your daddy? Bring him here, Mommy."

My heart felt pinched. My parents had warned me of much that had come to pass. Though Mom was gone, I wondered if Dad and his wife, Dolly, would be kind to Yousef.

Dolly had stolen my father from my life at almost the same age Yousef was now, but surely she wouldn't be unkind to a little child? She may not have cared about my brother and me when we were little, but she had my father now, and my mother was out of the way.

Even though Dad and Dolly thought religion was foolish and rebuked me for following one, surely we could be friendly?

From a Casswell-Massey catalogue, I chose a sampling of colognes to send to my father as a gift. He answered immediately. The rift began to heal.

I economized and could afford certain small extravagances—a pull toy of alphabet blocks, shipped from the USA, for Yousef, an ordered gift to be sent to my father.

Personal expenses were modest. For the first few years in Jeddah, we lived on lentil soup, boiled eggs, tuna, tomatoes and cucumbers and sometimes a roast chicken sent over by Mama Johara. The grocery store lettuce never looked too good. Cilantro withstood the climate better, as did *jurjeer*, a cheap local leafy green. I didn't need to buy many clothes in such a warm country. I went barefoot in the house, saving sandals for excursions outdoors.

By the time Yousef was two, I had a new kind of income. I wrote for the radio and newspapers. One series was for the English Service of the Saudi Broadcasting System of the Kingdom of Saudi Arabia. Radio. Another series was titled "Food, Facts and Fun." There were others.

An ability to churn out articles had gained me a steady small income. My boss at the radio station, an educated Palestinian named Yousef Salah, once commented that no one he had ever known could write more than six months' worth of a radio show called "A Leaf from Life's Notebook." He gave the show to me and I wrote it for years, until Saudi-ization of the workforce, causing a firing of freelance non-Saudi writers, caught me in its snare. Mr. Salah was most apologetic, and I will never forget his great integrity.

By the summer of 1987, when Yousef was three, I had saved enough money to go to California. During this first trip home, I visited my stepfather, Don, and friends. A year later, Dad and his wife, Dolly, invited us to stay at their house. It was Dad's first meeting with his grandson and the first time I saw my father since I had married, seven years earlier.

It was wonderful. My brother, Steven, Dad, Yousef and I all went to Disneyland, only half an hour from my father's house. Later, my father revealed that he paid my brother by the hour to accompany us. Steven did not want to appear with his scarf-covered sister in public. I am glad I did not know.

Kate visited us at my father's house. She was working in sales and management for a California newspaper. She was happily remarried to a Lebanese American, and soon they would have a son.

My father wished I would dress without a headscarf, and he said so. He kept his remonstrations to a minimum, not wanting to damage the mended bond between us—not, at least, while Yousef was small.

*   *   *   *

As the years passed, if Malik was given a work seminar in Europe, Yousef and I could accompany him—if I had saved enough money from writing, or if I could negotiate journalist discounts on air tickets from airlines and hotel rooms through tourist offices, offering to write and place future articles in the local press. Through such strategies, we could travel. On his own, of course, Malik could not pay our way.

No sooner did I come back from one trip than I dreamed of the next, even if a full year away. Yousef was so happy when he knew we were about to travel he kissed me repeatedly, hugged me, and danced for joy.

171

While Malik enjoyed traveling, it did not mean for him what it did for us. It took me a long time to realize that. He was a Saudi man going on a trip with his family, not people escaping, like Yousef and I.

Jaunts to the Red Sea coast's warm, turquoise waters helped maintain my calm during the non-traveling months of the year. At the beach one day, Malik suggested I don his white headgear over my big white shirt used for swimming and drive our car home. It was thrilling! I shared this adventure with my doctor, who told me about another woman who had been arrested, jailed and raped by the Saudi police when caught doing the same thing.

Scared, I never drove in Malik's country again.

The Red Sea was the only place to feel truly free. Its shores were home to crabs in sizes ranging from tiny little things I could pick up and watch crawl across my palm to the much larger ghost crabs. The ghost crabs created pyramid sand castles. They watched our invasion with protruding tentacle eyes.

The sideway- scampering crab of shallow waters that Malik caught for us to eat he called *Abu Mughass,* or "father of scissors." Malik taught us how to hunt *Abu Zroombuk*, the conch shell creatures, showing us how to boil them in their shells and then knock the cooked flesh out to eat.

To find *Abu Zroombuk*, we had to wade through clumps of sea grass where sea cucumbers lay in slimy inertia. "Don't ever pick up one of these," warned Malik. "When I was a teenager, one of my cousins dared me to pick one up. I did so and it squirted out a sticky goo that clung to and burned my skin. That's why some people call it 'Sea dick.'" He made a wry face.

To avoid stepping on the sea cucumbers, the sharp rocks, or get bitten by a crab, I wore sneakers that grew stiff, when dried, from salt residue.

If Mama Johara noticed us getting ready for the beach, she brought Miyaz out to the SUV and put him in the vehicle. We learned to leave quietly. Malik and I had an understanding: If his mother heard us and brought Miyaz out, we accepted with good grace.

He knew, however, I preferred our family be alone because my heart was sore from seeing Yousef ostracized.

172

One day, when we had both children at the beach, Yousef reached his arms out for his father to take him into the water. I picked up Miyaz and followed Malik. "We had better trade," said Malik. "You take Yousef."

"Why?"

I was stunned by his. Malik's eyes said he did not think Miyaz safe with me.

He expected me to seek *revenge*? *On a child?*

When the two children were happily digging in the sand and Malik took his usual solitary swim, I let the tears come. We did not speak much on the way home.

I learned that for a wife to complain—of injustice or loneliness or grief—is to weary one's Saudi husband.

The dilemma of finding a playmate for Yousef continued. When he was three or four, Malik and I bought him a battery-powered toy car that could drive at speeds of 60 inches per minute.

As it was brought into the house, it drew the attention of a visiting older cousin, Sultan. Sultan followed us upstairs and sat in the driver's seat. Malik left, pleased that Yousef had a cousin to play with. Every time Sultan visited, he was back in our two rooms to visit the car. I thought about turning Sultan away, but Yousef was ecstatic. If my son imagined he had a playmate, wasn't that all that mattered?

One day I steered Miyaz away from a toy he seemed bent on destroying. He recoiled from my touch as if shocked by an electric cattle prod. Miyaz rubbed his "wounded" shoulder and looking at with reproach at me.

At first I was stunned.

Then it happened again. I was being taken for a fool by a three year old.

When we first got to Jeddah, Malik wanted to build a house, using the money I had inherited at my mother's death. Giving this money to Malik for what he wanted was why I had to earn money for food, clothes and occasional plane tickets.

173

He also asked his own mother for a loan. He acquired a small piece of land so far away from town that it was wilderness. There was no water, no electricity, and no gas. But Malik was hopeful that the sellers' promise that all utilities would be "coming soon" was true.

Malik made a wonderful design. He drew a plan for two small houses, so that his mother could live with us.

He started teaching himself carpentry, including woodturning and carving. He made a beautiful bookcase. I knew that building a house would present him with an opportunity to demonstrate his talent.

While we still lived in the family building, Malik kept tools upstairs on the roof. Just as when he was a teenager, his brothers, nephews and his mother and second mother's drivers borrowed, broke, and forgot to return those things. Malik had reasons enough of his own to want to move away!

Malik was his own contractor, taking care of the entire design and the construction. Just as in the USA, all one needs for architectural designs is a stamp of approval, which of course costs a fee after the design has been inspected for code appliance. On-site inspections for code appliance take place as well.

Malik applied for a building loan from the government. Before it was approved, he began building a little bungalow on the new property. He worked on it every day for two years. It was a small abode, with a living/sleeping room, bathroom and kitchen.

We thought we could use it one day as a guest house. A noisy generator was installed for our electricity, and a one-family water tower. It was a peculiar empty neighborhood made of desert sand, divided by contractors' flags and asphalt-covered empty roads. Herds of camels grazed nearby and falcons circled overhead.

Malik worked hard and I admired him. He collected and carried stones and laid them out in a solid base for the bungalow. He mixed and poured cement and arranged bricks. Two tall arched windows were set in the main wall of the bungalow that faced into the garden. The little house counted on the wall surrounding the property for two of its walls.

Sometimes he could afford to hire immigrant laborers. Most were not very good. One carpenter's job had to be redone. The painters slopped paint and the bathroom tiles were a disaster. My husband patiently tore everything out and did the jobs over again. He learned a lot about managing hired construction crews.

On weekends and some weekdays, Yousef and I went with him to the site. It gave us a sense of freedom. What it didn't give me was a sense of ownership. Malik always referred to the land and house as "my land" or "my house."

"Would you mind calling it 'our' land?" I asked once. I never asked again.

It was not mine. As a foreign wife, I could neither buy nor inherit land. Our children could inherit. They would have to take care of me if I survived my husband. My rights would depend on their good graces.

I had put my fate in Malik's hands, believing he would always put my happiness firs

Western wives all do that. Then they have to decide whether the bargain is being kept. Malik was doing back-breaking work. He said he was doing it for us.

My husband could be kind, staying home from work to care for me when I was ill. He was a playmate for Yousef, allowing our son to do little projects with him.

I had to think of all of these details when appraising my circumstances. While Malik worked on this small house, I taught Yousef to enjoy the desert outdoors.

Kareema and her small children, a boy and a girl, came to picnic with us at the faraway land. Malik did not stay. Kareema's driver sat outside in the empty street. The children played and ate lunch. A couple hours later, as they were leaving, Yousef, crying for his new friend to stay, followed the older boy. That child picked up a large rock by the gate and threw it at Yousef's head.

Luckily, Malik arrived at that moment and drove us to the emergency room. Kareema went home distraught. "I wish I could take the gash on my own head," she wept to me on the phone, "instead of having it on your son."

How can any single parent cultivate tolerance in children when society surrounds them with discrimination? Kareem's children suffered too.

Like me, she was in a marriage that united two countries. She and her husband were Arabs from the Hadramaut. They were distant relatives. Her husband's branch of the family lived in Indonesia.

Her children were born in Saudi Arabia, but they could not claim Saudi nationality through their mother. Nationality is granted solely through the male line.

Yousef and I couldn't go to the faraway land when Malik hired laborers, or when he drove directly there after work. My husband's hands grew calloused and bruised. Winter gales blew down part of the brick garden wall twice. Each time the setback meant we had to cut something out of our budget, like interesting food or clothes.

The kitchen roof of the little house was very steep. I held the lower end of one upside-down V cross-beam while Malik climbed the ladder with the other end in hand. When he had hammered one side in position, he brought the other upside-down V cross beam into the crisscross angle, sliding the top into the middle notch.

Malik stood on flat boards suspended across the walls to do this. The hardest balancing act was when he hammered the boards in place and laid the red clay tiles. He was like a cat and never fell.

Despite the roads, that area remained wild desert. Neighborhood construction efforts were few.

Men came to knock on our gate and ask if a mosque was going up. They thought the tiny, domed chimney was a minaret. When they saw the big windows, they asked, "Are those the doors? Is this a grocery store?" Seeing the fireplace, they asked, "Is this where you will cook?"

"Yes," said Malik. He knew they would not have understood the concept of a fireplace built to make a Western wife happy.

Two years on, when the little cottage was complete, the city had still not hooked up the area to electricity and water. No one lived nearby because no one wanted to live with only baboons, vultures and vagabonds for company.

Still, we packed and moved. I was beside myself with joy. I would walk outside in a garden without being all covered up. I would be mistress of my own domain, able to play, jog, and have an outdoor life. Yousef and I were moving to a freer life, and Malik had made it happen. Our cat, Ramadi, would love it. We could get a goat if we wanted.

On the second night in our little desert haven, Malik turned off the generator, fearful it was overheating. Within minutes it was impossible to sleep in the hot, airless house. We couldn't go outside, though, because there might be scorpions or snakes.

"We can't stay," my husband said the next morning.

Maybe this was how Humpty Dumpty felt before he fell.

"Because of the generator?"

"And there aren't any neighbors. And no telephone. What if you or Yousef gets hurt and you need to get to a hospital when I am not home?"

He was right. Cell phones had not been invented yet. Ham radios were not used among Saudis. They were probably illegal, just like everything else. With broken hearts, we moved back to the main house.

Chapter 13

Shifting Sands

Ghazala disappeared from my life over a political disagreement. I told her a story about a young Saudi man named Abbas, who was killed for love of a princess. He had been my husband's playmate. A journalist called Abbas' mother to ask what she thought of her son's execution. She fainted dead away, having been assured by her brother, a high-placed minister, that Abbas would not be harmed.

Although Ghazala loved analyzing the distress of our common plight, she was not one to knock an apple off the royal cart, not even with a sidelong glance. She brooked no criticism of highborn families.

The next time I called her house, she would not come to the phone. "Madame is not home," said her maid. Madame remained "not at home" for the following weeks until I gave up.

It was not easy to find a Western woman married to a Saudi to befriend, certainly not before the Internet was invented. I was so cut off I did not know there were Western ladies' groups because I had never heard of them.

One day I saw a woman named Nicole being interviewed on Saudi TV. She was a beautiful young woman, the daughter of an English mother and a French father, she said. She lived in Riyadh and was explaining how she had become Muslim.

The interview was conducted and broadcast in English. As I wrote for the Jeddah Branch of the Saudi Radio Station, I just called up my main branch and asked for help in getting her number.

Nicole was very gracious and we became fast friends. She and her husband had recently moved from his home country of Lebanon to live with his sister, who had married a prince. Unfortunately, the prince had recently died, which was why she needed family around her.

Nicole was an interesting woman. When she fell in love with her husband, she not only converted to Islam but agreed to be a second wife.

She did not question her husband's continued marriage with his first wife. His departure from Lebanon put distance between herself and the co-wife. In Riyadh, she began working for the French Service of The Saudi Broadcasting System as well as Saudi Television's recently instituted English channel.

Although Nicole's new life had glamour, there were some humiliations. A mentally challenged sister-in-law was given to striking the lovely face I saw on television. "I cannot get mad or defend myself," Nicole explained. "She doesn't know what she's doing."

Nicole and I ended up writing a travel column together in the *Riyadh Daily* newspaper for several years. We reaped the benefits of scanty competition.

In fact, I competed with myself, writing under various pen names in all three English language newspapers. The *Riyadh Daily* newspaper was pretty nice about it, running my fake byline but issuing checks in my real name.

Nicole restricted herself to that one newspaper but she did a lot more work for the radio and television stations. In all that time, I met her only once, face-to-face, when she visited Jeddah and my house with her husband.

It seemed to me that some Western women I met were more accepting of Saudi life than I was. Not all of us saw eye to eye. I still wished that Malik, Yousef and I could go back to live in California.

One day Malik found, in the starry sky of possibilities, two ideas for our future that he plucked and laid in front of me in shimmering light.

"I will apply for a new scholarship to the USA, to get my master's degree," he said. "And you can work on a Ph.D. Maybe then you will be able to get hired from the States by King Abdul Aziz University!"

The thought of four more years in America not only brought tears of hope to my eyes, but getting a Ph.D. would open a world of opportunity. I might be able to get a job teaching at a college in the USA; then I could support our family while Malik looked for a job in the States. We wouldn't have to live in Saudi Arabia! I knew it would take some work convincing him, but it didn't seem impossible.

"Here is another idea," said Malik. "A friend of mine commutes from Rabiya to Jeddah every day. I could do the same. We could rent one of the new condos being built there. They are government subsidized for employees. All I need to do is put my name on the list of applicants."

Rabiya was a small coastal town to the north of Jeddah. We had gone there a couple of times to picnic and swim. Its waterfront coastline had not been confiscated by rich people as had the coastline of Jeddah, nor was it littered with trash.

It struck me as a Saudi version of a writer's retreat, where Malik and I could give daily swimming lessons to Yousef. The move would place distance between us and the extended family, lessening conflict. The idea was not as good as getting a new scholarship, but it was preferable to trying to cope with daily family friction.

Malik didn't tell his mother about his two ideas. Mama Johara had dreams of her own.

She was always trying to arrange things for her children, like the scholarships her three sons obtained. Mama Johara made sure most of her kids entered and finished college. That made them different from Madame Leena's children.

With Mama Johara spurring him, Malik might never have come to the States.

When he was in high school, Malik stopped studying. He saw himself, in a dream, clinging to a rope, swinging from one hand to the other. The rope was between two high buildings.

Malik told his dream to his father. His father looked somber. Muslims consider true dreams 1/46th of divine prophecy and his father was good at interpreting them: "You will fail in your end-of-year exams, but you will make up for it later."

Wow! Malik failed his final exams, just like his dad said he would. Mama Johara was furious.

Malik had built a little room for himself just behind the family bungalow to escape his second mother's children, who were forever getting into his belongings and breaking things. "From the moment I failed the exams, my mother visited my room ten times a day," said Malik.

"My cousins had been hanging out with me because they liked my room—it felt like a clubhouse. Once Mom started policing me, they all cleared out. If she didn't find me studying *each time* she stuck her head in the door, she snapped, 'You're going to end up as a street cleaner or a ditch digger!' She made me feel like garbage. I couldn't do anything but study, sleep and eat for a whole year."

In the following end-of-year exams, Malik achieved the highest marks for his grade level in the whole kingdom.

Saudi mothers expect that their grown children will support them financially. As soon as Malik returned to Saudi Arabia and became employed, at the age of 23, he gave roughly $250 dollars to his mother from the approximately $1000 salary he received every month. When he got a raise, he increased his mother's allotment. Mama Johara also received allowances from her daughters, who were teachers, and from her two other sons, Hisham and Haroun.

Before Malik finished paying her back for the loan he had taken for his land, his mother had saved enough money to buy a corner plot in a neighborhood called Al Bawadi. She wanted to break from Leena and be on her own. There were a couple of empty lots next to hers.

"Sell your desert land," she urged Malik, "and buy the lot right next to mine in Al Bawadi. Then we can request that the building loan you asked for be transferred to the property in Al Bawadi."

Malik told me what she had said over our lunch. I was horrified. Al Bawadi was a neighborhood of broken sidewalks and vagrant illegal immigrants scouting for work, handouts or an unguarded property to burglarize. The land was cheap there, but so what?

Compared to Malik's promises to me, Mama Johara's idea sounded like "Or you can live in a slum of Jeddah." I didn't hide my reaction.

182

"I agree with you," Malik said.

"We already tried building in Jeddah, Malik. Look where it got us: A beautiful little house we can't live in!"

My husband looked sad.

"I think your two ideas are wonderful, especially the one about going to America. You have no idea how happy I am to think that we might do either of those things!"

He nodded, eating.

"You didn't tell your mother you would consider her proposal?"

"Of course not," said Malik. "But I can't hurt her feelings. What she is trying to do will take a long time, and I have already filed for the scholarship. I also put my name on a list of applicants for the condos in Rabiya. One of those will come through before any sort of government building loan. Those loans take years to be approved."

So he humored her, pretending to listen.

Each afternoon, Mama Johara waited for Malik on the stairs, often with Ziyad beside her. He told me what she said when he sat down to eat.

"Why are you encouraging her? She'll be disappointed when we tell her our news."

"I'll deal with that when it happens."

On days my little Yousef particularly suffered, I couldn't wait to leave, and prayed for something to come through soon. Other times, I worried about hurting Mama Johara. She was a kind and generous woman even if her plans were not mine.

She often sent us meals--stuffed rabbit, *sayadiya*, lamb kebob, or anything she knew Malik and I enjoyed. Her generosity may have created guilt in Malik. In Islam, the mother takes precedence over the wife, and the most well-intentioned mother may unknowingly overlook the needs of a daughter-in-law.

One day Mama Johara glowed as she waited for Malik at the head of the stairs. She smiled at me when I peeked out.

As soon as Malik's khutra-covered head appeared around the corner in the stairwell, Mama Johara started talking. Malik's smile of greeting widened. They conversed for a few minutes, then Malik hugged and kissed his mother.

"What was that all about?" I asked.

"The building loan she requested for me has been approved."

"What?"

I was not really sure what he meant. He must have let her down with diplomacy. She hadn't looked sad.

Malik saw the lunch I had spread on a dining cloth. He put down his briefcase. "Let me wash up first and then I'll tell you what she said and how I answered."

"Okay."

Waiting for Malik, I thought about Mama Johara. When we moved out of town to Rabiya, or back to America on scholarship, I vowed to myself we would visit Jeddah a lot.

I just wanted to get my toddler away from psychologically damaging snubs, discrimination, and physical abuse. I had tolerated just about as much as I could stand.

Malik sat down to the food, smiling. He reached for bread, commenting, "I have decided to accept the loan."

"What?" His words made no sense. What was he talking about? He chewed on a mouthful of bread with some of the cucumber and tomato salad I had made.

"Explain what you mean."

He swallowed, "I'm going to take the loan."

I had no idea how to put my words together. I couldn't articulate.

"I am going to buy the land next to my mother's," he said.

His confession was like a sword through my heart.

"No, Malik."

He kept eating.

184

"I don't *want* to." My hands were shaking. "I want to go to Rabiya. Or to America on scholarship. I don't want to buy property in Al Bawadi. I don't like that neighborhood. You promised."

"You won't even notice it," he said. "Once you see what I build. You'll thank me."

"It's half *my* money," I said. "I do not agree. You may not use my money."

I wanted to throw up.

He kept eating without speaking.

"You decided this without asking me? You can't have the money. It is mine."

"I knew what you would say," he muttered, avoiding my eyes.

"I thought we both felt the same way."

He was quiet.

"Didn't you *care* what I wanted? About what Yousef needs? This is not right. I am supposed to have a say."

"Wait until you see what I can do. It will be better than the house I built on the faraway land. You won't even feel you are living in Al Bawadi." He forced a little smile.

"Decisions like these in a marriage are supposed to be made by both partners," I said. "I have some right in this. We are waiting for the scholarship to be approved."

"It has already been arranged. Look, Sylvia," his voice grew sharp and irritated. "The scholarship hasn't been approved yet, and moving to Rabiya would mean I can't build a house. By some miracle, my mother has managed to push this loan through. It must be a solution to our problems. Why don't you have *faith* in me? Why can't you be patient? Wait and see what I want to do for you and Yousef. I'll make you a house so beautiful you'll forget you're in Saudi Arabia. It will be more beautiful than any place we might have rented in Rabiya. More beautiful than any place we would rent in America."

"Bawadi isn't at the beach," I said. "And it isn't America."

My hands shook. The shock was severe. I was in a place where I had no rights, no one to intervene, no one to speak for me, and no blood relatives except for Yousef. Malik had appropriated my money.

Faith in my husband's word had been destroyed. I thought of leaving him forever even though I loved him. He did not seem to have any sense about what was good for me and our son.

Our happiness didn't matter.

Yet my little son adored his father. A boy needs his father. My own brother had been deprived of our father for years, when Dolly stole him away from us. That event had hurt Steven badly. He had been raised by a stepfather who abused him.

For the time being, it was impossible to forget I had been excluded from Malik's decision-making even as he spent hours, with growing excitement, drawing up his new house plans.

Abu Huraira quoted the Prophet as telling that when God created the intelligence, He told it to stand up and it did so, then told it to turn its back and it did so, then told it to turn its face and it did so, then told it to sit and it did so. He then said, "I have created nothing better, or more excellent, or finer than you. By you I shall receive, by you I shall give, by you I shall know, by you I shall reprove, by you reward will be gained and by opposing you punishment will be received." *Mishkat Al Masabih.*

Chapter 14

"The Cage"

Mama Johara moved into her new villa in Al Bawadi. It was a one-story, rectangular cement villa surrounded by a high cement wall with shards of glass cemented into the top.

She had goaded her contractor to all possible speed. Our house would be erected next door.

Malik and I moved into an apartment across the street from her house and Malik's new plot of land. A bitter gladness filled me to leave the Al Hamra building. Things had been getting very tense.

Cousins larger than Yousef led him off by the hand whenever they could, with smiles glued on their faces, into corners of the house so they could hurt him. I do not say they were bad children; I simply say no one paid attention. Children have to be taught to be kind.

Foreign maids from impoverished countries were "in charge" of these children, but they were given no authority. In fact, they themselves were often abused by parents or children.

Malik kept our visits to the family short, but he did not allow me to keep Yousef away. When I said I would not go, he took Yousef alone. I could not sit home alone more than a few minutes before I started worrying. Then I would throw on my *abaya* and run across the street to make sure my son was alright.

"Your nephews and nieces are indebted to you," I told Malik. "They think you married a Westerner just so she could give birth to someone for them to beat up. You've given them something to help them forget the boredom of their lives."

"If you don't like the way things are, then pack your bags and there's the door!" he snapped back.

Things had changed between us.

Malik's tongue had sharpened over the years. Even if my husband loved me, I didn't like the impact his culture had on him. The gap between us was widening. My upset remarks didn't gain his pity or understanding; they just made him aware I was neither Saudi nor Arab.

Part of me knew I should leave. Another part of me felt alien to my former culture. I was half a world away from my father's house and a car I could drive. I knew how to make a little money in Saudi Arabia; I didn't know how to do that in the USA.

And would I be accepted in America as a Muslim? My father and his wife made it clear they disapproved of my new faith, but that was because they were atheists. They thought all religions were stupid.

Could I go back to the USA completely on my own as a Muslim convert?

Oh, but I hated the way many of the Al Shamsi children treated Yousef.

Before moving to the Bawadi neighborhood, Mama Johara tried to appease me. "All children are naughty," she said. "It's normal. You've lived with us for five years. Keep your heart big."

"The children should be taught manners," I replied. "Their parents should talk to them and watch them, not leave them for maids to raise. These servants have no power. Some of your children and Madame Leena's children are mean to the maids or drivers. The maids are not respected and they can't teach the children anything."

Even Malik was appalled at the bad treatment of maids and drivers, for he commented, "Don't people worry that their maids or drivers will pray against them?"

That worry was not widespread. The children of one relative slapped and kicked their serving girl. I saw her sometimes standing with other maids at the front entrance to Mama Johara's house. She always had eyes brimming with tears when we hugged.

Not everyone was unkind to their servants, but there were enough instances to shock Western wives.

Instead of changing the way they treated their maids and drivers, many of my husband's relatives criticized the way he and I raised our son.

At family gatherings, some mean relatives looked at Yousef and said, "Doesn't he speak Arabic better than that? And he is so skinny! For shame!"

As for language, I had studied Arabic for only one year in California, but I understood well enough. I regret that Malik did not help me. He did not like teaching languages. He did not teach Yousef.

I spoke fluent French and a degree of Spanish. I was not too stupid to learn Arabic. However, Malik always spoke to me in English. I learned a few words of Arabic a month, if I was lucky. None of his family helped or offered to teach me Arabic. I had to repeat words I heard and demand someone tell me the meaning.

That didn't always work if no one felt like helping.

I guess everyone thought Malik should teach me. Malik was, by his own admission, a poor tutor. He said words too rapidly for me to hear properly. I needed to hear words pronounced two or three times.

I needed lessons, but I didn't have the money. Private tutors wanted 100 riyals an hour. There were free Arabic classes in the 1980s, but only for female Saudi citizens.

Because I was the parent with Yousef the most, I did most of the teaching. I have heard tapes of myself talking to him in Arabic when he was three or four.

"Why don't you speak better Arabic?" asked Grandmother Meriam, a relative from Mecca whose constant smoking of shisha did not impede her from reaching her nineties in decent health. She was an entertaining companion with her stories of travel as a bride from Mecca to Jeddah by camel and howdah, the curtained chair on the camel's back.

"I can't find a teacher."

Sitti Meriam knew I liked her. "Memorize the Qur'an," she suggested. "You'll learn that way."

Her logic was good. The Qur'an is in formal Arabic. By memorizing lines from that book and their meanings in English, I have

189

learned some formal wording. However, most people in Jeddah don't speak formal Arabic.

I never blamed Mama Johara for my lack of Arabic. She learned to read and write when her children did, using their books and allowing them to tutor her. She was not at all certain of grammar. As long as she could figure out what I was trying to say, it didn't matter to her whether I conjugated verbs correctly.

"Did I say that right?" was my frequent question.

"Yes, fine," she lied kindly.

Our move to Bawadi in 1989 took place around Yousef's fifth birthday. I led him to an Arabic kindergarten down the road from our new apartment.

"I want you to teach him Arabic," I said to the headmistress.

"We can't do that," she replied. "You have to teach him."

"I'm not an Arab," I said. "I'm American. You must have figured that out by my accent. My Arabic is not good."

"There's nothing we can do about that," she said.

I enrolled Yousef anyway. Maybe someone, like the teacher, might try to teach my son a little Arabic?

I was wrong. They showed him how to make butter, but no Arabic.

Life in our new apartment was more restricted than ever before. The roof was off limits. We found the windows covered in brown duct tape. That stuff was hellish to get off.

The apartment wasn't small, but it was dark and drab. One room had no windows. The layout coincided with the Saudi lifestyle and expectancy that male and female guests were split up.

We pulled off all the duct tape and cleaned the windows with solvents and scrapers. The former inhabitants had probably been from a small Bedouin town outside Jeddah, or maybe even as far away as Pakistan or Sudan. The poorer classes from all those areas use duct tape in preference to curtains. The point is not so much cheapness as the impossibility of peeping in at a woman.

The neighborhood had a handful of plain cement buildings with more duct-taped windows. In the center square, cats scrabbled in and out of overflowing garbage bins. Graffiti covered the wall opposite our new plot of land. Tractors had broken the sidewalks, which were always laid first in any neighborhood where apartment buildings were supposed to go up.

When Yousef asked, "Mommy, when are we going to the faraway land?" I answered, "I don't know, Honey. Look outside—there's Daddy!" Distraction was my best defense. I didn't have the heart to tell Yousef the faraway land had been sold.

In this apartment building I met Norah, a very young Englishwoman married to a Bedouin Saudi of Afif. She did not live in Jeddah, but came to visit her husband's relatives who did.

Her British parents were Muslim converts who had spirited their daughter out of London in order to marry her to a Saudi before she was 14. On the day she was smuggled out, British authorities stopped the British Airways flight they believed the girl and her family were on before the plane could take off. That reservation had been a subterfuge. Parents and daughter were on another flight already airborne.

Norah was a slight, pretty girl who had a small son by the time I met her. Though reasons are plentiful in history for young women to marry early, there is little sense today—even in the Middle East—in depriving a girl of a high school and/or college education or of encouraging her to become a very young mother. If she ends up divorced, how will that young woman support herself?

Norah's case was annoying, but I can't say unusual. After initially running into her on the stairs of the building and perceiving her to be British, I invited her over. That visit was followed by one or two more. At my door, the teen mom gave me her *abaya, turha* and face veils, and allowed her toddler to roll in, rather like a bumper car.

Yousef tried to play with Maimun, but the child was uninterested in polite company. While my four-year-old played with toys, the two-year old plodded on swift and unsteady feet from one bathroom to the other, splashing happily in the high, Western-style toilet and dropping everything he could find—soaps, vases, and hand towels—down the primitive floor hole toilet in the guest bathroom.

191

Yousef found him doing this and tried to stop him. Maimoon's high-pitched tantrum screams alerted me to the problem. His mother sat calmly thumbing through a magazine.

The bathroom doors were closed. I went back to making tea, and Maimun discovered small plants on the windowsill. He flipped them over to create his own dirt pile on my office floor. Norah sat glued to her chair, chattering away in a voice that would carry to me in the kitchen about the absurdities of all things American.

A combination of pity and boredom verging upon insanity caused me to invite Norah a second time, with more of the same comportment by the child and lack of interest from the high school-age mother. Norah's third and last visit would not have taken place had the girl not bribed me with the presence of a British mother.

I assumed the lady's presence would assure better surveillance of the child. I assumed wrong. Little Maimun came armed with the contempt of familiarity. Now a few months older and unintimidated, he went on his merry way, with no one but Yousef and I to look after him.

Maimun's grandmother was stamped with the same stoic immovability as her daughter. Digging under the surface of this heaviness revealed a lady who, like her husband, had accepted a dogmatic, indigenous Wahhabi version of Islam comprised of beards and female covering.

My reference to thinkers like Ibn Al Arabi, Rumi, or Ghazzali brought a blank look. She had never heard of them. By the time all the pictures had been pulled off my walls, the calendar ripped to shreds and various toys broken, I divined we had nothing in common save that we were all native English speakers and converts to Islam.

That should have been a great deal, but it was not. The many Norahs that exist throughout the Muslim world will melt into the veiled throng, accepting the version of Islam that is spoon fed to them.

In the quiet of my lonely apartment, I gazed through the window each afternoon at the cement foundation of the new villa. Malik oversaw every step of building. After lunch and a short nap each day, he donned overalls and went across the street to work. I couldn't stroll about the worksite because male workers were there. Malik was exhausted when he returned at sundown. After he ate, he fell asleep on the couch in the middle of blinking.

The man who owned a neighboring building sat on a chair outside everyday with his tunic hiked up to reveal his yellowing long cotton underpants. He smoked a shisha and stared at pedestrians. Sometimes he picked himself up from the chair to look for scrap metal, making forays onto our lot for this purpose. When he found a piece not hammered down or screwed in place, he dragged it back through the dust and scraping over cement to his own building.

He assumed my husband, attired in overalls, was a laborer.

"This is a complete waste of space," he said, his arm sweeping to indicate the courtyard, "You should tell the owner."

"I am the owner."

This neighbor was neither cowed nor embarrassed. "Why are you wasting all this space?"

Malik explained he was making a fountains in the courtyard, an inner sanctum. The man snorted. "You're crazy!" He stomped away.

Shortly afterwards, the same neighbor built cubical, windowless, concrete rooms between his building and his neighbor's. He must have paid off an inspector to get away with fire code violation. The airless cells were rented out to poor local workers.

The tenants hung the remains of their street-bought meals of rice and chicken in plastic bags on the half-dead tree in the empty lot just behind Mama Johara's villa. This was their own method of charity. Safe from scavenging dogs and cats, the rotting food could be found by starving vagabonds.

I often held Yousef at the window to show him the beginnings of the villa his father was building. My son saw a group of neighbor immigrant Syrian children playing.

"Mommy!" He wiggled in my arms, pointing at their antics. He wanted to play with them. Malik asked the group if they would mind a younger boy joining them for a little while. "Yes, bring him!" they said. "We will take care of him."

I dressed Yousef in his pintsize overalls and let Malik take him out to play. I returned to the window every minute or so to peer out, keeping my scarf on my head in case I had to run out in the street. I was not so sure about these children, but Malik said we had to trust people. He promised to keep watch.

Minutes later, I heard crying in the apartment hallway.

I threw open the door. The back of one of Yousef's pant legs was ripped and soaked in blood.

"I found the street kids throwing clods of dirt at him," said Malik grimly. "He fell against one of the metal spikes that sticks out of the concrete bases."

Mom ran for the first aid kit. So much for a brief hope that Yousef would have playmates in our new neighborhood. As the months passed, my eyelids began twitching and pulsing. When Yousef took his nap, I wandered around the apartment, crying. Sometimes I screamed with my mouth pressed into a pillow.

Knife pains began to stab at my kidneys—once so severely I crawled on hands and knees to the bed. Malik was not told. Perhaps I thought it might be mildly stimulating to drop dead. He would just repeat to me, again, how wonderful the new house would be.

On Wednesday nights before the Thursday/Friday weekends, Malik's brothers and sisters visited their mother. Malik went over to join them, taking Yousef.

"He'll learn Arabic by mixing with them."

It was hard to understand how. The children who came regularly didn't talk. If an adult said, "Peace be upon you," the little ones looked down and stuck their hands in their mouths. Then they were kissed, given candy, and sent to play outside with the drivers and maids. I stayed near Yousef.

Once I asked Malik to keep an eye on our son while I stepped into the restroom. Two older cousins led Yousef out into the space inside the wall surrounding the house. After a couple of minutes, Malik rose to see what the children were doing. He found Yousef backed up against a wall, crying, as his cousins whipped his legs with wires.

Mama Johara was angry when she heard about the incident.

"Hajr!" she called. Hajr was Mama Johara's maid. "Where are you? What are those maids doing?"

The maids had abandoned the children to have their once-a-week unacknowledged tea party in the kitchen while Hajr prepared dinner. The women were starved for friendship with others from their homelands, who lived similar lives of servitude. They heard Mama Johara's cries and quickly filed out the back door. Hajr came to the kitchen doorway, wiping her hands on her kitchen towel. She had a meal for thirty to get ready.

"I'm frying shrimp."

Tell Ali to get rid of those wires!"

"Okay," said Hajr, going to the intercom. Ali was the driver and her husband. He was outside in the street, smoking and chatting with the other drivers.

The next day Mama Johara bought new toys for Yousef. She tried to smooth things over this way when there were hard feelings.

Yousef's only true friends and safe playmates were children of other expatriate mothers. I had to knock at the door of a neighbor's house and borrow a phone if I wanted to invite over someone I had met. Mama Johara did the same thing when she needed a phone. It was embarrassing.

Finding friends was difficult before the internet. On a rare visit to Kareema at the university housing compound, I saw a sign in English advertising Afghani rugs for sale. The apartment number was given

That is how I met Mia, an American woman married to a Saudi computer programming teacher at the university. Mia's mother was an American convert to Islam and Mia's father was Egyptian. She had a little boy the same age as Yousef.

Mia was raised in Seattle and Kuwait. Her personality was bubbly and she was smart, with opinions. I liked her instantly.

One of her pet peeves was the shabby treatment of cats in the kingdom. She kept a cat traveling box in her car in order to pick strays off the street, take them to a vet, then adopt them or give them away. At her apartment, Mia had two dozen "outside" cats and several "indoor" cats, one of which was blind.

"Do you want a cat?" she asked me.

"I have a cat, and limited space. How many do you have?"

195

"Not as many as I did. The compound management has been poisoning them."

"What!? Why?"

"They think cats are rodents. The managers are leaving chicken meat laced with poison all around the compound. Nine of my cats have been poisoned. I found them lying in their own vomit and blood."

The hairs on my arms stood up. "Isn't that un-Islamic?"

"Of course it is!" she agreed. "These people are so ignorant they don't realize the prophet Muhammad, peace be upon him, said one has to pay a penance for accidentally killing an animal."

"Have you told them?"

"Do you think they listen?"

"No," I admitted. "They're not accidentally killing them, anyway. Wouldn't it be nicer to catch the kitties and vaccinate them?"

"Fat chance!" exclaimed Mia. "An American friend of mine who lives on another compound had a black cat for a pet. The gardener there told her that jinn inhabit black cats. She never saw her cat again after that day."

I shivered.

Mia's apartment had a sampling of old-fashioned wooden windows leaning against the walls.

"Where did you get these?" I asked.

"From Mecca, where my husband's family lives. They're left to rot when buildings are torn down. No one wants them. Aren't they beautiful?"

Everything Mia narrated was in an effervescent voice that radiated enthusiasm and determination. She had studied film making in Seattle and was trying to make a living as a photographer.

She assured her clients, who hired her for their daughters' weddings, that all the processing of the pictures was done by females. At first she worked freelance. When Mia opened a shop, she took on a female Saudi partner, operating behind the woman's wedding gown business.

Mia's contracts increased over the years, but not without troubles from her partner, the religious police, and contentious clients. Her greatest asset (she thought) was a supportive, easy-going university professor husband who did not mind if she came home from a job at daybreak or later. Saudi weddings are all held in the middle of the night. Mia learned to live the life of a night owl. (Mia has her own story to tell, in film form.)

My solitary life endured until another year had passed and summer was upon us. While Yousef and I stayed with a friend in San Diego, I visited a psychiatrist, at my friend's suggestion.

To the psychiatrist, I tried to explain my faith in Islam and my love for my husband and child, the reasons for enduring severe isolation in Saudi Arabia. Then I described my stomach pains, indigestion, eye and facial twitching, paralyzing migraines, eczema, and unending infections of the female organs.

My Jeddah doctor had already told me my pains were psychosomatic. He said I thought too much.

"What's happening to me?"

The psychiatrist had filled two pages with notes. "You are on the verge of a nervous breakdown. Why not ask your husband to move back to the USA?"

"Don't think I haven't tried! It may happen in a few years, but he is building a house for us right now in Jeddah."

"Then why not stay longer on your vacation? Your husband loves you. Explain you need more time to relax. He cares about you. Just tell him what you have told me."

"Will you write a letter to my husband, explaining your diagnosis?" I asked.

"Of course."

I sent her letter to Malik by express mail.

"Please, Malik," I said over the phone. "The psychiatrist says I need to relax longer here. You have the letter. May I stay a week or two longer?"

"Muslims don't believe in nervous breakdowns," he said angrily.

197

He contradicted himself. He was the one who had told me how Muslim doctors played the kanoon, a stringed musical instrument, to heal sufferers of psychological trauma.

What had happened to my husband? Why did his tremendous compassion not extend to me, his foreign, homesick wife, mother of his son?

My hand held the phone up but words would not come. One day later, I received a telegram:

"If you do not come back in five days, I will divorce you."

I had sacrificed a great deal for this marriage, as well as for my conversion. I was conscientious of all of that, as of Yousef's love for his daddy. If my husband was ready to call it quits, fine.

If we were at the end, I had arrangements to make and questions to demand of this man, face to face. I was not a coward.

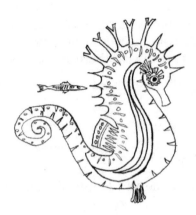

Chapter 15

The Hardship of Ease

It was a smiling and abashed man who met us at the Jeddah airport, not the brooding composer of the tyrannical telegram. Malik wouldn't kiss me at the airport. Couples do not embrace in public in Saudi Arabia. Instead he beamed and swung Yousef up in his arms.

"You both look so beautiful!"

In the car Malik kissed me, caressed my hair and tried to wipe away my pained expression.

"How could you?" I demanded. I wouldn't allow Malik's cruel telegram to be forgotten about simply because he was now happy.

"Why can't you be patient and let me visit my home for a reasonable period of time?" I pressed.

"Let's talk about it later," he pleaded with a conciliatory smile.

"Don't you understand that I had to work all year to make enough money to afford those tickets? You let me stay *17 days*. Malik, you used to go to *a full month* in Jeddah with your family when you were a student in the States." I was upset.

"I just couldn't take it," he said at length. "It's such a long time to wait for you. It's the life of a monk. I need a woman."

199

I stared. His manner was more embarrassed than apologetic. And it was unfairly adamant. Malik saw his physical "needs" as coming before my psychological ones. Was there any saving this marriage?

As he unlocked the door to our apartment, I held to my case. He had crossed a line.

"This is not my country. I miss my homeland. It is very hard living here, Malik. If you *refuse* to try and understand what my life is like, then there is no hope for us."

"I do think of that," he said gently. "Wait until you see what I got for you."

There was a very pretty new couch in my office.

"I know this life has been hard on you. I saw your mother's house after she died, when we went to visit your stepfather. This apartment is awful compared to that beautiful place. You think I haven't said to myself, 'Poor Sylvia, living in a suffocating apartment like this!'? But just wait, Sweetheart, until you live in the villa; you will feel so relaxed with your own gardens and so much space to decorate. I promise you, life will be beautiful. Look, this couch is really a pull-out bed. We can use it if your brother or your dad comes to visit us."

Malik was deftly pulling on heart strings. Yousef ran around the apartment, petting Ramadi, reacquainting himself with toys, then dropping everything to dive into his father's lap. Malik had bought fancy chocolates, a bottle of nonalcoholic wine that had made its way in the last year into Saudi supermarkets, boxes of European cookies, and fresh fruits. He had stuffed the refrigerator and kitchen shelves with everything he could think of Yousef and I might like.

He was trying to make up for ruining my vacation.

However, as days rolled by, he began to mention Western wives (whom I had never met) who did not feel the need to revisit childhood home or town or state. All the women I knew missed their homelands, (usually due to the offer of regained freedom and green nature) and they all found some way to scavenge enough money to go.

Every time he brought up someone I had never heard of, saying, "Mazen's wife's cousin knows an American who stays every summer with her husband in Taif. . . ." I boiled my response down to a formula— one that made sense to me.

200

"I am not this woman. I don't care whom you use as an example. Most women *are* like me."

Sometimes he was quiet; other times he disagreed vocally.

I was being cast as the villain, nine years into a marriage that had a very serious problem at its core--or perhaps in its surrounding hull. Was it the country or the husband? Would we be happier in the USA?

The claustrophobia of my caged life recommenced until a door swung open.

God says," "Lo, with hardship goeth ease" (Qur'an 94:6). We moved into our new villa some months after returning to Jeddah. It was 1990 and Yousef had turned six years old over the summer. The day of the move might have been more difficult if not for the kindness of Azza, manager at the female branch of the local Saudi French bank and a wonderful new friend.

Educated in England, Azza did not wear head scarves. She sometimes wore the long *abaya* loosely, as Western women did. She was an interesting and educated woman, reading science fiction novels, newspapers and the Qur'an. Azza traveled widely in Europe and the USA with her surgeon husband. Her spirituality was private and un-preaching. She made friends with all nationalities and did not try to convert anyone.

On the day that Malik and I moved into the empty villa, Azza sent her two maids to assist me. "They will help you get everything over to the house," Azza wrote in her note. "How can you do it by yourself? You have to look after your little boy and pack at the same time. Let my ladies help you and you'll be done in a few hours."

"That's a very nice friend you have," said Malik. "She seems to be a beautiful woman both inside and out."

I agreed, reflecting wryly that I couldn't make such observations about his male friends without being accused of lechery.

Our two little couches were swallowed by the new villa. My footsteps echoed when I walked through the empty, hot rooms. For the moment, we had but three small air conditioners: one for the bedroom, one for the family room and one in the kitchen. I rejoiced in hanging some clothes in my first built-in closet in Jeddah. Two cardboard boxes stood in for dressers for several months.

The villa was full of sunlight. I could walk through the empty rooms in the early morning when it was not too hot and dream of what they would be like filled with furniture, pictures and cool air. I could walk outside the house, protected from public view by the high surrounding brick wall. I did not have to shroud myself with an *abaya* or *turha*.

Even in the humid heat, I floated.

Mahogany-stained beams supported the high ceilings of Yousef's bedroom and the upstairs. Gothic-style wood-framed windows brought more light into the upper portion of Yousef's room. At eye level, we looked out upon new trees.

Malik was talented. I had never doubted that.

The house's rooftop had embattled parapets like a castle. Its red clay-tiled roofs were multi-level. The parapets baffled Malik's architect friends. He had to explain how he had poured the cement for them.

The salon (main guest room) had three wide French windows and sixteen small rectangular windows running below the ceiling, all beautifully hand-painted by Malik.

A year or two later, he hired artisans to paint the high salon ceiling deep blue with golden stars. From the center of the salon, he suspended a chandelier of Bohemian cranberry-tinted glass that he found, covered in dust, in a little downtown shop owned by a Syrian immigrant. Malik was not only talented, he was a successful treasure hunter who negotiated for undervalued objects at bargain prices.

The house was a wonder of open space. Every room had views upon the inner courtyard, the outer surrounding garden, or both. The main bathroom had a small, pyramid-shaped glass skylight.

Standing in a short backless sundress to look out on the street, I could look out the second story bedroom's bay window of reflective glass and no one could see me.

The house had cost less to build any house its size. If Malik had hired a contractor, the price would have been quadrupled. A

202

government loan, then available to all graduates who worked for the government, helped him finish.

The lovely house caused my in-laws to treat me with heightened respect. I was able to hold parties, inviting other expatriate wives. I was no longer embarrassed by my living quarters.

New acquaintances who had not witnessed my previous living conditions envied me.

One day when Yousef was sitting in the inner courtyard by himself, I snuck upstairs. Tiptoeing to the side of the roof, I looked down on my son through the battlements of our parapet. Yousef swung his legs, waiting for Mommy to return.

"Assalam Alaikum Little Boy," I warbled in a magical genie voice.

"Huh? Who is that?" He didn't sound scared.

"Assalam Alaikum Little Boy," I repeated. *"I am the genie of the house."*

Yousef was looking upwards. "Where are you?"

"Sitting on a cloud. Look straight up. Do you see me?"

"No."

" If you look really hard, you can probably see my feet kicking against the cloud."

"Oh, yeah! I think. . . maybe. . . Yes, I think I see you! Will you come down?"

"Ooooooooooh noooooooooooo." I tried to make my voice float. *"Genies are not allowed to do that. I just wanted you to know I am your friend and I like you. I hope you are happy in your new house."*

"Oh yes!" said Yousef. "It's great! Will you come back again? I want to talk to you every day."

"I won't be able to do that," I said, thinking maybe I had started a draining enterprise. *"I have already broken a law by talking to you today. Don't tell anyone. Just your mother. You seem like such a nice boy. I wanted to welcome you to your new house and tell you I am the genie of your house. Ooooooooooh, I am being pullllllllllllled awwwwwayyyyyyyyyy."*

"Don't go, Genie!"

"Good-bye, my young friend, I will come back some other day..."

"Goodbye Genie! Goodbye!"

Yousef was full of his exciting story.

"Mommy, didn't you hear? I thought you would hear us."

"No, I was in the bathroom. I didn't hear anything."

"He wasn't supposed to talk to me. He broke a genie law!"

"Who, Sweetheart?"

"The genie! I spoke to a genie! He was right here. I will find him for you!" Yousef called out to the genie, whom I very well knew wouldn't answer *now*, so I tried to distract him to tell me his story.

*   *   *   *

Yousef says he often called out to the genie, hoping for an answer. I felt a bit guilty, yet it had seemed if a child of mine lived in Arabia, there should be a bit of magic in the experience.

Would Santa come so far? My father brought the matter up. I had long thought Saudis did not do enough to make their big holiday—*Eid Al Fitr*--special for children. Children were handed money and taken to the toy store. How boring.

In Malik's childhood, Uncle Siddik had arranged sailors' dances on the beach. Old-fashioned wooden toys, comparable to amusement park rides, were erected in every town square. Given the disappearance of those things and the lack of traditional story tellers, acrobats, fire eaters, and snake charmers as in Morocco, there wasn't much to distinguish a Saudi Eid.

I wanted a parallel to the Christmas tree: a "flying" carpet strewn with wrapped gifts or visits from a gift-bearing genie.

The Christmas tree was transformed for my purposes. Yousef and my second son, Ja'far, were raised thinking the Christmas tree is an Eid tree. In Jeddah, we used a Ficus instead of a pine.

Santa began flying out to Arabia. He left gifts on the hearth of our unused fireplace.

"Santa Claus doesn't just visit Christian children," I explained. "He brings toys to all children who believe in him. He just gets more publicity in the West."

Santa got in through the chimney even though a glass covering had been cemented at the hearth to prevent geckos from invading our rooms. "Santa takes off the glass when he comes and then glues it back in place when he's leaving," I explained. *Easy work for a guy who flies through the air with reindeer*! Yousef's cousins ogled the brightly lit Ficus on their Eid visits. They were jealous.

In October, Yousef began first grade in an all-boys private school. I couldn't put off his entry into the gender-segregated world of Saudi schooling any longer. I had dragged my feet, knowing that by Saudi law, children who have one Saudi parent are required to attend a government-regulated, public or private gender-segregated, fully Arabic school.

It wasn't long before the Egyptian teachers at the school informed Malik our son was a genius. Malik and I basked in proud complacency until it struck us several weeks later that Yousef still didn't speak any more Arabic than when he started school.

He had, however, been developing an alarming number of stomachaches.

"Mommy, the boys hit me and throw pencils at my head when the teacher isn't looking!"

"You have to tell the teacher."

"You have to hit them back," said Malik.

"If he speaks English and they speak Arabic, why do they think he's a genius?" I asked Malik.

Too many things didn't seem right. The school representatives were schmoozing us for tuition. Without good Arabic, how could Yousef understand directions?

Malik visited the school and came back saying all was well. Another year rolled by and no one taught Yousef Arabic. My esteem for education in Saudi Arabia kept dropping.

During that first winter in our new villa, I negotiated trips, in my role as travel writer, with Swissair and the Swiss Tourist Department.

Malik enjoyed Switzerland as much as I did. We made friends with our Swiss ski instructor, Werner, and his American fiancée, Deborah.

Deborah sent me dried alpine flowers and long letters; the correspondence gave me opportunity to compare our cross-cultural marriages. Deborah described how she and Werner participated in road clean up after a spring storm. The Swiss paid female workers less per hour than male workers were paid. Such reminders of international marital culture clashes gave me a degree of patience.

In my seventh year in Saudi Arabia, several months after moving into the villa, we got our first telephone. Malik had found a "contact" in the phone company. In return, he had to find a job for the contact's relative.

On the exact day the phone was to be installed, two of Malik's brothers came to our house and offered to get us a phone. Malik figured they both had heard of our new phone and wanted credit for offering to help.

In a country where "I scratch your back, you scratch mine" is the barter system to obtain anything, they craved Malik's goodwill.

Malik used the phone to contact his daughter Yasmin, and ended up staying in contact with Jean and both her divorced parents. Jean's mother was studying to become a lawyer, maybe to get her daughter out of legal scrapes. Jean's father told Malik that Jean was now a high class call girl.

On one of Malik's subsequent visits to Yasmin, he found Jean had a new boyfriend. Jean's father said he was a pimp. Malik found Yasmin's younger brothers watching porn on television. Things would only get worse.

Prices for international phone calls from Saudi Arabia were exorbitant before the introduction of the internet. Still, the phone was useful for spreading news of the August 2, 1990, Iraqi invasion and annexation of Saudi Arabia's neighbor, Kuwait.

The rest of the world knew days before the Saudi media announced the invasion by radio and television. Most people found out first through the grapevine. False information got mingled with truth. Saudis panicked. Kuwaitis flooded into Jeddah. Kuwaiti women were easy to spot; they acted freer than Saudi women.

Many shops and businesses closed. People wanted to leave before the Iraqis invaded Saudi Arabia. Western wives of Saudis kept in contact with their embassies. The embassies would inform us if we needed to leave. Friends called me from the States, begging me to come home.

I never did believe Iraqi soldiers stormed a Kuwaiti hospital and tore premature babies from their incubators to cast them upon the cold floor. Arabs love babies. I was not surprised to later hear the public disclosure that the story of the incubator babies was contrived, rehearsed and delivered by the daughter of the Kuwaiti ambassador to the U.S.A.

By the following summer, Malik and I resolved our private battle with a truce. As soon as he saved enough money, we would go to America to live as a family.

"I don't know how many years it will take to save the money," he warned. "But if I start a business on the side, which I have been thinking about a lot recently, then I can retire from my government job and concentrate on running that business, whatever it is. I am thinking of starting a woodworking or import business. If need be, I can travel back and forth between Saudi Arabia and the States and you can live in California. This villa will be our home base in Jeddah when you and Yousef come on vacations."

The plan was 100% acceptable to me. Education in Saudi Arabia was completely unacceptable for preparing a child for life. Malik agreed that Yousef and I should travel to California for a summer holiday. Yousef and I were indebted, once again, to friends and family who put us up.

The day after our return to Jeddah, Malik attacked me. "How could you have gone out with any other men before we married?"

"What?"

I used to be able to tell when my husband was nursing a grudge. This time I had not seen it coming. He was referring to a period ten years earlier, when he had broken up with me and was dating other girls.

"Malik, we had broken up. You were dating too."

207

Nothing I said mattered. After a little while, I realized Malik secretly thought I should not have gone on vacation at all. Why? He had built "me" a real house in Jeddah. In his mind, I should not have left, but he never said it.

This lack of communication was seriously damaging to our marriage. He did not tell me what he was thinking and punished me when I couldn't figure out.

I served Malik's meals in silence and took mine on the floor of the empty foyer. My anger was real; I was angry he would ruin my vacation once again. I wondered why he didn't divorce me. Why did he like to toy with me?

After a couple of weeks, Malik reverted to speaking of the time we would move to the States. Then one day he arrived home with a full set of new furniture and an air conditioner for my upstairs studio. His subdued demeanor belied the excitement one might expect from a man surprising his sweetheart.

It was an apology in a vicious cycle, but I had been isolated for so long I didn't see the pattern.

*   *   *   *

The first Persian Gulf War was formally declared in January of 1991, when a coalition of 32 nations including the United States, Britain, Egypt, France and Saudi Arabia began the process of regaining Kuwait for the Kuwaitis. When the first U.S. military jets flew over my house in formation, I felt the cavalry had come. Over the phone, Mia cheered, "Hooray for the Red, White and Blue!"

Saudis were worried about their bank accounts and chemical warfare. They began transferring money, stockpiling food and buying gas masks as well as guns, legally or illegally. B-52 bombers, employed as cargo planes, shook over our house on a nightly basis as provisions were flown to the US troops.

Kate, my old friend, was now business manager of a Californian newspaper next to a U.S. military training camp in Palm Springs. She asked me to write a column that would help soldiers know what to expect when they came to Saudi Arabia. The U.S. armed forces began to radio broadcast my articles. When I found out, I switched to a pen name.

208

My writing place was my upstairs office. On windy, overcast days during the seasonal change from summer to winter, I looked out at the swaying eucalyptus tree and bougainvillea plants, telling myself I was in the West. It was deliberate cultivation of delusion.

Chapter 16

Stolen Treasures

In the center of our courtyard, with its patterned tiles and gypsum engravings executed by Moroccan craftsmen, Malik had devised an electric water fountain that, with the flip of a switch, sent water rippling down two tiers of marble bird baths. Velvet-textured yellow and purple pansies looked festive in clay pots. Tubular pink and white blossoms bloomed on the slender Nicotania tobacco plants, emitting fragrant aromas towards sunset. Air circulated in the courtyard, although the blazing sun did too, prompting Malik to design a long canvas on a roller that he fixed in place to one side of the inner roof. The canvas could be drawn overhead to shade the flowers.

Busy construction of villas and apartment houses in our neighborhood quickly packed the neighborhood. Within a year, air stopped circulating. Most of the flowers died. Yet Queen of the Night, an Arabian vine that erupts in delicate, fragrant blossoms infusing aphrodisiac into the evening air, was sturdy enough to survive the daytime exposure to Arab sun as well as lack of breeze. The tendrils snaked upwards toward the red clay tiles, and Malik carefully secured their routes.

Malik had woven the scent of Queen of the Night into the tales he told during our college days. In those early years of our marriage, I

211

had but to close my eyes to capture the intoxication of exotic fruit and flower scents wafting over the walls of a royal garden in Jeddah belonging to then-Crown Prince Faisal.

One special story contained the smell of guavas, custard apples and tart tamarinds ready to burst from ripeness:

"My brother Tarek and I were nine years old that day," Malik liked to begin, and when Yousef was old enough to listen with me, we knew what day Daddy meant. It was a morning that found Malik and Tarek wandering through downtown Jeddah. The boys had paused in the shade of a building, wondering where to go next.

"A hand grabbed my ankle. I tried to run, but the hand held me. Tarek ran away and then stared at me from across the street.

"'You, boy!' I heard a rough voice coming from the ground. 'I could snap your leg off.'

"'You'd go to hell' I told him. I looked down at my leg and saw a huge hand and a hairy, muscular arm.

"'I *am* in hell.' Iron bars held the thick male arm in.

"'That's the prison!' Tarek yelled at me, but I could see it too.

"'Who's that little girl telling you it's the prison?' the prisoner asked me.

"'Nobody,' I said.

"'If you were a kind boy, you'd bring a poor soul some delicious mangoes and guavas. That smell is driving me insane. My head comes off tomorrow, but I want fruits before it does. These jailors only give me beans and bread.'

"I told him I didn't have money, but he said, 'Who needs money?' And that's when I saw his glazed yellow eyes peering at me from the hole. He still didn't let go. His hand was like iron.

"'Isn't there a garden wall you can climb over? A strong boy like you?' he asked me. 'Sure,' I told him. The prince's garden was near our house.

"'I can feel your big leg muscles. Run off and get some mangoes and guavas. If you promise, I will let you go'

212

"I thought as soon as he let go, I would run like the wind. I wasn't going to bring fruits back to that prison. But then this guy said, 'Swear by Allah!' And he wouldn't let go. I think maybe I started to cry.

"'I can't let you go until you swear by Allah,' the prisoner said. 'You know what that means.'

"I was thinking God would understand if I swore by Allah just to get free from that criminal, but then the prisoner asked, 'You know what Allah does to boys who swear by His name and then don't keep their promise?'

"I asked 'What?' and he said, 'Their tools drop off. Then they have to be eunuchs. You know what eunuchs are? Fat men without willies who guard the king's women. They were once boys who swore by Allah and broke their vow. Their tools dropped off. No use for a wife after that. Now *Swear!*'

"He scared me to death. His hand held me harder than ever until I cried, 'I swear by Allah!' That prisoner still wouldn't let go. He snarled, 'You swear by Allah that you'll bring mangoes and guavas to me as fast as your legs can run, or you hope Allah makes your tools and that other boy's tools drop off so that cats eat them!'

"So I swore again, all the words he said. Then he let go of me and we ran away. Tarek asked where we were going. I told him about the swear and he knew we had to do what I promised.

"I cupped my hands for Tarek's foot, and then I grabbed a tree branch and climbed over the wall after him. We picked mangos, papayas and guavas as fast as we could. We were throwing the fruits back over the wall so we could gather them there. Tarek kept saying we didn't need so much, but I thought we needed as many as we could get in our *thopes,* because of the swear.

"Then, at the far end of the garden, a caretaker noticed us. He was jumping over flowers, running for us and he had a big stick in one hand. I told Tarek to come on. I pushed him up over the wall and started to go after him.

"But the caretaker caught my ankles and pulled me down. Even though I hit my head, the caretaker didn't care. He was shaking me, calling me a thief. He said, 'If you ever climb into this garden again, your head will be chopped off in the public square. We'll stick it on a spike here at the garden gate where your mother can come kiss it. That's the penalty.'

"Tarek was crying my name from the other side of the wall.

"The caretaker started beating me with the stick to the garden door, yelling, 'Never show your faces here again!'

"We still got the fruit and raced as fast as we could back to the prison. We rolled the fruits through the black bars of the low windows. The prisoner didn't say a word. I don't know if he was there anymore."

Malik always remembered that in a single day, he had been threatened with losing his two most precious possessions.

*   *   *   *

In the summer of 1991, Malik went on a work seminar to Florida while Yousef and I visited my father. My husband agreed to join us in California when his seminar had concluded.

On the second day of Malik's seminar in Florida, he asked me by telephone to come to Florida. My polite refusal unleashed more hard feelings on his part, thereby subjecting me to now-accustomed fear and worry.

He recovered his good humor before flying out to California where he joined us in visiting my father. Then we returned to Jeddah.

At work, Malik was promoted. Consequently, he offered my father a tempting, lucrative position as design engineer. Dad thought about the offer. The salary was breathtaking—one hundred thousand dollars a year—demonstrating the esteem in which American engineers were held in Saudi Arabia.

Finally Dad turned it down. "Sylvia, I am so happy with my life here—my independence, my private business and the way I have my garage set up—I would just miss it all too much."

I was disappointed, but I had worried Dad might not be happy in Jeddah. Malik's offer meant a great deal to me, although I realized it did not guarantee our relationship would be without continued shocks. My father and his wife Dolly seemed to fight a lot. I began to think this must be the way all marriages were although I did not dare fight or attack the way Dolly did with my father.

In October, 1991, I turned 35 and became pregnant. Malik slipped into a severe depression, barely speaking. He reacted to the pregnancy as an announcement of death in the family. His attitude was shocking.

"You'll never travel again. Our lives will be miserable," he said. I could not understand him at all.

Yousef wanted a brother or sister. I wanted another child. Malik, however, never reacted in joy to the news of children.

He had been unhappy when I was pregnant with Yousef. When I had asked about the possibility of having another child, he repeatedly answered it was "too soon." Now I was 35, Malik was 37 and Yousef was 7 years old.

Malik insisted I get an abortion. Abortions are illegal in Islam and in Saudi Arabia. That didn't matter to my husband.

A thick pall of gloom covered our house. I was treated like a criminal. From the moment Malik went to work each morning, anxiety grew in me over the resentment and depression he would carry back in the house at lunchtime. Then he refused to speak to me, lying upon the couch with one arm over his eyes, doomed to the unbearable torture of a new baby.

I was his number one enemy, the source of his hell. The whole situation was so absurd and wrong that I could not explain to Yousef why his father acted like we were on the brink of nuclear war.

The stress was unbelievable. I began considering a trip out of the country for an abortion I did not want. I confided these morbid thoughts to my friend, Azza.

"If you could see the tiny fetus that is inside you right now," she said. "You would stop thinking about your husband's immaturity. Most of the men here are childish. Forget about him, Sylvia! This is your decision. Don't get an abortion, just take a trip back home to visit your father. Go get some peace."

She had pointed out the shackles I had helped place around my own ankles. I had to stop thinking of Malik as the person who needed to be happy before I could be. I booked a flight for California, intending to stay near my father.

"I am going to the States because you don't want a pregnant wife around," I told Malik. "I need to be with my family. If you don't want another child, then I will raise this baby alone."

"Do whatever you want."

"I will."

Yousef loved the five weeks we spent in the U.S.A. My father constructed boats, cars and airplanes out of wood, batteries and tiny engines; Dolly drew pictures with Yousef and showed him off to her friends.

Uncle Steven chased Yousef through the house in hide-and-seek games until my son had giggled himself into hiccups. I reveled in seeing my firstborn accepted by my own family.

Getting involved in a junior basketball team at an elementary school down the block from my father's house brought great happiness. I admired the well-behaved children and thought about how much Western society nurtured me, especially as a woman, in ways not adequately appreciated when I was younger. It was hard to believe I wouldn't have dared to have come back to California unless an educated Arab woman had talked me into it.

I took Yousef to my father's barber.

"Do you know what your grandson did, Ray?" the man asked my dad at their next meeting.

"No, what?"

"He slipped me a quarter as a tip when he shook hands with me."

One attempt to call Mrs. Galbraith revealed music had slipped out of her life as liberty and a great deal of sanity had out of mine.

"Funding for music stopped, so I teach English writers in remedial classes," she groaned over the phone.

"Writing is fun."

"No it isn't. It is horrible. Where is Ann? What happened to her? Do you ever see her?"

Mrs. Galbraith was not cheered by hearing from me.

I am not sure Malik was either, even if our phone calls were long. Sometimes he held the phone without speaking as five or ten minutes ticked by. I worried about the bill, which would be mine alone to pay. More than once it was time to take Yousef to basketball practice, but Malik didn't seem to comprehend that information.

Yet he claimed he missed us.

Malik promised happiness and no further outbreaks of temper. He wanted us back. Five weeks had passed. I sighed and made reservations. It shocked me, soon after we were home, that he could not remember why I had left in the first place.

Chapter 17

Neck Rings of the Doves

The Saudi oil boom brought wealth, facilitating a flood of scholarships for study abroad to Saudi students, most of them male. One could tell where men when young had been sent to study in the West by their wives' passports. In the 1950s and 60s, foreign wives came from Germany, Italy, Denmark, Norway and Italy. In the 1970s and 80s, they came mainly from the USA, Canada, and the British Isles. Permitted foreign scholarships waned in the 90s, either for reasons of attempting to force national students to go to Saudi institutions or from fear of oil and so did the number of Western brides. In the early 21st century, there has been a resurgence. So long as young Saudi men go to the West to study, stories of love will blossom, contacts *("wastahs")* will be found to obtain the elusive permission getting around the ban on marriage of Saudis to non-Saudis and foreign brides, most of them Western, will accompany their bridegrooms back to Saudi Arabia.

Some women marry Bedouins (originally nomads) and some marry Hejazis—the people of the Western province who were generally sedentary (mixed with pilgrims over generations) or sedentary/tribal Saudis from the East. Saudis are very much aware of their blood roots. Their wives will become aware, as well, of their husband's lineage, (although in truth the Western wives may not in their hearts care). However, that lineage, along with the family's financial status, will impact the treatment the ladies receive.

My dear friend Isabel has milky white skin and sky blue eyes that her Bedouin husband, Rashid, must have found otherworldly when he first met her in the States. Though from England, Isabel's mother had married an American when her husband died. Isabel met her own handsome future husband in the USA. He was studying to be a pilot and she was studying air traffic control. Her exquisite voice rippled like a pure mountain stream through his headphones. He would have been lost forever in the sky if she hadn't talked him down to earth. Even I, a woman, tear myself away from her voice with regret. Her fair vowels can calm a storm or create one.

With typical Arab generosity, Rashid gave Isabel a sports car when they were dating in the USA. She and the car were shipped to Saudi Arabia, where the car was sold. There was no great fight over that decision: Isabel couldn't legally drive the car, and the young couple needed the money. Rashid's job as a government pilot, like all Saudi government jobs, paid precious little. However, the couple was given a couple of rooms in the family house while Rashid's mother took Isabel under her wing.

This Bedouin mother-in-law was inheritor of a refined oral tradition. Nomads once recited poetry to each other over desert campfires. They pierced their tongues with the ornament of classical Arabic poetry. Therein lies one of the great differences between the modern nomadic and the modern sedentary people of the Arab Peninsula; the old timer Bedouins revered classical Arabic and wished it to be revered by others. Um Rashid—Rashid's mother—taught Isabel perfect Arabic as painstakingly as Isabel's girlhood teachers had cultivated her Etonian vowels. If anyone calls Isabel on the telephone and she answers in Arabic, the caller assumes her to be Saudi.

Isabel's bilingual abilities and melodic voice did not gain her access into Saudi Arabia's air traffic control towers. She was obliged to seek income at a lower level.

She lived in the extended family building with her in-laws, much as I did with mine. Like similar buildings in Jeddah, it had three floors. The first (street floor), whose foyer shimmered with tiles from ceiling to floor, was for receiving guests. Two apartments were on the second floor and two on the third. Each apartment was accompanied by a kitchen. In Isabel's building, all manner of toys, tools, furniture and boxes were left on every staircase landing. Mounds of broken toys migrated with the wind and the maids' sweeping on the rooftop from a right corner to a left corner and perhaps to the center of flat rooftops. (The rooftop of my own

220

building was identical.) Downstairs, at street level, scattered car parts demonstrated the passion beloved to Isabel's husband: working on cars. A moonlit drive to the junkyard in search of a car part was an excursion my friend often partook in with her husband when she wanted to spend more time with him.

At first, to make money, Isabel did nothing but tutor in English studies. She accepted students in a room of a second family building located behind the villa she resided in. However, there was no walkway to that residence. She would have had to walk around the block, except that women did not do that—not by any obedience to an Islamic rule— rather, by observation of Saudi culture. Well-bred Saudi women do not take walks on the street, although they will walk in malls and from the Atlantic to the Pacific Ocean when on vacation. In Saudi Arabia, however, their husbands would rather women be crushed by a bulldozer than take a walk in public.

Rashid obliged Isabel to wait (sometimes for hours) for a driver to take her on the 15-second ride to the house behind the one in which she lived. Meanwhile, her sisters-in-law were resentful of the beautiful Western interloper. When Isabel finished her lessons and went back to her own rooms, they snuck in to destroy. They broke chairs, ripped up English books, and tore language posters off the wall. Isabel could not directly complain, save to her husband. To complain directly to the relatives would have been a breach of etiquette.

In her own building, where most of the extended family live, there were few boundaries. Children wandered in and out of apartments. Isabel might often find various in-laws waiting, unannounced, in her sitting room at dinner time on any given day. This was particularly the case during Ramadan, the month of fasting, when it is always easier to let others cook. She told me that in her household, she had to be prepared to feed whoever showed up. She got used to it, but it must have worn her down.

Outside the home, she embraced convention, covering from head to foot in black, including her face. I always thought Isabel observed this dress to please her husband, and not necessarily God, for never did I hear her tell any of our friends to do as she did. One thing (among so many) I loved about Isabel was her willingness to discuss the presence of Western wives in Saudi Arabia philosophically. "You have to be a little twisted to get here," has been her conclusion.

A decade into her marriage, Isabel discovered Rashid in the midst of quiet arrangements for a second marriage. Something in her snapped. She ripped apart her wedding photos and marriage certificate, sold her wedding jewelry and withdrew into a shell. Perplexed, Rashid took her on a trip to England, thinking to cheer her up.

As soon as they were on Western soil, she announced she was remaining and would not return to Saudi Arabia.

"If I had known you would be so hurt, I would never have thought about getting a second wife," he told her, sincerely sorry. After all, they were supposed to be on a romantic holiday, weren't they?

She didn't believe him, and viewed him through eyes narrowed to a slit: "You have a twisted sense of humor."

"For God's sake, I won't go through with it," he told her. "Stop thinking about it."

"Someday I'll stop thinking about it. Have a nice life."

"Your children need you!"

"Tell them I died."

She meant it.

Rashid was stunned.

In a country of male privilege and entitlement, second and third wives are as normal and essential to female unhappiness as every other type of male favoritism. (Spoiling male children works well, as a secondary form of torment, as the more spoiled boys are, the more careless of and likely to scream at a mother they will be when she is old.) Members of the good old boys' club raise eyebrows when a man married a decade or more doesn't start thinking about bringing in new female blood.

Rashid had, after all, been exercising his male privilege, no doubt after having been harassed by the jokes and derision of his male friends. Now not only did he have to renounce the endeavor, which certainly had its subtle allure, but he had to re-woo his own wife, whom he had forgotten was not Saudi. (She had such a good accent.)

Courtship was expensive and a little scary with Isabel's beautiful face suddenly unveiled and her in jeans, boots and a Gucci silk headscarf that kept slipping off her new styled locks, and that big art bag on one shoulder with decorative brand name paper bags from the other. Only twice could he get her over to the Arab restaurants and shisha houses on Edgeware Road, London, so that he could sit down and puff a bubbly smoke.

"Well, that's not very romantic," said Isabel, and he would find himself paying for it next day, standing in line for Fortnum and Mason's fancy pastries and trying to hurry her past the fashion departments with their hellish price tags. At last, Isabelle agreed to go back to Jeddah. Overall, she said, she benefited from his aberration. By the terms of her return, Rashid had to allow more freedom in her movements around the city of Jeddah.

"What I have resented most about my life here," Isabel confided to me one day, "is after getting here, I never had a choice. As a woman, I discovered I was barred from the sort of options I would have had living in England or the States: pursuit of education, a wide range of jobs, even divorce."

Isabel's subtle revenge and life project became adoption. Although adoption does not formally exist in Saudi Arabia, the process goes by another name and children are benefited in the same ways, save that they retain their family names or choose their own when they are grown. Isabel adopted two Arab boy infants, announcing, "The more boys I can adopt, the more Saudi men will have to say they had an English mother!"

She has a devilish humor.

Her older children sought out scholarships and universities in the West where Isabel visited them on the tickets they often purchased for her with their scholarship money. For Isabel, patience paid off. She no longer cared what Rashid did and he knew it.

Some wives fare rather well at first. Joyce, whom I met through Isabel, was also lovely and brilliant. Her husband, Essam, participated in all their babies' deliveries, which took place at private hospitals so that he could attend. When I met her, she and her husband had rented a building big enough for her to start a small ceramics art and sales business.

Running it and raising her children occupied her for several years. I enjoyed her company; she was widely read and well spoken. She

223

made strong arguments for the inevitability of Western wives ever integrating in complete harmony, with peace in our souls, into Saudi society—not even if we were Muslims or became nationals. "How can we, being females?" Had we been rich females, or Saudi royal females, our chances might have been greater. Like me, Joyce had to embrace massive restrictions in job potential, transportation and communication as soon as she got to Jeddah.

With the advent of the internet, she registered for online postgraduate studies, acquiring her degree faster than most people. She traveled back and forth to England and finally graduated. Like many a Saudi husband, Essam did not think Joyce had any particular goal in mind with her studies and travels. When she spoke of their moving back to the U.K., he treated the topic as shadowy as a woman's desire to have a honeymoon on a steam liner. Perhaps one day. . . . .

Five categories contribute to the shattering of many Western wives: a growing sense of violated rights, a husband's ambivalence to the same, his lack of acknowledgment of his wife's sacrifices, and a dearth of mental stimuli or career opportunity. The last and fifth category is the ban on being able to move around without a car and being beholden to an imported non Arabic speaking male driver with no better than a first grade education. The smarter the woman, the more likely she is to break down.

After Joyce acquired her degree and had managed as many kindergarten businesses as could be done in 15 years, she became strangely undone. Joyce turned to drugs, meeting dealers on open roads despite her knowledge of the fate she would face if caught. Dealers are beheaded. Users are imprisoned and subject to all manner of abuse, including rape. When the face that stared back at her from the mirror grew haunted, Joyce realized—with a superhuman return to reason, that she had to save herself.

How can Saudi husbands be blamed? They are living in their own culture. Their mothers and sisters exist within the parameters of restrictions and they are female. Logic follows that all females should meet the same expectations. Perhaps some Western women manage for the rest of their lives. I never met any.

She brought her children, two boys and two girls, back to England for the yearly summer visit, there leasing an apartment. At the end of the vacation, with some heartbreak, she sent the three younger children home to their father. She would not let Essam or his family say that she was depriving the children of an Islamic upbringing or their paternal family's love. Joyce calculated that her self-sacrificing act would demonstrate her trustworthiness. Only her eldest son, Ibrahim, a tall strapping young man enrolled in college, stayed in England with his mother.

Essam became unrecognizable when his wife failed to return home. Outrage rose up in an vicious swell against her as an individual. "You will never see your mother again!" he screamed at the three returned children.

"Let me go to Jeddah!" cried Ibrahim to his mother. "He can't say that! I will change his mind."

"Do you want to be trapped there for the next four to five years?" Joyce asked.

Essam forbade the children in Jeddah to speak to their brother Ibrahim by phone. It was not a terribly original plan; other fathers try it. The plan always backfires. It is no surprise to me that now, years later, the grown children all live in their mother's country save one young female who married a Saudi. She visits her mother regularly.

If Western wives ever think of leaving their marriages and the country, a tide of obstacles block their way, the strongest often financial. If such wives came to the kingdom without university degrees, they face the knowledge that without better education, they will not be able to support themselves back home. In marriages that have deteriorated, Saudi husbands may prevent wives from traveling with more than one male child, assuming mothers will not risk never seeing their other children until they have become adults, should the mothers opt not to return.

Not all Saudi-Western marriages have sad endings. Some endure for decades in love and harmony. In those marriages, the husbands endeavor to enable their wives and children to visit the wife's country of origin at least once a year. If such men are capable, they foot the bill. If they cannot, they erect no impediment to their wife and children's happiness.

Marital successes are hard to measure, for years count. One happy Saudi-American marriage was cut short by the death of the wife, Cindy. Adrienne brought her to my house when Cindy came from Riyadh.

I had heard much about how Cindy's husband, a well-to-do, educated Najdi, adored his wife. Whenever they had a dispute, he afterwards kissed her hands and entreated forgiveness. He financed an art and gift boutique for her in Riyadh.

When this tall, beautiful lady developed breast cancer, her husband took her to the one of the finest medical facilities in the USA. Adrienne and Cindy stayed in telephone contact for some months. As the condition worsened, Cindy stopped returning Adrienne's calls. Then Cindy died. Her husband's devastation touched all who knew them. He was lost for a long, long while, hardly knowing how to help his little girls or himself. Finally he remarried, though he continued to grieve and carry his dead wife's picture with him.

Maria, who came from Caracas, Venezuela in the late 1980s with her Saudi husband formed a small Hispanic support group with other South American wives. After twenty years in the kingdom, the ladies in the group—like so many foreign women who spend any number of years in Saudi Arabia—had all been diagnosed as clinically depressed.

Far too many other women are waiting for husbands to take them back to the West, waiting for the society to change, waiting for more money to travel with, waiting for a *life*. "We all thought things would get better," said Maria. "We saw a little Westernization, like the introduction of businesses and restaurants we recognized from our countries. But as the years have passed, we realize life is just as stagnant and oppressive now as it was in the beginning. We've lost hope. My friends and I are panicking." Maria worked as a kindergarten teacher, making much less, in ratio to the economy, than she would have made had she remained in South America.

Unless they take Saudi citizenship or get a special visa through a contact, foreign wives may not lawfully work, so any job they take is under the table. Their salaries as teachers are embarrassingly low. Mia, who created a business for herself as a photographer taking pictures of unveiled brides at weddings, was one of but a handful of female friends who carved a lucrative niche for herself in the Saudi job market.

When she first came to Saudi Arabia, she taught in a school, but moved swiftly to her great love, film and photos. As a photographer, she was regularly harassed by the *mutawiyyin* or religion police. Every so often, they threatened legal action if she did not limit herself to passport pictures. Since the *mutawiyyin* possess power that ebbs and flows with the mood of the government, their threats are not to be taken lightly. Mia must continually pull strings with contacts in high-up places.

Yolanda, the southern Californian bride of an enormously rich Saudi, took her husband's nationality after a decade of marriage, with the private sanction of the American Consul General. She retained her U.S. passport. The U.S. government officials recognized that she had no rights to Saudi inheritance were she not to take the nationality.

Conscientious Western mothers feel overwhelmed by the idea that to liberate themselves, they must deprive their children of their father's closeness. This has played a role in keeping the majority of Western wives locked in place. A few who made the break to their homeland were followed by husbands on best honeymoon behavior. The women were persuaded to return, sometimes to their detriment. Rita is an example. When she worked as a manager for Mia's business, her reputation was as a sharp-witted business woman. Something went terribly wrong with Rita's marriage. Love turned to war. The war extended to Rita's mother, a cultivated and beautiful Pacific coast lady who visited her daughter and grandchildren regularly. Mu'ad's treatment of his mother-in-law was so contemptuous that when she tried to verbally defend her daughter, he dragged his mother-in-law out into the street by the legs.

Mia helped Rita return to the USA with two of her four children. Having two children should have been enough for Rita to negotiate seeing the other two. However, Mu'ad followed Rita to the USA, showed contrition, paid all her bills, and promised to release her savings to her— half a million dollars she had either brought into the kingdom or had helped make as his astute and hardworking business partner. Feeling that he was truly sorry, Rita accompanied Mu'ad back to Saudi Arabia. Immediately her daughters were taken from her and sent to live with their Saudi grandparents in Medina.

Worse, she discovered her bedroom was gone. In her absence, a second wife from Morroco had moved into the villa. Rita's possessions had been moved into a smaller, upstairs bedroom. She herself was put under house arrest by her husband.

Rita often went hungry from lack of money. Sometimes Mu'ad allowed Rita to work teaching English in order to make a few riyals. Abruptly he would force her to quit, and she would go back to bouts of starving.

227

Rita was by nature independent, a fighter. She did not try to escape the country because she wanted to be near her children. The boys were allowed to live with her, but she saw her daughters only once or twice a year. The grandparents kept tightening restrictions, hoping the girls would forget about their mother. Submitting to life as the less-honored wife, Rita became pregnant and miscarried while her co-wife delivered a healthy baby. Rita was lactating and offered to nurse the baby. Her friends were shocked.

"I like children. Our living situation wasn't the baby's fault," Rita explained. What she knew as a Muslim was that a woman who nurses a child not her own is considered that child's "milk mother," deserving of proper respect. Her offer had no underlying deceptive motive, but it was a clever and noble move nonetheless.

Rita finally left Saudi Arabia for good when bouts of hunger became too frequent to endure. She feared for her life and stable health. She traveled home to her parents with her oldest boy, Omar. At first, Mu'ad forbade Omar speak to his brother or sisters. The paternal grandparents brought Rita's daughters to her house and smugly told them all their mother's things were going to be thrown away. The girls insisted on appropriating every single item—down to the last plastic comb—and made a shrine of the objects in their own bedroom. About six months later, Rita's eldest daughter sent shock waves through the kingdom by running away—successfully—to the US embassy in Riyadh. By sheer coincidence, another daughter of a departed American wife of a Saudi also successfully escaped to the US embassy in Riyadh at exactly the same time. The two teens were in sanctuary, but frozen in place.

Friends of both mothers sent an avalanche of letters to the White House before a planned U.S. vice presidential visit to Riyadh. As a result, the Saudi government allowed the girls to leave, and Rita's daughter came to live with her mother. The diplomatic pressure was to good effect: Mu'ad's restrictions on his remaining daughter loosened considerably, and he has had to allow phone calls to take place between his two remaining children and their mother for fear of diplomatic intervention and his own children's revolt.

A healthy mother is better for children than anything else. This is the reasoning behind the break made by those Western wives who leave Saudi Arabia, even if they find themselves separated from children by an angry father. The kindest men understand this need of Western wives, even if they are upset.

Before Rita left Saudi Arabia, her son Omar came home from school with the news that there was another boy in his class who also had an American mother. Next day, she sent a note with her son for that mother, writing, "Hi, my name is Rita. I hear you are American too. Give me a call; let's meet." She put her phone number on the note. That evening, she got a call. She heard a child's voice. "Hello," he said. "I am Fareed." "Where is your mom?" asked Rita. "She's in Oregon. I haven't seen her in two years," he replied.

There *are* happy marriages. The happiest one I ever heard of may also have been the strangest. It was of the woman who arrived well before my time, a woman from Norway who married two Saudis, or to put it more correctly, who married a jinni inside a Saudi man's body.

In the 1950s, a well-born Saudi named Saleh (others say he was named Samir) traveled to Norway, not realizing he shared his body with a good jinni. The Arab human was handsome, with flashing deep eyes like two wells in a desert oasis. He had money to burn, so he bought a slick black sports car in Oslo.

The jinni who co-habited the body was a Muslim who wanted to see the cold Northern lands. As jinn do not look like humans at all, they either assume the shape of humans or animals or co-habit a human body when they want to partake of the human realm. It does not happen often. (Angels can also take on human form, but they do so only in complete obedience to God.)

A Norwegian co-ed named Maarte was appointed to show the Saudi around the university town. She was a tall, stunning blonde—from the tip of her head to her feet. She had ice blue eyes and blonde eyelashes. Her refined nose was a perfect accompaniment to the dainty chin, and her mouth was like two rose petals.

She took Saleh to see famous sites like the Oslo Palace, the Akershus fortress and of course a Viking ship exhibit. Maarte acquiesced to picnics off the beaten path, as at the waterfall at Grünerlokka and to moonlit walks after romantic dinners. She found the young Arab's accent and manners fascinating.

Saleh was smitten and thought only of getting what any other hot-blooded male wants. He did not think of marriage.

The jinni inside him did. The jinni fell deeply in love with Maarte. He proposed to her and procured the necessary papers (with the help of the human body) for her to enter Saudi Arabia. While still in Norway, the jinni taught Maarte to pray as a Muslim. Sometimes when she recited Quran, even alone in a room far from Saleh, she heard a male voice recite with her. The voice had an unusual timbre, with the tone and resonance of a bell.

Being of brave Viking stock, Maarte was startled but not afraid. This was the moment she began to suspect there were two beings in one body.

When in possession of that body, Saleh did not recite Quran with Maarte. If she asked him to pray with her, he laughed at the idea of a Norwegian praying like a Muslim. She thought he was teasing.

Returned home to Riyadh by evening, Saleh woke up the next day shocked to find Maarte living in his house and acting married. He suspected he married her drunk.

On the occasions that the jinni slept, Saleh was in command of his body. The human was not usually kind. Sometimes Saleh returned expensive purchases "he" had made for Maarte and told her she would have to leave the country.

When the jinni took control, the purchases returned to the house and Maarte was happy. The jinni gave her his true name and taught her how to pronounce it.

One day, Saleh died in a helicopter crash. Maarte was pregnant with her first child. She attended the human husband's funeral. He was placed in the ground by male attendants.

Maarte continued to live in their house, praying and reading Quran. Allegedly when she read out loud, a voice accompanied hers.

The baby was born with an American (female) doctor attending. Maarte and the doctor became friends. That is how her story circulated. Maarte made sure her son learned to read the Quran well. She said he had his father's voice.

There is no way to substantiate a story like this one, but Muslims do believe in jinn. I believe in them, just as I believe in angels.

Western wives married to Saudis are subject to many variables, one of the most difficult being the chance that a husband may be more or less than he seems.

Any young woman who is in love with a Saudi should think of and prepare for that possibility if she makes the decision to live in Arabia.

Chapter 18

Sanctuary of Trees

Pregnant with my second child back in Saudi Arabia, I wrote several newspaper columns, including one on gardening. There was about a meter of arable soil on three sides of the villa, and two meters on the fourth. The rest of the area was covered in cement.

Malik planted eucalyptus, mango, tamarind, Indian nut and banana trees. Because the eucalyptus reminded me of California, I was particularly fond of it even when the roots of one found their way into a downstairs toilet. A Pakistani plumber came to solve the problem.

Madame, we must chop this tree down," he advised. "Let me get my axe."

"Over my dead body."

The plumber stared at me. "But Madame, the tree and the bathroom are too close! The tree will grow roots into the toilet again. It is no use."

"The tree never did that before," I argued. "It might *not* do it again." I was talking about the tree as if it were a child, but so what? I loved it. "It's my tree. And it's my house. Just make sure the roots are cleared out of the pipes. Don't you hurt that tree!"

I convinced Malik to give the eucalyptus another chance. He did, and it never grew roots into that toilet while I lived there.

Behind our house was a one-story villa that went through a series of inhabitants. One family built a long chicken coop. The coop was noisy and stank. Of course, I noticed the stench most while I was pregnant. A pair of eucalyptus trees buffered out the noise, sun and stench to a degree.

A fellow from that one-story villa came over one day and asked if he could cut off our tree branches that extended over his yard. We had to agree. It was his air space. He had been polite enough to ask.

I was home the day a workman was on the job. The racket drew me outside. Straddling the wall between our two houses, a worker had a power saw posed as far down the *trunk of our tree* as he could reach without falling off.

"Are you crazy?" I exclaimed. "What are you doing? We didn't say anyone could cut the trees down!"

The nasty tree assassin threw himself off the wall, into his employer's yard.

"What is *wrong* with you people?" I shouted. "You pray to Allah to grant you the gardens of Paradise, but you don't like trees. Don't you understand Paradise is full of trees?"

There was a total silence. I had a sobering mental image of neighboring housewives listening at their windows to the shrieking American woman.

Sometime later, all the branches extending into the neighbor's yard disappeared. Our trunk and branches remained. If this was a win, it was exhausting. It seemed to me I was constantly treading water against the undertow of a multiple-culture gap. It was impossible to second-guess what was to come.

During the first years in our villa, I tried everything to coax lush growth from our various trees. By that I mean I talked to them. Malik planted Indian nut saplings in the corner of the garden off the kitchen, promising me I would love their fruits. "You're doing a great job! You look wonderful!" I told the trees.

I loved the trees. Every foot they grew made me happy and brought that much more greenery into my life. The Indian nut trees began producing scores of small, red fruits, the size of apricots, but kernel shaped. The flesh was firm to chew, yielding a sweet-and-sour flavor. Birds liked to eat them. It was a good idea to cut into the Indian nuts with a knife and not just bite in as they were easily infested with worms.

The Indian nut trees were so hardy in Jeddah's hot, humid climate it didn't take many years before their branches gave ample shade to the side of the kitchen which would have been subject to the harshest sun rays. After a time, the lower branches (the only ones that could be plucked by hand) became overgrown.

Malik asked Hadaya, the driver, to prune the branches a little; my husband was afraid the laden branches would break off from the trunk. If they broke, we would no longer have shade.

Hadaya did not ask for specifics. "Yes" was his answer to everything. It didn't matter if he understood or not.

That day, Hadaya was strangely keen to do whatever job he imagined Malik had told him to do. Using a tall ladder, he sawed off all the branches of the Indian nut trees he could reach. He cut them off where they met the trunk, leaving the amputated trees surging into the sky like manicured palm trees. Only a few branches mocked the sky at the top. There was no shade left.

Unlike eucalyptus trees, branches cut from Indian nut trees don't grow back.

I remember approaching the kitchen that day, wondering why the full force of the Arabian sun beat upon the kitchen windows. Why did everything look so much *hotter?*

Then I realized there was no shade. Shock. I threw on my black *abaya* and *turha* and ran outside. The incisions on the trunks told the story. Some nitwit had amputated their limbs.

Hadaya!" I called out. "Hadaya! What have you done?" I wanted to throw myself on the ground and sob.

Hadaya came ambling around the side of the house from his room.

"Did you do this?" I pointed up.

"Yes," he said, smiling.

"Why?" Tears spilled down my face. I had waited so long in that horrid apartment before moving to this villa. I knew the branches would never grow back. They had shaded me while I made dough for apple pie or wrapped up rice and meat in grape leaves—things I always sent to Hadaya. I had been nice to him. I had cooked delicious food for him.

"Baba told me to." By Baba, he meant Malik.

"No. Baba *didn't* tell you to cut *all* the branches off."

Hadaya blinked, sweating under the brutal sun. He frowned, looking uncomfortable. Not only was I not praising him, I was crying as if he had done a bad deed.

I was sweating too. Half the year in Jeddah, people are hot and sweaty. I stared at this man whom I tried so hard to treat with consideration. Seeing I was just going to keep complaining, he started walking back to his part of the house.

"Why did you hurt my trees?" I called after him, tears spilling down my cheeks.

He stopped, turned, and repeated his insane story about Baba telling him to do so.

"Why couldn't you *ask* if you weren't sure?"

Hadaya's sullen expression announced he was sure. Baba had been clear. My sorrow did not sit well with Hadaya. He looked more offended than sorry.

I tried not to look at the trees as I returned to the kitchen door. I realized Hadaya's ignorance was as much a part of the elements of Arabia as the heat and humidity, but it didn't make it any easier to accept.

The outer garden kept changing. When the giant eucalyptus by the front gate threatened to grope inside our water supply with its fearless roots, Malik had to have it taken out. That left a hole and a chance for a new dream. We could afford a tree that had once been beyond us.

Malik arranged for a Bedouin, a horticultural trucker, to bring us a palm tree. Palm trees are not only expensive in Saudi Arabia, they are difficult to transplant. The roots have to be kept moist in transportation. Being stopped *en route* can seriously diminish chances of a successful transplant, as can the length of the drive. Our tree was brought from a village a few hours from Jeddah.

I watched the planting from the bay window in the tower. No one could see me.

A crane hoisted the palm tree over the street-facing wall while the Bedouin yelled orders. He had a checkered headscarf flopped over his head and wore a grimy, long robe that must have been white when first sold at the market. A lit cigarette dangled from his mouth.

Just before the palm tree was lowered into a hole, he peeled the cigarette off his lips and tossed it down into the hole.

That palm tree died.

Mr. Robinson was a British horticulturist under Malik's authority at work. Malik asked Mr. Robinson if he would mind overseeing the next palm tree transplant into the same gaping hole in our front yard. Curious for the sake of my gardening column, I watched that transplant too.

I wanted to be able to describe for my English readers what made for a successful palm tree transplant in Arabia, especially as the first one had failed. I was sure that Mr. Robinson would succeed where the Bedouin had failed.

By chance, Mr. Robinson had a smoldering cigarette in his mouth. I thought nothing of this until the crane held the palm tree dangling in the air above the newly-opened hole. At that moment, Mr. Robinson removed the cigarette from his lips and flicked it into the pit. The palm tree was lowered.

My limbs tingled. Here was a rite! Malik had shown me a sketchbook full of Mr Robinson's drawings of plants he had seen in Arabia. Mr. Robinson reminded me of English botanists I read about who traveled throughout Africa, India and Arabia in the 19th century.

I told Malik about the burning stub of a cigarette. Was this a coincidence? He promised to get Mr. Robinson to reveal the truth.

Mr. Robinson laughed and swore it was a coincidence. Ah, the jealousy with which explorers guard their little secrets!

Epilogue: The second palm tree died just like the first one.

In my gardening column, good advice helped expatriates setting off on holiday outside the kingdom. Readers learned how to place potted plants in the bathtub upon bricks or pebbles, leaving the tub a few inches full of water.

The columnist never followed her own instructions; she was too excited and busy packing.

In the seventh month of pregnancy, travel plans for having this second baby became my primary focus. Climbing stairs brought on contractions and bleeding. Malik wanted me to consider giving birth again in Jeddah.

"The hospitals in Saudi Arabia are much better nowadays," said Malik. "Why don't you have the baby here? The wife of my friend, Mazzan, just gave birth in the Ghassan Pharoan hospital. He said it was wonderful."

I had firm thoughts on that: "My second child is going to be American by *birth*," I countered.

If I had learned anything from being on the U.S. consulate's phone list during the second Gulf War, it was that non-Americans were willing to turn themselves inside out to have a mother give birth in the States and ensure a US passport to an offspring.

My first child's citizenship wasn't quite as stable as mine. Yousef would have to live in the U.S.A. for two years before he was 18 in order to retain his American passport or to pass that nationality on to his own offspring (I was never sure which). To complicate my understanding, every inquiry at the consulate seemed to yield a different answer.

As the years passed, and we had made no headway to moving back to California, I grew more concerned for the future of my son and potential grandchildren. What if Yousef married a Saudi and his children were not American? Would such grandchildren be allowed to inherit from me?

Wisdom dictated that my second child obtain American citizenship through place of birth as well as his mother's citizenship. The doctor said travel would be contingent upon the extent of spotting or bleeding. Yousef and I managed to fly to the USA two weeks before my due date. No doubt a silent, nonstop inner prayer to God throughout pregnancy helped deliver me safely in every sense. Thanks be to our Creator!

During the short flight from L.A. to my destination, the Monterey Peninsula, pockets of air sucked our small plane into sudden drops. The children onboard laughed themselves breathless.

"Do you need an upchuck bag?" asked a lady. "You look a little green around the gills."

Before I could answer, the plane dropped straight down into another pocket. The children shrieked.

I wanted to kiss the ground at landing, but that would have entailed getting back up on my feet. I believed I was being very conscious of not getting myself into a situation that would be physically demanding, but I had a brain lapse when I took Yousef to the beach the next day.

Carmel's beach front shifts every year. In some years, there seems to be very little descent required from the street to the shore; in other years, there can be high sand dunes requiring a steep climb back up to the car from the beach. I also forgot how excited children get when they see the beach.

As soon as the water was visible, Yousef dashed down the steep slope to the water's edge.

"Wait!"

My son was out of earshot. The sound of the waves and the seagulls filled the air. I didn't think going downhill would trigger labor, so long as I didn't fall, but I was worried about Yousef getting swept out by a wave. Ocean foam was rolling over his feet where he stood, entranced.

Riveting my eyes upon him, I began my slow way down. Luckily, a couple strolled near me.

"Could you do me a favor?" I called out.

"Sure," the man replied. He and his lady looked inquisitively at me.

"My son just ran out to the waves. Would you mind looking at him for a minute while I get out there and grab his hand? I can't move very fast."

"No problem," they agreed, and stood surveillance while I inched down.

It was worse going back up of course, but Yousef was a good boy. It took near forty minutes as he waited for mommy to rest three minutes between every two steps up. He amused himself playing with sand.

Ja'far was born at the Monterey Peninsula Hospital, in a forest between the cliffs leading to Pacific Grove and the deeply wooded area of the 17-mile drive. Before delivery, I took breathing classes and found a certified nurse to act as labor coach. While the pain was as significant as in the first delivery, I felt neither scared nor alone. I felt gratitude, thinking, *this staff will do all it can to make sure I do not die.*

"What juice would you like to drink?" the hospital nurse asked me when I was resting in my room after delivery. "We need to keep you hydrated."

"What is there?" I replied, astonished at being offered a choice. I had been served tea at the public hospital in Jeddah after a dinner of pungent boiled mutton served with white rice.

"Cranberry, Orange, Pineapple, Apple . . ." she recited.

"Cranberry!" I cried. "I adore cranberry juice!"

"Cranberry it is."

"Can I have more if I get thirsty again?"

"As much Cranberry or any other type of juice you want!"

I was in heaven. Yousef sat up on my bed with me. We watched TV and gazed at little Ja'far, whose "long" eyelashes the nurses had been exclaiming over.

"I don't see any eyelashes," said Yousef.

"He has long ones for a newborn. Don't compare them to yours!"

American ladies had sometimes asked my son if they could have his eyelashes. He hid behind my skirts for fear of scissors, thinking they wanted to cut his eyelashes off. All the children of Saudis were gifted with eyelashes models would kill for.

Yousef went home with Kate, who had come to help me until Malik arrived. Four days later Malik showed up bearing flowers. When I saw him play lovingly with his new son, I found it hard to understand why I had been forced to suffer so much when I became pregnant.

Yet the puzzle continued. Twice more I became pregnant. In both cases, Malik was relieved when I miscarried. His reaction was not common, and my grief went unnoticed.

We ask God to forgive us.

Chapter 19

"The World Opens and Shuts"

We brought baby Ja'far home when he was five weeks old. It had been strangely easy to exist as a family for that first month after Ja'far's birth in the tree-filled, European-flavored town of Carmel-by-the-Sea on the Monterey Peninsula.

Our little rental house had a distant view of the ocean; I had made sure it would, to please Malik. I took care of Ja'far, Malik lifted weights, shopped and cooked for us, and Yousef played outside with a neighbor boy or accompanied us on errands. It was a charmed, short life.

The tiniest glitch had been fleas stirred up by Yousef's raking before his father arrived. Fearing for the wellbeing of my imminent newborn, I contacted the rental agency.

"Fleas have never been reported before," they said.

"I didn't bring them in my suitcase."

An exterminator visited and the fleas disappeared.

Malik contemplated buying a small plot of land in California. This should have thrilled me, but his insistence on an ocean view was always beyond our finances. I didn't understand why it was so important to him since our home in Jeddah was an hour's drive from the Red Sea. He explained he worked too hard not to see the ocean in California.

Our return to Saudi Arabia seemed calm at first. Malik had new male Saudi friends at work. He told me about their Filipino girlfriends.

Why tell me these stories? Why explain that this man or that man loved the smooth as silk skin of his mistress?

I guessed the men were sharing their stories of sexual conquests and I honestly did not know what to say. Malik passed no judgment. Maybe I was one oe boys?

Every so often, he spoke to his daughter Yasmine by phone. Yasmine had eaten some poisonous berries a few years before, and the result had been brain damage. She insulted her father over the phone and Malik forgave her.

In Jeddah, I rocked Ja'far's cradle with my foot and wrote weekly radio shows and newspaper columns. When Ja'far was awake, I gave Yousef his school lessons.

I used the Calvert School in Baltimore, Maryland. They sent all the books for 2nd grade lessons. When Yousef found out he would no longer be going to Saudi school, he proclaimed me the best mommy in the whole world.

For the first two weeks back in Jeddah, Malik brought lunch home from various restaurants. I did all the housekeeping and laundry I could manage while caring for the baby and giving lessons. By the third week, my husband said. "It's time for you to cook for us again. You are being lazy."

I was embarrassed when Mama Johara came over unannounced because the house wasn't very tidy. Yousef did well in his studies but goofed off if I wasn't standing over him. Malik washed dishes after I cooked but went off to sleep in the upstairs bedroom where the baby's crying didn't keep him awake.

When Yousef was lonely at home for want of playmates, Malik got upset. "See? I told you he needed to be in school! He would have had friends in school!"

"Really? He was in an Arabic school last year and he didn't have any friends because you haven't taught him Arabic."

"You have to make sure he socializes with other children. That's your responsibility as a mother! Let him be with the children of your friends," retaliated Malik in fury.

I refused to send Yousef back to Saudi school. Aside from the real danger of male teachers sexually molesting the boys, I could not forget how my son had cried through every weekend in the first grade, wet his bed, and begged me not to force him to go back.

As a woman, I was not allowed to knock at the door of the school or talk to a single teacher.

My friend Mia was providing home education to her older son, Zac. Like me, she had recently given birth to another child, a boy. She knew more about Western women's activities in Jeddah than anyone else.

She helped me sign Yousef up for swimming lessons from an American woman instructor at a Western compound and then for horseback riding lessons from an English woman instructor, at stables an hour's drive into the desert. Malik had to arrange transportation for me, which he did through his office, sending one of the drivers who drove around those wives who didn't have live-in drivers.

Every solution demanded I add to my duties. I couldn't mention I was tired to Malik or he would point out he hadn't wanted another baby. According to Malik, it was my fault that I was overworked and that my oldest son was lonely.

Like new mothers everywhere, I felt pressured to keep everyone happy but myself. On top of these daily struggles, I became emotionally wrung out by the slaughter going on in Bosnia-Herzegovina.

Three months before Ja'far was born, in April of 1992, Bosnian Serbs began a siege of Sarajevo. Anyone in Bosnia opposed to a Greater Serbia was being cut off from food, utilities, and communication. We had our first satellite dish at about this same time, sold by Saudi princes. (Technically, satellite dishes were outlawed by religious authorities.)

Satellite provided my one tenuous thread to the West, and as it happened, the only English station available then was CNN. That channel opened a blood-splashed window on Sarajevo to me.

Concentration camps had been mushrooming in Yugoslavia. Women were raped while their men were castrated and shot against electricity pylons. The predominant number of executed were Muslim, although Christians came in at a close second.

I could have been Bosnian: they looked like me. They were Caucasian Muslims. The first mass graves held the most educated of these persecuted people. Granted, this was a people who had converted to Islam centuries earlier, but the bond I felt was charged with emotions.

The Bosnian president, Alija Izetbegovic, thought the West would stop the ethnic cleansing. Then he thought the Saudis would.

Victims' heads were used by callous young Serbs (brainwashed to hate) as soccer balls. Babies born to raped Bosnian and Croatian women were abandoned by their mothers. The situation was ghastly.

"You will not believe," said the Prophet Muhammad, "until you wish for your brother what you wish for yourself." The Saudis had just moved heaven and earth to help their brothers and sisters in Kuwait, who were Arabs.

The main response in Saudi Arabia to the genocide in Bosnia involved sending blankets.

A handful of Saudi English-language columnists wrote editorials seeking to wake up their compatriots. They asked a lot. In Saudi Arabia, so long as the religious police enforced the closing of businesses during prayer, the segregation of children from the first grade onwards and the covering of women in the streets, all was well.

I made an appointment with Hazzal, the editor-in-chief of the paper I wrote for, one of the very few Saudis to write movingly of the Bosnian crisis. I wished to discuss the recent shelving of my work by male copy editors. He was the only editor to employ Saudi women at his newspaper.

I met a man who spoke excellent English and who professed views as strongly in person as he did on paper, sympathizing with the plight of those unjustly treated. It occurred to me during the meeting that I had never met anyone before in Saudi Arabia who spoke up in a public forum about the error in Saudi attitudes.

"Rest assured your articles will be published," he told me. "I will see to the matter and keep in touch with you. I am glad you came to me."

He assigned me research topics that his copy editors could not dispute. Not many conversations elapsed before Hazzal professed he was in love with me. "I am your slave," he said. "Ask of me anything. The newspaper and I are at your disposal."

Emotionally vulnerable women don't need much of a nudge to fall off the cliff of sense and morality. I had been worn thin by Malik's jealous rages. If he wanted to punish me for flirting, maybe I should really do it.

I was easy prey, having been subjected to years of blame, demands, and games. I had been cut off from my culture and the normal opportunities of career and hobbies my high school friends enjoyed.

It was a mistake to listen, but I did, may God forgive me.

My in-love boss believed I deserved all kinds of good things that coincided with what I had been yearning for: frequent trips to California, a maid to help me with the housework, publication of each of my articles without a finicky copyeditor to shelve them, and naturally, his profound, undying admiration. It struck me as reasonable to leave Malik and marry Hazzal. As a prominent Saudi, Hazzal would protect me against Malik should the latter turn vengeful.

Hazzal had a wife—a lovely, kind, and educated woman. I knew her, had socialized with her. That Hazzal could turn from her and romance me did not penetrate my consciousness.

How I went from self-sacrificing to self-aggrandizing in a split second, I will never know. It scares me to death to remember, and I am ashamed. Without remembrance of God, any one of us can go to the dark side.

What I had forgotten was Malik mentioning, just about the time we moved into our new villa, that our phone was tapped for government security purposes. Noting my sudden distance, Malik decided to listen in on my phone conversations.

Thus did he discover my secret.

After an initial rage, Malik surprised me. He offered to let me go. Maybe he wanted someone new as well.

Hazzal balked. "I want you to patch things up with your husband!"

My world shattered again.

Malik's calm dissolved when I didn't leave. He didn't know whether to throw me out or let me stay. "Should I let a whore take care of my baby?" he screamed.

I wasn't a whore, but I didn't say that. I just looked in the mirror and wondered who that person was. I did not recognize myself.

I had ruined my life. Why hadn't I left Malik when I was pregnant with Jaf'ar?

Every day, Malik swung wildly from hating me to loving me. Paradoxically, a few little things changed for the better. He stopped calling me "the old woman," something he had called me since I gave birth to my first child.

"No one will love you as much as I do," he said a few times. But then he would be horrible again.

One night, I found him weeping. "Everything I worked for is in ruins!"

Other times, he flung, "What are you still doing here? Why don't you leave? I keep waiting and you don't get out!"

I was the enemy.

I learned to hate myself.

*   *   *   *

I gave up writing—first, under my name—then, under *any* name. All the articles I had submitted to the various newspapers and that had been shelved by editors were eventually published.

Khadra, a Somali woman who had once been my maid for a short while and was now a friend (and who visited as much to socialize as for charity) picked up the checks at the newspaper headquarters and brought them to me so I could sign them over to her.

She had a little daughter Jaf'ar's age whose Saudi father had died. This man's death had thrown Khadra's life into turbulence and despair. She had been taken as his second wife over a year earlier, he being a Somali-Saudi of growing means.

Khadra had a son by a Somali from whom she was divorced. Normally in such circumstances, with a boy child, it is hard for women in countries like Somalia and Saudi Arabia to get remarried. Once they have a child, the chances of becoming anyone's wife are halved.

The new Saudi husband's first wife was displeased with Khadra's arrival, but taking a second wife is what many men do in Saudi Arabia when they are financially successful. Khadra told me that he brought her mother and son to live in Saudi Arabia too. He must have loved Khadra!

Like so many of us, Khadra's husband made no legal preparation for his dependents after his death, which came all of a sudden in a car accident. She wailed when she saw his lifeless body carried to the house. No sooner was he buried than his first wife and grown sons threw Khadra, now pregnant, out of her house and into the streets along with her son and mother.

So she became a maid.

She was at first employed by my friend Mia, and then by me, but she was not a good maid. Khadra was, however, a sweet woman, one I was happy to call friend. I managed to find little ways to help her, as with the newspaper checks.

The only way I could publish, which lasted for about three months, was by using my friend Kareema's name to write a column on Muslim Spain in another local newspaper. The Spanish ambassador to Saudi Arabia was intrigued by my column. He wrote to Kareema on the subject, and she passed the letters to me.

But I had to stop talking to Kareema. My phone line was bugged. I was terrified Malik would go to her husband and create distress in Kareema's life.

In fact, I stopped seeing *any* friends for that same reason. Friends have to be protected from a vindictive husband. His rage was so intense, I had no idea how far it would spread.

I was increasingly confused and scared. It took a few years, still living in Jeddah, to have friends again.

My greatest lesson from that period is to be decisive when right is on one's side. When right disappears, we must pray for God's forgiveness.

*   *   *   *

One day, many years later, in California my doctor looked at X-rays and asked quietly, "Did you know you have a fractured rib? It was done a long time ago."

No, I didn't realize. Yet I know what day I was kicked in the ribs. Given my low self- esteem at the time, I would have said, then, that I deserved it.

Chapter 20

Changing Seasons

24-to-48-hour-long sandstorms churn up the sky when seasons change in Jeddah. Everything above ground is swirling soup. Tree branches whip against walls and lash against the metal casings of air conditioners.

Street cats climb up into the engines of cars to escape choking grit and dust. For some, the sanctuary is an illusion when impatient drivers start engines without looking under their hoods. Then the cats are mangled to death.

During sandstorms, the dark sky feigns winter although air conditioners continue to fight off the heat. People stuff rags underneath doors and in cracks around windows. The fine dust sneaks in, laying coats of powder upon indoor furniture, the floor, the rugs, one's hair and clothes.

During sandstorms, we wore scarves over our noses, even in the house. The desert's voice howled outside for days, railing against man's efforts to subjugate it with palaces, compounds and watered gardens.

The weather's harshness reminded me the only true refuge is the sanctum created in our hearts. It was a sanctum I had difficulty holding onto. My emotional life had come to represent the sandstorm, and I couldn't see a way out.

Yet in the midst of my daily trauma, a woman appeared who was so much worse off than anyone else.

Grace and Mia found this American woman, Michele Chambers, who had, like us, fallen in love with and married a Saudi. She had moved with him to Saudi Arabia many years earlier. The similarities ended there. Michele had few, if any, choices left. Meeting her made me realize how many were still mine to make.

As president of the ALJ, Grace brought Michele's case to the attention of all members. She explained an American nurse had come across Michele and contacted the ALJ.

As a sufferer of Huntington's, a neuronal cell disease, Michele was no longer able to care for herself. When her symptoms first became unmanageable, Michele sank into severe depression. Her Saudi husband abandoned her in a government public hospital. Few knew who she was. She screamed if anyone tried to touch or bathe her. When I told Mama Johara about Michele, Mama Johara gasped.

"I know who you mean!" Her eyes widened. "I was visiting my brother, Siddik, when he was in the hospital, and I passed by the ladies' ward. A woman was crying and shrieking in English. Her voice echoed through the corridor. I begged the nurses to tell me who it was, but they could only tell me she was a Westerner. No one knew her name. The patient couldn't walk or get out of bed on her own. She wouldn't let anyone touch her or make her bed. She wouldn't eat! She kept weeping and crying out Arabic boys' names.

A lump formed in my throat. Poor Michele. My hand squeezed Mama Johara's. "That's because her children are Saudis. She was calling for them."

"Oh Most Merciful!" Mama Johara's eyes reddened at once, filling with tears. "May Allah help her!"

Grace explained to me how Michele had met her Saudi husband in a U.S. discotheque. Michele was young and healthy then. She believed there was a chance the disease might pass her by although she accepted there was at high risk of developing it.

She told her Saudi fiancé. Deeply in love, the young couple chose to marry. That was not so bad, but then Michele got pregnant (although she had been warned). The young couple thought that threats of the disease in the future were far away.

They were wrong. Michele began to show signs of Huntington's right after the birth of her first son. Her hands shook and she dropped things. Refusing to accept the truth or the risk, Michele became pregnant again and gave birth to a second son. By this time, her disease was so advanced that it had become dangerous for her to hold either child.

Huntington's afflicts both muscles and brain, and it plunged Michele into abysmal bouts of depression. During one of these, she told her husband she didn't want him to take care of her. She wanted to be left alone. He took her at her word, drove her to a public hospital, and walked out. He did not return.

Grace, Mia and Rita were the trio who took personal routine responsibility for Michele. They cared for her physically and financially. They learned about her disease and located her husband, badgering and shaming him into bringing the children to visit their mother. Mia gave Michele baths, shaving her legs.

The three ladies invited me to Michele's "birthday party" at her new residence, a place where terminal patients had rooms. When I walked in, my eyes were drawn to colorful children's drawings taped to the wall around Michele's bed.

Though Michele pronounced her words with difficultly, there was a sense of pride and joy in the way she showed off her sons' drawings. Her mood must have improved a great deal from what it had been before for her to look so cheerful. None of us would have wanted to be where she was. I could only imagine how dreadful her circumstances had been prior to this.

"How often do her children visit?" I asked.

"Every week or two. Every time her husband brings them, Michele asks him when she can come home," whispered Mia.

"Why can't she?"

"He doesn't want her to know he is remarried."

While Mia, Grace and Rita never were able to acquire Saudi government assistance for Michele, the ALJ made monies available to her, as did the three ladies though they were shy to admit it. They paid for a private nurse named Hawa ("Eve" in Arabic), a wonderful African lady who tenderly looked after Michele 24 hours a day, seven days a week, like she was her own child.

Michele lived into her forties although she eventually could no longer communicate, had to be carried from the bed, and gained nutrition through a feeding tube.

Her mother in the USA had no contact with her. There was a time, when Michele was first found, that her mother asked her to come home. Michele refused, unable to bear separation from her children. Then Michele's mother requested the US Consulate in Jeddah have her daughter declared mentally incompetent. There was a problem concerning a small inheritance left to Michele by an aunt.

Michele's sons were not tested for Huntington's disease although their chances to inherit are 50% or more. Their father did not wish them to know. [7]

Recognizing how much better off I was than Michele encouraged me to write again. I worked on children's plays, directing plays for my children and their friends. Some of the mothers joined in, helping to direct, costume and organize. We presented one play at my home, and the other at a big Eid picnic Mia used to arrange at a hotel at the end of Ramadan. The children were thrilled to be actors.

It seemed to me that when mixing with a group of half Saudi-half Western children, Yousef felt at ease, even pleased with his bicultural heritage—especially during play rehearsals. At those moments, I did not get any sense of his resenting my nationality. Ja'far was in the second play I directed, having not been more than an infant during the first. Unlike his older brother, Ja'far had plenty of English-speaking friends in the years before first grade. Because he did not grow up as isolated as Yousef, he did not demonstrate trauma.

Yousef returned to Saudi school when he was 9 for third grade, and then again at 10, for another year of third grade. No one taught him Arabic. The system was barbaric.

---

[7] In 2009, one of Michele's sons died in one of the frequent car accidents that claim the lives of so many young male Saudis, who typically race the streets to celebrate high school and then college graduation. No one told Michele. I could not help but think she would notice that son's absence when the other one visited her even if she was unable to make her comprehension known. However, Michele herself died about a year afterwards. May God grant Michele and her sons reunion and peace in the Hereafter.

Naturally, we thought he was being taught.

"How many times does he have to be in the third grade?" demanded Malik of Yousef's school principal.

"Until he learns it," said the principal grimly, "even if it takes ten years."

Malik complained the Saudi resources for education were very poor. "I did not even know what I was 'reading' until the third or fourth grade," he admitted.

I found the situation increasingly bizarre and alarming. This concerned my son's future career. Malik was too impatient to teach our son Arabic, his family didn't care to teach him or talk to him (or Jaf'ar) and we lived in Arabia. We had hired private tutors in the past, all of whom seemed singularly ineffective.

Our son was learning very little at school, and the schools seemed to be the world's worst, which made no sense in such a rich country. Yet he learned fine with me.

The books were made of poor quality paper and were produced by poor quality printing. Many school teachers and principals screamed, insulted and beat the children's hands with rulers or slapped them on their heads. These underpaid instructors were recruited from poor Arab countries outside Saudi Arabia.

Educated male Saudis shun the lowly distinction of elementary public school teacher, and for good reason. Public elementary schools for either boys or girls pay lousy teacher salaries. They beat the lousy salaries paid in the West by a mile. In Arabia, immigrant teachers were poverty stricken, forced to work until midnight.

Some of my friends who are teachers in Jeddah have continued that lifestyle of grinding poverty well into the 21st century.

The impoverished Arab instructors at boys' schools were often bitter. A few, sadly, were pederasts. The main problem for sons of mixed Western/Saudi marriages is discrimination. One English friend related that she removed her boys from a school where they were whipped with wires.

I knew how unhappy Yousef was in the first grade and again in the two years of third grade. I could not help. Mothers cannot go inside the schools or talk to any of the male teachers. We have to leave everything to the fathers and chew our nails in worry. Saudi fathers are products of this system. Acceptance, they think, is the best way to avoid further punishment of their sons and a way to make "men" of them.

Malik hired one of the teachers at Yousef's new school to tutor our son in Arabic after school. The man quietly did Yousef's homework in the salon for two years. Being an impoverished, hard-working soul from Egypt, the tutor looked around at what was, to him, immense splendor, and began scribbling notes in pen on our just-purchased turquoise-colored couch.

Yousef knew this was wrong. He told the man to stop. He could not defend the couch too bravely, however. He risked losing the teacher's protection from the other teachers—and students—at the school.

I noticed the ink writing on the couch and asked Yousef what had happened. He explained and I was frustrated because I could not, by Saudi Islamic standards, talk to this tutor face-to-face. That also is the reason I did not discover, until years later, that the tutor used to bring toys to keep Yousef quiet while he, the teacher/tutor, did my son's homework.

My son did not realize the relevance of what happened the day he was crouching on the floor to play with some toy cars brought by the tutor until much later. Apparently, my son's white cotton Saudi pants, commonly worn by all boys around the house, had slid down to reveal the upper portion of his buttocks.

"You have beautiful buttocks," said the tutor, tracing his finger over the curve of his cheek in a gesture symbolizing admiration of beauty.

The first tutor's tenure came to an abrupt end following a series of small events that started with Yousef being asked in class one day by another teacher, who happened to be vice principal of that school, to write something on the board.

"*Tikdeer?* Can you?" asked the vice principal.

"*Tikdeer,*" agreed Yousef. No one had even taught him to conjugate simple verbs. He should have said "*Ikdeer.*"

"Can you?" repeated the teacher, louder.

"Yes, can you," said Yousef, smiling.

Slamming his hand down on the desk, the teacher stood up and roared, "Can you?"

"Can you," whispered Yousef, his smile evaporating.

"You dog!" cried the man, leaping forward. He walloped Yousef on the side of his head, knocking him down.

This same vice principal was asked by Yousef's tutor to fill in while the tutor was out of town. When the vice principal came to our house, he realized my son really did not know Arabic. Although he had hit Yousef, he was not, essentially, a bad man. He had imagined the boy was being disrespectful.

It was from this moment on, according to my son, someone actually began to teach him Arabic. (I pray God reward that man in this life and the Hereafter, ameen. I forgive him his anger, for he did not know.)

Yousef learned to hide in order to survive these years. He hid, as much as he could, his lack of Arabic and his American identity at school. At home, he hid his school day from us. Once, when Yousef was the new boy at a school, the teacher, who was leaving the classroom, told the other boys to shake Yousef's hand. Yousef thought they were rising to beat him. He began swinging with his fists. The boys dog-piled on top of my son.

Frequently Yousef was trapped in the school bathroom by bullies. On the most dramatic of these entrapments, the arrival of the Caucasian-looking boy brought about intense questioning, from which emerged the nasty fact that his mother was American.

For this outrage, Yousef was shoved into the floor toilet hole. Excrement smeared onto his white tope. He tried his best to clean himself, and came home with wet clothes that day. He made up stories to explain getting wet, getting clothes ripped, and losing things.

Malik decided to construct a tiny room with a tinier bathroom in the garden, where Yousef could take lessons. It was a great place to hang out as he grew up.

After seven years of after-school tutoring, five to six days a week, Yousef could speak, read and write good Arabic. We probably had four or five tutors in all. Each one made the same speech every so often:

"Remember that you are an Arab! You are not American. Do not call yourself that."

Yousef would wander in to the kitchen to collect the tutor's tray of tea and cookies. "He told me not to call myself American, Mom,"

"What? Another one? Tell him you are lucky to belong to two cultures! Tell your teacher I teach you to think of yourself as a citizen of the world."

Yousef grew fond of his very last tutor. One day, after the tutor went through his "Be glad you are an Arab" speech, he added a request.

"Guess what he asked for, Mom!"

"What?"

"He wants me to help him get a green card."

I should have been ready for that.

Most of the tutors did not help my son accept *me*. Having been stigmatized since babyhood for being the son of an American woman, Yousef grew to see me, in a strange way, as the enemy, especially when he overheard his father insult or yell at me.

I was the reason his cousins looked down on him. The teachers and tutors confused him more. At school, directly or indirectly, the lesson was that non-Arabs were to be disdained. The irony of this lesson is that the teachers were Egyptian, themselves recipients of Saudi condescension. Nonetheless they were indoctrinated to spew out the concept that only Wahhabi Sunni Muslims were true believers and that everyone from Shiites in eastern Saudi Arabia to my friends in the USA were all going to hell. In a nutshell, Saudi school contradicted almost everything I taught my son.

As he entered his preteens, my eldest son became conscious of the fact that his father could have married a Saudi rather than an American. Yousef did not resent his father for marrying me. He just wanted his pain to stop. He wished me off his radar while we were in Jeddah, which was most of the year.

At school, Yousef tried with all his might to be an Arab. He spoke no English. His tutor kindly (and confusingly) did not let on. Yousef was placed in a beginning English class along with his classmates. The heavy accent of the countryside Egyptian "English" teacher (a *fellaheen* with very little English under his belt) colored the phrases that were repeated in a chant after the teacher pronounced them in class:

"Ay weell go to duh storrr [I wish to go to the store]."

"Ay weell go to duh storrr."

"Ay weesh to abuyah Bebssee [I wish to buy a Pepsi]."

"Ay weesh to abuyah Bebsee."

In a moment of revelation, Yousef slipped and jokingly poked fun, for his little brother Ja'far, of the "English" teacher's accent. Ja'far was thrilled to be laughing with Yousef about "big boy" school.

"You sit in those classes?" I demanded, appalled. "Why don't you tell them your mother is American? Why don't you tell your teachers that you study in the Calvert home school system?" I had been spending all my extra time tutoring him, from second through the sixth grades and halfway through the seventh grade of American studies during all the years he attended Saudi school in Arabic.

"I can't do that," Yousef answered. The gaiety of the moment was gone.

"Why not? You're wasting your time! You could be teaching those classes!"

"Mom, you don't understand."

I didn't. Yousef disdained me so greatly that I had taken my woes to the Calvert School coordinating teachers. They replied to my dazed, sad letters with compassion and counsel. When we went to the mall, Yousef walked on the other side of the corridor. If I tried to talk to him, he dropped behind and pretended not to hear. The first time he veered off on the opposite side of the mall walkway, I called,

"Yousef! Why are you over there?"

"Oh, no reason," he mumbled. He wandered back to take five paces with me, then veered off again.

Yousef did not want to be seen with me in the Saudi public. Ten years earlier, the same emotional distress had overwhelmed my brother when I first visited California with four-year-old Yousef and a scarf covering my hair. My father had paid "Uncle" Steven by the hour to go to Disneyland with us. My father loved me enough to be willing to be seen with me no matter how I looked. My brother, however, didn't want me to look Muslim. Now I understand how Steven felt, given that my own son was ashamed of me for who I was.

There should be a big warning sign on the cultural bridge some of us choose to cross: **Attention to all those who pass. You will be shunned on both sides.**

Yet on summer trips to America, Yousef reverted to such filial love and kindness I wondered which boy I had with me. In Jeddah, he was only content to acknowledge me as his mother when we were alone or with other half-Western children and their Western mothers.

A number of Western friends married to Saudis have had similar problems. Sons of such mothers don't wish classmates to know their mothers are not Saudi. They wish their male cousins didn't know. If such boys lose their mothers, then everything changes. That pain is even worse.

Yousef yearned to be friends with the male cousins who were the most hotly anti-Western. He discovered that if he tolerated their ridicule of me, they accepted him.

"You don't understand, Yousef," I tried to explain. "They are jealous of you *because* of me. They are conflicted. They wish America didn't exist and they wish they had an American passport."

He didn't believe me. Then the eldest of two cousins who were brothers quietly began trying to get a scholarship to America.

"I thought Mithak hated America!" said Yousef, incredulous.

"He is jealous of America, Yousef," I repeated. I hated to say "I told you so." When Mithak finally gave up in his quest and submitted to attending university in Dharan, he stopped speaking to Yousef. Mithak's younger brother, Muthenna, later succeeded in obtaining a scholarship to the States. He moved to Louisiana, relocating after Hurricane Katrina hit.

Those two boys wanted Western freedom. They wanted to learn English, date a Western girl, and feel significant as travelers in the eyes of their friends and family.

In Jeddah, boys are banned from meeting anywhere except their homes. They are chased out of malls and family restaurants by religious police. They are bored. They end up racing cars on public roads, sometimes crashing the cars and killing themselves. After every high school graduation, such news fills the Saudi newspapers. Western mothers of Saudi children have lost sons in this way.

The only boy of Saudi-American heritage living in Jeddah I could find near Yousef's age, when my son was a preteen, was Abdur Rahman, the eldest son of an American friend named Renee. Renee was a talented artist and aerobics teacher who later separated from her husband though she remained in Jeddah. When I first introduced Yousef to Abdur Rahman, it took Yousef awhile to get over his prejudice towards Abdur Rahman for being half American.

Like Yousef, Abdur Rahman showed strong signs of insecurity when he was growing up. He wanted to be part of the life of his older Saudi cousins. His in-laws allowed him to go in the car with the driver to take those cousins to school when he was four years old. One morning his mother woke up and found him missing. She was frantic and searched all over, finally calling police. The in law's driver meanwhile took the cousins to school. At the school gate, they found the four year old waiting with his father briefcase and wearing a thobe like his cousins. He had walked 2 miles to get there.

Renee said both Abdur Rahman and his younger brother Soliman were known to abandon their beds, without telling their parents, to walk the streets and even the highways, to be with their male cousins. They were so small, and the urge to be part of their cousins' world was fierce. They too were embarrassed of their American mother.

By the time we met him, Abdur Rahman was trying to show the world how very 'Saudi' he was by tormenting his sister, a year older than he. When he acted as her driver, he berated her if a strand of hair escaped her scarf. He had the back and side windows of the car tinted the darkest shade of black possible so that no one could look in at her. Eventually, both struggling to be Saudis, Abdur Rahman and Yousef became friends.

Many years later, Abdur Rahman apologized to his oldest sister for the way he once treated her.

*   *   *   *

Because Ja'far spoke very little Arabic, he did not know when his cousins were mean to him. By the time Yousef was 13, his Arabic was quite good. He was a translator for his brother and buffered out much cruelty.

I got to witness this. One day, on our way to the beach, I heard Ja'far say, "Miyaz, look at my action figure!"

"Get your stupid toy out of my face," snapped Miyaz.

"What did he say?" Ja'far asked Yousef.

Yousef hesitated. "He said it's very nice."

The only truly kind male cousin was Yousef Tarek. Yousef Tarek, son of Malik's half-brother Tarek, was a bit of an outcast due to Circassian forebears (white-skinned, mountain-dwelling people of Russia) who had bequeathed him fair skin. I liked him for his gentle manners.

"Let me see your toy," Yousef Tarek said to Ja'far, trying to undo the wrong.

On another occasion, Malik and I took these four boys to a beach zone to the south of Jeddah where rental motorbikes and camel rides were available to the general public. I played with Ja'far while the Yousef and his two cousins rented motorbikes. Miyaz cut loose like a mad camel. He headed erratically towards cars parked at the far side of the beach, rammed into an open car door and fell off his bike.

"Miyaz hit a car door down there, Malik!"

"Good Lord!" exclaimed Malik, running in that direction. A lady seated just inside the car with her legs stretched out on the ground had been hurt, though not badly. Malik apologized and returned with the boys.

"She might file a police report," I said in Arabic, when we were all in the car. "The police may come visit you tonight, Miyaz."

"So what?" demanded Miyaz.

"Do they put people in jail for that, Malik?"

"If he goes to jail, he'll have to miss some school," said Yousef Tarek with a little smile.

Miyaz looked alarmed. "Mama won't like that," he said. It had not occurred to him that Mama Johara might find out.

"I don't know," said Malik in answer to me, unaware that Miyaz was getting scared. I could tell, watching his expression in the rear-view mirror.

Miyaz's face crumpled. He was weeping. I wasn't sure if he was more scared of the police or of Mama Johara. She had become very strict about disciplining him. She wanted him to make something of himself. My son Yousef and Yousef Tarek swapped smiles. After half a minute of watching Miyaz cry in terror, I felt sorry.

"Don't worry, Miyaz. You are young. Even if they file a complaint, no one will put a child in jail. Be careful of other people after this."

"Will Mama find out?"

"No," I said.

"You can't be sure," Malik said. "She seems to know everything."

*   *   *   *

For some time, I had been trying to refrain from burdening Mama Johara with my marital problems. Miyaz's father and stepfather traumatized her sufficiently.

By the time Miyaz was 10, Abdu had reappeared to legally challenge Mama Johara's custody. The Saudi courts favor fathers. Abdu had court connections. What he really wanted was money, and he had discovered that Mama Johara would pay him every time he threatened to take his son away from her. Whenever Abdu felt short of cash, he requested a visit from Miyaz. Mama Johara always paid, and heavily.

Miyaz knew that his real mother's husband, Jameel, hated him. He probably did not know how *much* Jameel hated him. Mama Johara

263

attempted to shield her grandson from this knowledge. Miyaz had done nothing specific to enrage Jameel except exist.

Shahidah had done nothing to offend her second husband save be married before him. In Saudi Arabia, many men consider that a sin. Jameel beat her regularly and locked her in rooms for long hours. To relieve his ravaged ego, he took Shahidah's savings to Egypt at least once a year, where he could watch belly dancing spectacles and tuck his wife's earnings into the sash of a dancer's undulating hips.

She followed him to Egypt, with their children, wiping out any savings she might have and to keep him true to her. I wondered why she cared.

When Miyaz was 13, a family council was called on behalf of Shahidah's sufferings. Ghassan, one of Leena's sons and therefore Shahidah's half brother, was sick of Jameel's obsessive hatred. Ghassan made a proposal no one would ever forget. Normally a convivial and entertaining man, Ghassan looked somberly at Jameel.

"I propose this," he said darkly. "We call your eldest son, Barak and give him a gun. You command Barak to shoot and kill his brother Miyaz. That will finish the matter and your honor will be avenged. No one will be punished because Barak is a child."

The room quivered in silence. Jameel, given to bipolar fits of piety which he demonstrated by growing beards and shaving them off, had a beard that day. His hand held onto it, but he couldn't formulate an answer. The proposal symbolized what he most yearned for in a foggy sort of way. Jameel's desire conflicted with everything Islam teaches to people of understanding. The Al Shamsi family waited, forcing Jameel to mull over the indecency of his attitude.

I cannot say his outlook improved or that he stopped abusing his wife. Barak did not shoot Miyaz. Jameel found less violent ways to express his irritation.

Abdu, Miyaz's real father, had a non-financial change of attitude before he died, quite suddenly, of a heart attack. He took Miyaz for an outing with his new wife and children one day when Miyaz was 14, and for the first time, did not demand money from Mama Johara. It was a good day. Miyaz was encouraged to hold onto that memory and discard the others.

The kindergarten I chose for Ja'far was owned by a Saudi woman of the infamous Bin Laden family. The school held classes in both English and Arabic. I overheard the Bin Laden owner mention that she had an American passport.

To me, she remarked on the necessity of my little boy's conforming to Saudi culture: "He will have to get used to the way things are here. He is going to live here for the rest of his life."

"You don't know that," I said.

"Yes, I do. He is Saudi, isn't he?"

Being a rich Bin Laden with an American passport, she could live wherever she wanted. To bluntly state that my child, not possessing her wealth, was fated to stay in Saudi Arabia forever, struck me as abrasively arrogant.

The Bin Ladens did not yet have to cope with the disgrace of being related to Oussama, mastermind of the Taliban.

When Ja'far was ready for first grade, I flatly refused to put him in Saudi school. Isabel told me about a small international school that she co-directed with an American wife of a Saudi. These two ladies offered children like my Ja'far unofficial education. Not for the world will I write its name on these pages! I wish other expatriate mothers to benefit from its mercy.

Isabel explained that if I were to seek a job there, the director would be more likely to take Ja'far in. The files of the illegally enrolled children were kept in an underground safe of a kind Saudi prince. That prince protects the records from belligerent administrative officials who descend in 'sting' operations to root out students with a Saudi parent. Such kind and brave Saudis try to soften the harshness of their world.

Chapter 21

Farewell Pilgrimage

A beautiful young French woman with dark hair and dreamy hazel eyes came seeking a job as teacher at the same time as I did at the school where I intended placing Ja'far in first grade. Madeleine looked like a cross between a 19th century Jumeau doll and Mata Hari. She was from La Haye en Touraine and had married the acclaimed Saudi fashion designer, Yassir Al Balad. I was stunned to discover she had almost become my sister-in-law.

One evening several years earlier, Malik and I had been at The Palm Oasis Restaurant, which was managed by Malik's brother, Ghassan. Ghassan held up photos of three lovely girls. "Which one?" he asked in his jolly way. He was struggling between choices of brides: a Saudi/Yemeni distant cousin, a deposed Sudani princess, or a young French woman.

"The French girl, of course!" I cried, thinking how delightful it would be delightful to have a French sister-in-law whom I could practice the language with. Ghassan had met Madeleine through her sister, Veronique, whose husband had come to the kingdom on contract. Ghassan finally chose the distant relative (who looked a little like actress Sharon Stone, only brunette).

Later I learned from Madeleine that she had met Ghassan but once, and very casually. "Saudi men!" She laughed. "No wonder they are so dizzy -- the world never stops revolving around them. He never asked *me* if I would consider marrying him."

Madeleine later met and married Yassir, a Saudi fashion designer whose picture she had cut out from an international fashion magazine. She was an intelligent, romantic, college-educated young woman who yearned for the exotic. It seemed to be a family trait. A second sister also found her way to the Middle East. Thus two sisters were in Jeddah and one in Lebanon out of four sisters.

Madeleine's father was a brooding and strict man. It may have been that trait which encouraged all his daughters, once grown, to escape to distant parts. When Veronique, who was in Jeddah with her husband, met and then introduced her visiting sister Madeleine to Yassir, Madeleine saw a Westernized Arab fashion designer who spoke good English and tolerable French.

His clothes were shown in a yearly Paris fashion show. As the internet took on, he developed a masterful online presence. His line has become world famous. Even then, he was at ease amongst a vibrant circle of Western fashion lovers and of course, the ubiquitous female models, most of whom paraded nude behind stage and semi-nude on the catwalk.

Madeleine's romantic heart was stolen. Here was a man of the exotic East who understood the West and seemed as tolerant as any Western male!

She had not yet seen the metamorphosis act so many Saudi men excel in. It takes place on Saudi soil. When Yassir put on the Saudi *khurta*, everything changed: he became consumed with social traditions and stigmas.

On a visit with her new husband to a wedding held in the Saudi mountain village of Abhaa, Madeleine needed to pass in front of a tented pavilion where male guests thronged in order to reach the main building where female guests were being entertained. Yassir put his hand on her arm.

"You cannot walk in front of those men without being veiled." Madeleine is nothing if not headstrong. She was 19, but unintimidated.

She would have kept walking, but Yassir pulled her forcibly back into the car.

They began bickering.

"Finally," she told me, "I agreed to hold the veil in front of my face. It was like I disappeared as a human being behind it." Madeleine looked distressed as she related her anecdote: "I hated the way it made me feel. I had already started to realize I did not count for much to Yassir. He cared more for what people said than he cared about me. He got a French wife because he is a fashion designer and his Western affiliation is mainly with France."

Madeleine had been living in Jeddah for over ten years when we found each other.

"Why haven't I met you before?" I asked.

We shook our heads at our cocooned lives. A woman in Saudi Arabia can have a hard time meeting people. Now that there are secret social media groups, there is a little more support. Before the internet developed, many of us lived as if in caves.

Madeleine was sick of her day-to-day life. Seeking a job, she was trying to get out in the world and prove herself. If she and I hadn't gone to the same private school to find jobs as teachers, we would not have met each other.

When we shared our experiences, she said she had tolerated her fashion designing husband's double standards long enough.

"My husband gives exhibitions every year in Paris. His models are half nude when they put on a gown or bikini, and he surrounds himself with naked women. But when he has dresses made for me, he covers me with fabric from the neck and down to the wrists and ankles. What hypocrisy!"

Madeleine's romantic dreams of falling in love with a talented, open-minded Arab artist were ravaged by Yassir's discriminatory attitudes. True, he was rich, but as a man from a small mountain village, his standards at home were as conservative and rural as his standards at work or at leisure for himself were liberal.

Simply put, Yassir exemplified a case study of Saudi males, who are allowed to live in two worlds, changing their ways to adapt to either.

The Saudi females I have known have tried to be consistent with themselves, but what does it matter if they allow raise their sons to be duplicitous?

Foreign wives, like Saudi wives, are expected to tolerate Saudi men's adaption of the double standard. Obviously there are exceptions to every observed behavior, but it is important that newlywed foreign wives of Saudis understand this problem before they get to the kingdom.

Ironically, conservative Saudi families are not inclined to believe that any morally conservative families exist in the West.

"I married my husband as a virgin," Madeleine said. "That is the kind of family I came from; My father wouldn't let my sisters or me out of his sight. He was a small autocrat in his own right.

"Yassir saw that when he met him. But within a year, my husband claimed, 'Oh, you couldn't have been a virgin because you're French.' You can't win with them, Sylvia!"

Before her wedding, Madeleine had wanted to learn about her fiancé's religion and had read parts of the Qur'an. "His manner of insisting I be Muslim was to fault me for every little thing. He would imply that *everything* I did was wrong. If I didn't eat dates in Ramadan, I was not a 'good' Muslim."

Like most Western girls who are not raised to bite their tongues when men have temper tantrums, Madeleine lashed back at Yassir.

"When my husband called me a donkey, I said 'If I am a donkey, then you must be one too.'"

The most important thing Madeleine did for me was make me laugh. I had almost forgotten how. One day she said she had painted her bathroom blue. When her famous husband mocked her efforts, she told him, "At least one of us has taste."

Yassir was speechless with rage. Offended beyond measure, he moved downstairs in the building he owned. His decision suited Madeleine just fine. She immediately had a French countryside painted on one wall of her dining room and told the painter to bill her celebrated husband.

She took her meals in restored peace.

Her entry into my life helped me make comparisons. Though she was younger, I found her more courageous about being who she really was. She was inspiring.

We had a lot of in common. Both of us had two sons, and we both loved history, travel, reading, art, and fashion. It was fun practicing my French, but my talking to her on the phone in French irritated Malik.

"Every little Moroccan speaks French," he said. I realized that was supposed to be a dig, but in fact only underlined Saudi attitude towards other Arab nationalities.

"Yes, Moroccans are talented!" I was learning to answer like my new friend.

"You torture yourself," she told me. "Stop! Saudi men are spoiled. You have to see the humor in the way they act."

"I don't want my boys to be that way," I said, thinking how Yousef seemed no longer to value me.

"What can you do?" Her voice made the question into a challenge rather than a defeat.

At the end of 1999, in a particularly foul mood, Malik announced, "Sylvia, you are leaving at the end of this school year. I cannot tolerate you here anymore."

This was the same man who had not long before bought me a piano and discussed our buying property in California. His pronouncement was brutal and I took it seriously.

I had tried to overlook Malik's moodiness and vacillations because he was artistic, generous and kind when he wanted to be. Now I suffered an emotional collapse.

For seven years, Malik had attributed his black moods to my romance. I had tried hard to redeem myself, working diligently, spending vast amounts of money—all I could afford—on my husband and the boys.

Throughout the seven years, he verbally flayed me, again and again. Breaking my bones would have been kinder. Many women tolerate oral abuse, thinking that *not* to do so makes them bad mothers or unfaithful to God.

"It's too bad you quit your family and homeland, converted to Islam, came to Saudi Arabia, and then screwed up your entire life. Everything good you did was for nothing. All your efforts are wasted. You're a failure."

I would not have survived without the Western wives who taught at Jaf'ar's school. They too were married to Saudis. They tried to stop me from hurting myself, which I taken to doing to make my husband stop castigating me. He mocked the faith which had brought me to marriage and his land, making me feel I was worthless.

"Crazy women are better than you are," he said.

Friends worried about me.

Yet some also shocked me. "I hope my husband burns in hell," said one American woman of her Saudi husband. I pointed out she wore a scarf on her head, She affirmed she was Muslim. "I still hope he burns in hell," she said. "I count on it."

"What?" I asked, aghast.

"He has tortured me. I want him to burn."

Racial prejudice and male chauvinism had ripped apart the beautiful fabric of faith that had drawn me to this country. Did anyone else see the damage?

Though I now had a deep bond of love with Mama Johara, I could no longer seek her comfort for fear of worsening her health.

Madeleine visited me the evening of the day Malik made his proclamation that I must leave. She brought as a gift the CD soundtrack of *Shakespeare in Love* and hugged me while I wept.

Malik wanted our end to come in the summer. I redoubled my prayers for the only thing left to do in his country: make pilgrimage.

The thought of pilgrimage had long scared me. There are hardships involved like severe heat and lack of clean food or bathroom facilities. There are yearly reports of death from fires, human stampedes, and sometimes riots.

I had lived in Saudi Arabia for almost two decades without performing this holy rite. Malik had never had free time from work to take me on pilgrimage with him.

Many Muslims wait until they are old because they want the pilgrimage to "erase" all their life's sins. That was Malik's attitude.

Azza had made a pilgrimage so uncomfortable that hearing her accounts of stinking, overflowing bathrooms that had to be waded through had given me shivers.

"How can one stay clean for prayer?" I asked.

"You can't," she said grimly.

Mama Johara had narrated her last pilgrimage to me, which she made with her grandson Miyaz. They boarded a full bus. The bus driver said to a seated man, "Move your suitcase off the seat and make room for other people."

"That's not my suitcase," said the Bedouin. "That's my wife."

"When I looked more closely," said Mama Johara, "a poor woman covered in her abaya was doubled over in her seat. Her husband had put the suitcase on her back and was leaning on it."

My friend Shirley, met through the American Ladies of Jeddah, who had married a Saudi and now served as a doctor at a hospital in Mecca, called me with a proposal.

"I have a patient who, with her family, runs a pilgrimage company called Al Qaswa. It costs roughly 7000 riyals[8] per pilgrim. She told me there is space—would you like to go with me?"

"Yes!" I said. "Tell me more!"

The company had a bus with a bathroom in it and offered clean, comfortable lodgings during the pilgrimage. I asked Malik if I could go.

"Do what you want." He did not have the right to refuse.

I would never have so perfect an arrangement for my children—their father would take good care of them while I went to Mecca and Arafat. I would be gone only five days.

Before I left, Uhood, my beautiful, darling niece-in-law, had a dream. "I saw you," she said. "You and Uncle Malik. Your house was open, like a stage. I was watching everything happening in it. You were

---

[8] Approximately 2000 dollars

talking to Uncle Malik, pleading with him, and he turned away from you. Your skin was beautiful, Sylvia, translucent, like water. When Uncle Malik turned from you, you begged him to look at you. You tried to pull on his jacket. He wouldn't look or listen."

Uhood's dream encouraged me. I think my unloved state—and Madeleine's--scared Uhood. She once said, "If two such beautiful women in Jeddah are so unhappy, what can I hope for in marriage? How will I ever find a kind man?"

She refused suitor after suitor until a doctor of kindness and intellect finally presented himself, though to accept him, she had to distance herself from family prejudice. [9]

I counted the days to my pilgrimage, yearning to go.

"How will I get to the Jeddah hotel from where the bus leaves?" I asked Malik.

"Hadaya will take you," he said, referring to our driver.

I kept a stiff upper lip. When the day came, however, Malik relented and drove me to the hotel. He wished me a good pilgrimage.

Maha and Farida, the two sisters who ran the ladies' section of Al Qaswa, both spoke English. Their faces shone with smiles. Their sons, who helped serve drinks during the bus journey, were the humblest, sweetest of helpers. They did not act like I was a leper because I was a woman. Everyone was kind, informative and cheerful and welcomed Shirley and me into the group.

Maha and Farida helped everyone by reminding what prayers to make at certain times. I loved the chant, "I am here, My Lord," as the pilgrim sings—the females in softer voices than the males, but women *do* chant or sing with the men. Not since my mother's death had I felt God's hand upon me so palpable that the hairs of my skin stood on end. I felt love for all mankind.

At the campsite outside Mecca, all the female pilgrims slept on floor mats. Amongst us were immensely wealthy women who had palaces to call home. They and the others—women like me and women

---

[9] She chose a Saudi of Asian background and was jeered at by younger members of the family for doing so. A permanent rupture in the family took place.

who had come from North Africa, China, and Pakistan—slept like girls at a slumber party.

I made friends with a retired airline attendant from Algeria named Malika who had traveled from her country to make the rite. I introduced myself after hearing her ask one of the Saudi female scholars a question founded in Sufi mysticism, having to do with the power of God's one hundredth name.

"We do not embrace this kind of thought," admonished the scholar, annoyed. "It is not part of Islam." Malika was stilled and did not ask any more questions publicly.

I remembered North Africa, even if I had never been to Algeria.

After we had chatted a little, she asked, "Why did that woman get so angry?"

"They don't understand the concept of God as the 'Beloved' in this country," I explained. Speaking in French allowed me to explain what I had figured out without having anyone break into our conversation and cut me off.

"Saudi Arabia's perspective on Islam is basically Wahhabism after Muhammad Abd Al Wahhab, the scholar from Najd. If the Saudis favor any other perspective, it is that of the ancient scholar Ibn Taymiya, and mainly because Ibn Taymiya's point of view supports the Wahabbi perspective. The people are immersed in that. They just don't 'do' analogies or allegories. You can't expect them to understand."

"But you do," she said.

"I like to read," I explained. "And I like the writings of mystic scholars like Al Ghazzali and Ibn Al Arabi. I cannot get as close to God through fear as I can through love."

She was happy to have found a kindred soul. That evening, we walked out amongst the pilgrims, who came from every point of the planet. Russians, Chinese, Malaysians, Africans, Arabs, Indians, Pakistanis, and rare Westerners all slept, rose, ate, walked, sold and bought merchandise and mingled together.

It was a microcosm of mankind gathered in a hot, barren desert spot where there was nothing visible—no golf courses, swimming pools, movie theaters, restaurants or world cups—to have attracted them. There was nothing to entice everyone except God's command to Muslims to remember Him this way once in a lifetime if a human being is able.

Malika bought gifts for both my sons and invited me to her home in Algeria. At the women's camp, I was invited to speak before the ladies and explain, in my poor Arabic and a little English as I pleased— for most of the Saudi women spoke English—what had persuaded me to follow the path of Islam.

"It's not the only way to God," I explained, knowing many would disapprove, "but the more I learned about Mohammad, over 20 years ago, the more I was convinced he is a prophet just like Jesus, Moses, Abraham, and all the other prophets whose names we know and don't know, peace be upon them all. It is the path I chose for myself."

Maha came up to me, beaming. "I love you," she said. She had two pretty, young Chinese girls with her. "They want to meet you. They are converts too."

The Chinese girls and I smiled broadly at each other. All we knew of a common language was "Assalam Alaikum" meaning "Peace be upon you." We smiled at each other for five minutes and they wrote their addresses for me in Chinese script.

When I wanted to call Ja'far and Yousef on the phone, a rich Saudi woman urged me to hurry. When I was off, she sought me out. "Please forgive me," she begged. "I shouldn't have hurried you." She looked ready to cry. I was dumbfounded. No Saudi woman who was a stranger to me had ever been so apologetic about anything, ever. Then I remembered that not a single angry word is allowed during pilgrimage if one wants one's effort to be accepted by God.

During the symbolic "stoning" of the devil at the pillars, Farida guided me through by the arm, telling me when to duck. Getting hit by overly enthusiastic pilgrims who are throwing stones was a danger I had heard about.

Shirley and I were both embarrassed on the day of Eid when the female pilgrims pulled out cologne, jewelry, and pretty new dresses from their bags.

"Oh, my! Did *you* bring anything nice to wear?" Shirley asked me.

"Not a thing," I admitted. "I kept thinking of the pilgrimage as a time to pray and think of the Hereafter!"

"Me too. Did you bring any cologne or perfume oil?"

"You're lucky I brought deodorant."

For all the fear I had nursed of this religious duty, I was amazed at its ease. That we were in the hottest of barren deserts did not matter; that a government-sponsored workforce labored hard in the streets to clean up rubbish strewn by the ignorant was a mere footnote; that three million human beings of every race and language all vied to go to the same spots at the same time on foot or by car did not bother or alarm me.

My female co-travelers could have been angels for their sweet smiles, good manners, generosity and gentle graces. Not a hint of arrogance fouled the words exchanged, the only harsh ones those addressed by the fundamentalist scholar to the Algerian lady. The female pilgrims with me were so careful of themselves, so loveable and accepting, they seemed like my sisters. Here was a new sensation after two decades of confusion.

After the pilgrimage, the emotional roller coaster of my home life recommenced. Mama Johara underwent an out-of-body experience she recounted to me in detail. "I was awake," she told me. "My soul slowly pulled out from body with a mild pain, like tearing, and then it hovered. I could see myself in the bed. I waited there, looking down. Then a strong hand, as large as my entire body, compressed my soul back into my body. I was no longer above, but back inside my body and utterly astounded."

I did not know what her experience meant, but I steeled myself to never show her a sad face. Unfortunately, though the pilgrimage was a pillar of Islam accomplished, it did not immediately give me the strength to stop inflicting self-punishment when Malik vented his anger. In my own defense, I was divided from friends who could tell me I was not a bad person. All I heard was descriptions of how evil I was, over and over and over. I was sorry and presumed I deserved it.

It was during a night my head throbbed so painfully sleep was impossible and the fear of having a concussion, after hitting my head against the cement wall in front of Malik (hoping he would stop saying horrible, mean things), that I realized killing myself—even by mistake—was a very strong possibility and one which, moreover, could break the bond I had been trying to forge with the Beloved. Pain killers did not help.

"Oh Most Merciful," I prayed. "I am sorry. Forgive me if I die." Every week was the same cycle of fear, tip-toeing and recriminations alternating with seeming family calm. I believed I was losing my mind.

In a society where women are pressured to adopt their husbands' reasoning rather than develop their own, I cannot see how female suicide can be avoided. Only at moments of critical analysis—which I had not totally lost—did I realize the wisdom of creation. It was God's choice to create me a Westerner, an American. To accept prejudice was ignorance at best, ingratitude at worst.

Prejudice in the form of racism and hatred exists everywhere. To be healthy, we must see the beauty of what we are and the good God has provided us. If one set of circumstances is too hard and we are able to find greater ease elsewhere, then we should do so.

Those are attainable blessings.

My foray into doll making had caused me to marvel at the spirituality of other doll artists, whose interviews I read in *Dolls* magazine. Every time I returned to the West, I came across good, kind, generous people who—without attempting to convert me to their personal beliefs, and no doubt fathoming my sadness—swept me into their love and mercy, not allowing me to leave them but somehow strengthened.

The West taught me independent thinking, and independent thinking had allowed me to see Mohammad as a prophet.

Western freedom of thought allowed me to see there had to be many paths to spiritual enlightenment.

The Qur'an says, "Believers never despair of the mercy of God." My mistake was in too long seeking Malik's mercy rather than God's. I had to forget about Malik's pain and save myself. His pride would never be assuaged. Even *he* told me so.

For very brief moments, Malik managed to disconnect from his angry Saudi persona and become again the man I had first met, though no longer in love with me. At those moments he said, "Why do you care what I think? I'm just a guy. Go home and live your life the way you want to. Take the boys. They'll be happier in America. Stop thinking of me! You'll feel better."

If I loved my sons, it was more important for me to care about what kind of men they would grow into than worry about the pain divorce might bring. I dreamed of improving the relationship between Yousef and me and wanted to help assure Ja'far did not fall prey to resenting me because I am American.

Yousef was sixteen years old and Ja'far was eight. Ja'far wanted to be with me, though he knew he would miss his father terribly. Yousef did not want to go. He had struggled hard to fit into Saudi Arabia. Malik was hero to both boys, but to Yousef he represented the only Saudi acceptance our eldest had every truly felt. People of that society had ostracized and abused Yousef as a child, and there was nothing Yousef wanted so much as to be identified as a Saudi. Ja'far never felt that dilemma except when his brother tried to pull him into it.

Yousef, who struggled many years more to accept and finally grow into his bicultural heritage, had a duty at 16 of which he was yet unaware. When he was first born, Malik said to me, "Now you will have someone to take care of you." In prophetic tradition, it is the boy's job to care for his mother. One afternoon, Yousef approached his father in the privacy of the beautifully furnished, airy salon where Malik sat sipping tea under a painted night sky.

"I'm *not* going to America!" he told his father. "I'm going to stay with you, Baba."

Malik patted the couch so Yousef would sit. He hugged his son. "No," he said quietly. His voice caught.

"Why? Why not!" demanded Yousef, his eyes growing red.

"Your mother needs you," said Malik.

Yousef narrated this conversation to me several years later. I was moved. For every post office poster of half Middle Eastern/half American children who have been kidnapped and taken to the Middle East by angry, self-righteous fathers, there is the graciousness of Malik's gesture. Our marriage may have left us both scarred and weary, but in his response to Yousef, Malik made his own sacrifice.

There is always struggle in life. Malik remarried a Syrian woman the same age as Yousef. I have never met her, but I know she thinks ills of me for reasons I fail to grasp. My heart goes out to her, for her country has gone up in flames. I have instructed my sons to be kind to her and to their sisters.

For my part, I found what I guessed would come true: I have re-found myself in the West. For howsoever long God may grant, it is still a realm of freedom, with rights won for women, by women. Whenever I am depressed, I walk outside my door and look at a tree. No one harasses me, no one chases me, and I am considered completely normal.

It is amazing.

Epilogue: the Death of my second mother

For many years, I accompanied Jaf'ar home to Saudi Arabia in the summer to see his father.

My children's stepmother, Muna, has had but a sixth grade education. I do not know why she hates me. I have tried sending her gifts, but she throws them in the garbage.

It unnerved her to have me visit Mama Johara, who lived in her own separate apartment downstairs in Malik's villa. Muna threw tantrums when she heard I visited, but Malik explained it had something to do with her later diagnosed disease, multiple sclerosis. He said multiple sclerosis afflicted her brain and caused her to throw things and scream. I am so sorry for her.

I did not realize how much I would miss Mama Johara. When I returned to sit close to her, kissing her hands and cheeks, she would beg me to live in Saudi Arabia. Each time I explained to her I could not do that, and she accepted quietly, though sadly. She did not enjoy Malik's new wife because Muna disliked Mama Johara for no particular reason. Perhaps it was due to the M.S.

However, Malik was as good a son as any woman could ask for. He cared for his mother and provided all her needs. Others of her children contributed in varying degrees. Mama Johara was much loved by everyone.

After a lifetime of back pain and lack of exercise due to the extreme restrictions placed upon women, Mama Johara developed diabetes and a heart condition at a relatively young age. She tried to take the weight of all her daughters' troubled marriages, including my own, upon her shoulders, and the stress was formidable.

She had heart surgery after I left, and the toll was significant. Nonetheless, she moved about, seeing to her daily tasks to the best of her ability. She had one, and later two, Indonesian maids live with her since walking became more and more difficult. She was not steady on her feet.

One day she slipped and fell on the wet bathroom floor. She went to her doctor at Erfan hospital, one of the older hospitals in Jeddah whose reputation has swung widely between good and horrible. Her medical insurance was through her youngest son, Hisham. Soon she was hospitalized, with many an X-ray taken.

Apparently no qualified person at Erfan ever read those X-rays.

After well over a month, with no improvement and a great deal of suffering on Mama Johara's part, Malik decided to physically remove her from Erfan and take her to a hospital where royal family were wont to go. There were American doctors and nurses on staff.

At that hospital, one of the finest in Jeddah, he was told there was no room for her even as she was laid upon a gurney. He knew that if he insisted and did not remove her from the hallway, they would be forced to take care of her.

He was right. They found her a room.

An American nurse told him Mama Johara's fall had broken her pelvic bone, and shards had penetrated the bladder. She might have been saved, said the nurse, if action had been taken quickly.

No surgery was ever done at Erfan because no one ever read the X-rays, or if they did, no one cared. In fact, the Al Shamsi family was told on a daily basis that Mama Johara was getting better.

Yousef went to visit during the winter and tried to cheer her up. He told me one of his aunts stayed with Mama Johara every hour of the day and night. His grandmother had infections throughout her body as well as horrid bed sores. Mama Johara was in so much pain she could not sleep, and eagerly awaited the gas tank and mask brought to her each night so that she could lapse into a state of unconsciousness.

She died of septic poisoning. Yousef called me to tell me in February of 2011. It was a blow almost as severe as the losing of my own mother.

One touching memory of this darling woman who took my cause and who never, ever thought of me or treated me in the manner Malik said she would, who never thought I was dirty, was formed one day on a summer visit to Jeddah. I looked at her face for a long while and saw the orphan, and then the co-wife, and then the female deprived of a yearned-for education. She often said she wished she had been born a man. What honesty.

I tried to burn every detail of her beloved face in my heart, letting my devotion show so she could see it. Love speaks a language the eyes can translate. I promised to see her the next year. I did see her one more year, but only one.

She told Malik I loved her more than some of her own children did. That may or may not be, but I have never been able to hide my feelings. I pray for her as if she were my own mother. Malik has been kind to me since I left, and that is partly due to the love shared between his mother and me. I wish all his family well, for they are all dear to me and I consider them family, no matter what. May God have mercy on us all! Ameen.

Goats on a Jeddah beach

A rare, mixed-gender private elementary school
in Jeddah

Sylvia and her mother

Muhammad, Ziyad, Malik

283

Yousef and his Baba in Morocco

Kate and daughter

Grandmother Zainab

Madeleine

Sylvia and Ja'far

Jar'ar with his Baba in Morocco

Saudi-Western children actors

Mama Johara

CPSIA information can be obtained
at www.ICGtesting.com
Printed in the USA
LVHW01s1621010418
571883LV00018B/187/P

9 780998 177502